THE RUSH LIMBAUGH STORY

Paul D. Colford

THE
RUSH LIMBAUGH
STORY

TALENT ON LOAN FROM GOD

AN UNAUTHORIZED BIOGRAPHY

ST. MARTIN'S PRESS   NEW YORK

Production Editor: David Stanford Burr

Library of Congress Cataloging-in-Publication Data

Colford, Paul D.
 The Rush Limbaugh story : talent on loan from God / Paul D. Colford.
        p.   cm.
 "A Thomas Dunne book."
 ISBN 0-312-09906-1
 1. Limbaugh, Rush H.   2. Radio broadcasters—United States—Bibliography.   I. Title.
 PN1991.4.L48C65   1993
 791.44'028'092—dc20
 [B]   93-24164
                                                              CIP

First Edition: September 1993

10   9   8   7   6   5   4   3   2   1

Contents

Contents

Acknowledgments

Mammoth biographies of Harry Truman, Henry Kissinger, and John F. Kennedy were published during the writing of this book. They earned justified heaps of praise from the critics for the breadth of their analyses and the exhaustiveness of their research. At the same time, I envied the biographers for having access to voluminous files, public records, and archives.

For in the case of Rush Limbaugh, there are obviously no such troves to sift through. As a result, this biography became a reporting job with ample doses of detective work. Being able at long last to locate an old tape of Limbaugh working on the air as disc jockey Jeff Christie was a thrill exceeded only by the satisfaction of finally tracking down his first wife, Roxy.

I am grateful to her and to all of Limbaugh's friends and colleagues through the years who agreed to be interviewed. At the top of the list is his radio syndicator, Edward F. McLaughlin, who added to my understanding about how the show developed and how the network-radio business works. The book also profited from the copious reflections offered by two of Limbaugh's heroes, his friend George Brett of the Kansas City Royals and former Chicago disc jockey Larry Lujack.

Special thanks, too, to Millie Limbaugh, who welcomed me into her home in Cape Girardeau, Missouri, late on a winter day, to talk about her son. And especially to Rush's brother (and attorney),

David S. Limbaugh, who patiently answered hours of questions in his Cape Girardeau office and on the telephone thereafter.

I also thank president Gary W. Rust and librarian Sharon Sanders at the *Southeast Missourian* in Cape Girardeau for opening the newspaper's clipping file to me.

My friends Mike Barson, John Williams, Lonnie Hanover, Gabriel Gluck, and *New York Newsday* columnist Dennis Duggan offered invaluable encouragement and advice from the earliest stages of this project. My longtime mentor, James C. G. Conniff, raked his ever-helpful pen through some of the weed-choked copy, as did Jerry Agel, valued friend.

To Doug Knopper, thanks for helping sort out the vagaries of the radio ratings. To Sister Mary Downey, thanks for the prayers. To my agent, Jane Dystel, thanks for putting it all together so painlessly. To my editor at St. Martin's, Tom Dunne, thanks for the direction along the way.

At *Newsday*, my colleagues Verne Gay and Ben Kubasik were generous fonts of small personal favors and large lessons about how the TV business works, while David Firestone and especially Susan Brenna doubled as valued boosters and editorial sounding boards. All you guys are great.

To librarian Christine Baird, who moonlighted on research, you are the best! To Anthony Marro, *Newsday*'s editor and senior vice president, a big thanks for streamlining the book-writing leave, and to my editors Phyllis Singer and John Capouya (now with *The New York Times*), thanks for making it all work out in the end.

To my parents, Joseph and Catherine Colford, loving thanks for the cheers in the grandstand and so much more. To my big brother Joe, thanks for those eleventh-hour insights.

Finally, I could never have completed this book without the love and understanding of my wife, Jane. She heard me out time and again, and she read through the chapters with her schoolteacher's eye. But most important of all, she managed to keep her sanity (and mine) on countless evenings and weekends while tending to our Catherine, four, and Liam, two, and steering them away from the attic office that became my Limbaugh Lounge.

I love you, Jane. You, too, kids. And look, it got done after all.

Introduction

When Rush Limbaugh reached New York in the summer of 1988, there was little reason to take a close look. At least not immediately. As the radio columnist at *Newsday*, I had seen so many conservative talk-show hosts come and go from the local dial that his arrival at WABC-AM seemed about as permanent as a manager's job with George Steinbrenner's Yankees.

There might be a column to write if Limbaugh and his "talent on loan from God" lasted more than a few months. But fat chance, right?

Wrong.

Limbaugh's chest-thumping style inspired a column five months afterward and other stories followed. Now, five years after his arrival, he is the cult figure who became a national phenomenon who became a conservative icon. As many in what he calls "the dominant media culture" tsk-tsk his polemics and ignore his role in the country's political debate, millions of Americans have bought into his Reagan-right message and his mischievous, bombastic persona.

The program on WABC and a second national broadcast that he launched later that summer on a few dozen other stations have grown into a one-man media conglomerate. On radio, "The Rush

Limbaugh Show" was being carried by six hundred stations and attracting more than sixteen million people a week in the spring of 1993. On television, his late-night session was third in the ratings behind "The Tonight Show" and "Nightline." His book, *The Way Things Ought to Be*, had sold more than two million copies and was still going strong. His onstage appearances around the country were drawing thousands of fans.

Limbaugh seemed to be everywhere. On the radio and on the tube. As host and as guest. ABC newsman Sam Donaldson speaking to the National Association of Radio Talk Show Hosts, told the broadcasters: "I listen to you all the time. But when I'm home in the Southwest, I merely hear Rush Limbaugh." His show blanketed the map. There was no escaping him.

It was no wonder that George Bush sought him out, put him up in the Lincoln Bedroom, and eventually asked to address his radio audience during the 1992 presidential campaign.

But who is Rush Limbaugh and where did he come from? How did he get here from there?

Except for a few in-depth pieces published in recent years, notably an insightful profile in *Vanity Fair* written by Peter J. Boyer, most articles have dwelled on his more recent success instead of his personal story. As that story is typically abbreviated, the son of small-town Missouri started out as a disc jockey, worked a few years with the Kansas City Royals, returned to radio and hit it big.

But these skeletal facts overlook Limbaugh's struggle early in his radio career, when creativity offered no protection against the whims of station managers. Some of them were so unimpressed with Limbaugh that they completely forgot about him until I pointed out that he had been on their payroll.

This book also describes the pivotal roles played by Rush H. Limbaugh, Jr., his domineering father; by Edward F. McLaughlin, the visionary and mostly unsung radio executive who took an unknown and turned him into a superstar, and by Roger Ailes, the combative political adviser who introduced Limbaugh to President Bush and also produced the TV show that has become the broadcaster's second front.

When Limbaugh has been asked how he managed to avoid military service during the Vietnam War, his plausible answer is repeated in most cases without challenge. But on that subject, too, the details spell out a different story.

Same thing with his political passion. Limbaugh has praised the conservative legacy of Ronald Reagan, but the laudatory remarks have masked a startling indifference. He did not register to vote until he was thirty-five years old, by which time he had sat out both of his hero's successful runs for the White House.

This book seeks not to judge Limbaugh or his ardent conservative views, but to illuminate his background, chart his bumpy road to respectability, detail his tremendous success, and document the unexpected impact he has had on broadcasting. It also endeavors to identify his place in the evolution of talk radio.

Is this book unauthorized?

The short answer is yes. But there is a longer answer, too.

In August 1992, about twenty minutes after I dropped off a note at WABC telling Limbaugh about the book and seeking an interview, he opened his radio broadcast by reading my correspondence. His voice brimmed with sarcasm. "Imagine my shock," he said. "Unauthorized bio, heh-heh-heh, gee . . . I think what I better do is think about anything that might embarrass me and admit it, you know, here. Go public with it so that nothing in this book is a surprise to anybody, but the thing is . . . I'm a dry ball. I've led a pretty ordinary, dull, uninteresting life."

On two other occasions, he told his listeners that this book would never come out because there was no dirt on him to interest a publisher. Even off the air, he stated so confidently that the book would never see print that his closest friends and associates believed it as well. Some of them looked shocked on hearing from me that the book was, in fact, under contract. How could Rush have been wrong?

Curiously, however, Limbaugh also conveyed the impression that he wanted the book to go forward. Although he never contacted me directly in response to my first note, or a second one weeks later, he made no effort that I could see to turn away potential sources or to end my continuing exchanges with others.

In a significant concession, he allowed his brother and his mother to be interviewed during my visit to their hometown of Cape Girardeau, Missouri. The hours spent with David Limbaugh, who also serves as his brother's attorney, were extremely helpful in understanding their boyhood and the deals that launched the radio and TV shows.

According to David, his brother did not want to speak with me because he intends to write an autobiography at a later date. In the meantime, it was as if the autobiographer-to-be wanted me to unearth the old stories and get them out there. A good friend of his surmised that Limbaugh welcomed this book simply because its publication would give him plenty to rant about.

I'm not so sure. For somewhere between Limbaugh's gypsy years as a disc jockey and the success that now earns him millions of dollars a year, the "dry ball" from Cape Girardeau came to embody a myth only partly of his own making. His bashing of liberals, his assaults on "feminazis," and his expanding role as a Republican party apologist came to obscure the soul within. I think this bothered him. "I am not a bigot. I am not a racist, a homophobe, male chauvinist pig, or any of that," he complained to an interviewer.

If there was a chance for his character and sincerity to break through all the controversy—for Limbaugh himself was by now ill suited to introspection—then I think he wanted that to happen. Even if the book exposed some dirt in the process.

This is no "harmless little fuzzball," as he would have us believe. Nor is he "the most dangerous man in America," as some of his ideological foes have argued.

The real Rush Limbaugh, controversial though he is, stands somewhere between those two poles. But far be it from me to call him a centrist. Front and center, yes. But centrist? Never.

THE RUSH LIMBAUGH STORY

Chapter 1

"RUSTY"

Cape Girardeau lies nestled in the southeast corner of Missouri about one hundred miles south of St. Louis on the way to Memphis. It's a town set apart by rolling hills, flat farmland, and a wide and treacherous expanse of the Mississippi River; a tidy city of older homes, dozens of churches, shopping malls, and industries that through the years have produced everything from crushed rock to breakfast rolls to Rush Limbaugh.

As the story goes, the community took its name, but not the correct spelling, from Jean Baptiste Girardot. He was a French ensign in the early eighteenth century who either left his station and crossed the Mississippi to establish a trading post with the Indians on the promontory now known as Cape Rock—or he made it there after being tossed overboard during a brawl. Years later, the Spanish occupied the settlement, and Don Louis Lorimier, the representative of the crown, persuaded East Coast farmers to move into the area. In 1806, three years after the Louisiana Purchase made the territory a possession of the United States, Lorimier laid out the town of Cape Girardeau.

The Limbaughs brought other colors to the regional mix. They were of German and Dutch extraction. The distinctive name Rush came from family member Edna Rush, whose descendants sought to keep her maiden name alive by giving it to her grandnephew more than a century later.

Rush Limbaugh, Sr., who turned 101 years old in 1992 and continued to practice law in Cape Girardeau, was the youngest of eight children born on a farm a few miles south of Sedgewickville, in adjoining Bollinger County. His father died when he was seven, so that he credited an older sister with engendering the love of oratory that he passed down to his son and grandson. She gave him a book of speeches that he read and committed to memory.

Rush Senior first moved into Cape Girardeau to attend the Normal School, now Southeast Missouri State University, and later went on to the University of Missouri's law school. When he returned to the city in 1916, it was to work with a local firm and to moonlight as a city prosecutor at the rate of three dollars per conviction. Eventually, he also served as an elected member of the Missouri House of Representatives and as chairman of the Cape Girardeau County Republican Committee. In time, he came to be recognized as one of the wise elders of Missouri.

He and his wife, Bee (Seabaugh), had five children, two of whom would make their own deep marks in civic circles.

Stephen N. Limbaugh was a partner in his father's law firm until President Ronald Reagan named him a U.S. District Court judge in 1983 (and his own son, Stephen N. Limbaugh, Jr., who had been a circuit judge in Cape Girardeau, was appointed to the Missouri Supreme Court in 1992). And then there was Rush H. Limbaugh, Jr., a wide mountain of a man who exceeded three hundred pounds much of his adult life as he impressed Cape Girardeau with a force of leadership and a gregariousness that swept up all those he set out to meet.

Rush Junior, the father of the conservative broadcaster and the single greatest influence on his life and politics, had already graduated from law school when he began military service in World War II as a flyer of fighter planes in the China-Burma-India theater. His experience with the Army Air Corps instilled a desire to introduce the wonders of aviation to his hometown as well.

In 1946, Cape Girardeau acquired Harris Field, a fifty-seven-acre army training facility. A $115,000 bond issue, whose passage

he strongly advocated, was used to develop the space into a municipal airport with a Naval Air Reserve unit attached to it. A two-
thousand-foot runway was doubled in length, and Rush Junior,
who was secretary of the airport board, helped convince Ozark Air
Lines to make Cape Girardeau Municipal Airport a stop on flights
between Memphis and St. Louis, beginning in 1951.

"CAPE LINKED WITH NATION," the local newspaper proclaimed,
noting that air mail reaching the afternoon flight from Cape Girardeau would be delivered the next day in either New York or Los
Angeles. "In a similar manner, air express can be received here in
a matter of hours, aiding the commercial life of the city." Salesmen,
contractors, and doctors added their own planes at the airport with
an eye toward extending their services well outside of town.

Rush Junior again squeezed himself behind the controls of a
plane. After meeting Mildred (Millie) Armstrong while the outgoing
native of Arkansas was studying in town at Southeast Missouri
State University, Rush Junior married her in 1949. He then taught
her how to fly.

In Cape Girardeau, as in many small towns, people have long
espoused an ordered, conservative view of the world, and none
more passionately than Rush Junior. A lawyer in a family full of
lawyers, he went on to head the Cape Girardeau County Republican organization—and beamed with satisfaction when he led vice-
presidential candidate Richard M. Nixon and his wife, Pat, in a
campaign swing along Main Street in 1952.

Rush Junior also was a pillar of the American Legion, the Veter-
ans of Foreign Wars, and the Rotary Club. He addressed local
groups on the evils of communism, taught Sunday school at his
Methodist church, coordinated naturalization ceremonies at the federal courthouse, and presided night after night over lively dinner-
table discussions in which he imparted unshakable political beliefs
to his two sons.

Rush Hudson Limbaugh III, known as Rusty, was born in 1951.
David Scott Limbaugh arrived two years later.

"David and Rusty weren't troublesome kids," Millie Limbaugh
recalls. "They both walked early, but they were about two years
old before they started talking. Rusty was two and a half when he

would look at the cars going down the street and identify each of them by name. 'Ford, Chevy,' like that. Now how in the world would a child pick that up?"

They read the Hardy Boys, *Robinson Crusoe* and other classics, and Rusty amassed a library in his bedroom. Outside their modest home at 412 Sunset Avenue, the action centered not on the Mississippi River, which had been long since hidden behind an ugly wall to protect against flooding in the downtown shopping district, but on an open field up the street. The tract, now occupied by the parking garage of a nearby hospital, was the scene of game after lazy summer game of baseball.

While most boys in the neighborhood loved the Cardinals—and on summer weekends Rush Junior used to fly his two sons up to St. Louis in the family's Cessna 182 to see the team play—Rusty favored the Los Angeles Dodgers. Specifically, the chubby Rusty liked the Dodgers' lean and bullet-fast Maury Wills, who stole a then-record 104 bases during the 1962 season. He corresponded with Wills and in 1965 he finally got to meet the ballplayer before a game in St. Louis. As the local newspaper reported the encounter, Wills told him "that in the art of stealing you must think and go at the same time."

Rusty also played baseball in the Babe Ruth League and later joined the jayvee football team at Cape Central High School. Coach Ryland (Dutch) Meyr remembers it well because "how many kids come up to the coach and give him the terms under which they'll play?" Meyr says he recruited Rusty in his sophomore year after seeing footballs "just explode off his foot" during gym class. "He had that natural pop, but he told me that he didn't want to do anything but kick. He was a good-looking specimen, a chunky guy, so I figured that after a while we'd put the pads on him and turn him into a defensive tackle."

Sure enough, Rusty kicked field goals for a few weeks before switching to the line in a season of five wins and a loss. "He participated reluctantly, but I think he learned to like it," Meyr says.

Rusty was not an outcast, but he was introverted and shy. He lacked confidence. He once hid himself in the backseat of a car so that he could steal a peek when a friend necked with a date up front—and thereby learn how to do it himself.

But when he got a sterling opportunity to grab a kiss of his own, the results were devastating. It happened during a game of spin-the-bottle. Round and round the bottle wobbled until it stopped and pointed to Rusty as the one who would now be kissed by one of the prettiest girls in high school. But she looked at him and gasped. Couldn't do it. Not with *him*, that is. And everyone in the room witnessed his humiliation. It was a wound he would nurse forever after.

"He did have a weight problem growing up, and being heavyset like that seemed hard on his self-esteem," recalls David, who went on to become a lawyer like his father. In fact, it is not so farfetched to imagine that this feeling of being separated from a hipper crowd was a factor in Rusty's ardent embrace of the Republican party later on. Speaking on the radio in 1992, he seemed to suggest that the GOP offered a haven from a sense of exile: "The Republican party is like a microcosm of those of us who are conservatives. Every day we are inundated by what is supposedly natural in this country, what is supposedly normal, what is supposedly in the majority, by virtue of what the dominant media culture shows us, and most often it's not us. Most often, what we believe in is made fun of, lampooned, impugned, and put down. Then, we don't want to feel that way. We want to feel as much a part of the mainstream as anybody else."

It was as if the GOP became a metaphor for the way he saw himself growing up: "made fun of, lampooned, impugned, and put down." Indeed, he returned to the image at other times on the air. What he saw as scorn for the party he recognized all too clearly in his own life. He seemed to identify with the GOP for reasons above and beyond those his Republican father held close.

In a similar vein, Rusty's affection for radio, which began when he was young, was propelled in large measure by a desire to win acceptance. He wanted to be the one "playing everybody's favorite songs." Or as he elaborated in an interview: "The initial allure [of radio] was that I hated school and I'd be getting ready for school every morning and my mother would be fixing breakfast, and I regretted that I had to go to school, and I'd be listening to the guy on the radio and he was having fun. And he didn't have to go to school, as far as I knew, and that's the first allure. The second allure was, I love music. And I wanted to be the guy playing everybody's favorite songs that they would listen to. And then, I wanted to stand out. I've always had an ego that wants to be up front, not background. And it just evolved into, I mean, radio is so much fun."

A personal favorite was Larry Lujack, a lovably irascible disc jockey whose shows on WLS, the 50,000-watt Chicago station, reached Cape Girardeau loud and clear. Lujack would influence Rusty's own radio style to a much greater degree than the future talk-show host would acknowledge years later.

Rusty also used to imitate sports announcer Harry Caray, who was then doing play-by-play for the Cardinals and pumping extra excitement into the best of games. Turning down the volume during telecasts, Rusty assumed the Caray role as he supplied his own play-by-play. In addition, a toy electronics gadget allowed him to transmit his voice on the AM dial inside the house, thus inspiring him to broadcast entire "radio shows" of music and banter into the kitchen. And some of those programs he put on tape. One day, his mother went to play her reel of songs featuring the King Sisters, only to find that Rusty had erased the music by dubbing over his own domestic broadcasts.

As a teenager, Rusty filled the gap between himself and his more confident peers, between a drudgery that he felt at school and the lofty expectations of his father, with this love of broadcasting. He came to like broadcasting much more than baseball and football. It belonged to him. It was his refuge.

"He was precocious, but he was also proficient," David says. "He was always walking around practicing with his voice. I always thought it was affected when he practiced his 'radio voice,' when he enunciated every word. But it was almost as though he knew that this is what he would be doing later on in his life."

Fortunately for him, a real-world opportunity presented itself early on. His father owned a small piece of local station KGMO-

AM (now KAPE-AM) and that connection allowed Rusty to get his own radio show while still in high school. "That was luck," he said later. "I fell into it."

Calling himself Rusty Sharpe, because almost all disc jockeys adopted names snappier than their own, he took to the airwaves at the end of the school day and played rock music while the other kids were off being kids. Although the late sixties were a pivotal time in rock and roll, with the emergence of the Doors, Jefferson Airplane, the Byrds, and other lyric-minded acts from the West Coast, Rusty didn't inhale. "I never really listened to the lyrics," he said. "Rock to me was never anything special. It's all about rebellion and blue jeans . . . I have never owned a pair of blue jeans."

His parents clung to the hope that the radio thrills would give way to a more serious appreciation of school, but Rusty would have none of that. He became absorbed in radio and hated school all the more because of his passion. He gave up football and the debate club after only one school year's involvement because he had no more time for them. In addition, in the summer of 1967, when he was sixteen years old, his mother and father let him study at the Elkins Institute of Radio and Electronics in far-off Dallas for the government license needed to operate a radio station during the hours when he would be alone on duty.

He stayed in a rooming house run by a woman who heard from a concerned Millie Limbaugh throughout the six weeks he was away. Nevertheless, he took advantage of his freedom and started smoking cigarettes, to his parents' horror when he returned home. He also headed further down his own road by disc-jockeying on KGMO not only after school, but on weekends, too.

"I knew the boy had talent," Millie says. But to his father, radio seemed like such a fleeting occupation that he feared for the youngster's financial stability later on. However, it was already too late. Rusty was hooked, doubly so because he believed that being on the radio gave him a sure shot at popularity among the other kids at Cape Central High School—though it didn't happen that way.

His classmates came to consider him a snob. With his retro flattop, which grew awkwardly out of shape in his junior year,

Rusty also never looked the part. Adding stress to the struggle, he ended up in a hospital emergency room when the glass in a door at the high school gave way as he was pushing on it. A dozen stitches in each arm, and who would believe it?

He hated being a kid because only adults seemed to care about what he had to say. "Rush was never much of a kid himself," David recalls. "He preferred adults. It was his choice."

"My father was constantly stressing the importance of education, and he would educate us," David adds. "He was a student of government and politics. As the evening news was running on television, he provided a running commentary. He was consumed by politics and patriotism. My father also forced you to think. He gave us discriminating minds, he trained us to think logically and to justify our reasoning. If he heard a statistic on the news, for example, he'd say, 'Now why should I believe that?' "

The father's fascination with politics prompted him to read about communism and Karl Marx so as to better inform the talks he was often asked to give before local groups. He told his audiences that communism was bad and he challenged the notion that communism in its purest form offered a utopia. Meanwhile, he advanced a law practice that represented numerous corporate clients, including out-of-state companies that he served as local counsel. His success enabled the family to move from the small house on Sunset Avenue to a far more spacious dwelling at 846 Karau Lane, an upscale neighborhood in a wooded corner of Cape Girardeau's north side.

Although Rush Junior wanted to make Rusty recognize the error in his choice of radio, the father was blind to the knowledge that his son had learned well from his namesake and shared his views. Rush Junior failed to see that Rusty's wish to make his own decisions was a rebellion without rebelliousness; he was an iconoclast who did not wear blue jeans. What's more, just as Rusty's desire for acceptance fueled his entry into radio at an early age, the hope of pleasing his hard-to-please father no doubt went a long way to harden his support of the conservative Republican cause—his father's cause—which held added appeal as a haven from slings and arrows. Nevertheless, it would be two contentious decades before

Rush Junior realized that his itinerant son had been following in his path all along.

"I really consider the greatest education I ever got was from my dad," he told the Cape Girardeau paper while his father, one of its readers, was still alive. "I never told him that. But I really think I learned more just from the times that we would sit down and talk and argue than I did in any other way."

His father was his hero. "I would get mad at him," he said. "Nothing was ever good enough for him, and I got very angry, but the desire to please eventually took second place to the desire to actually do my best."

And the community outside the Limbaugh home reflected the father's views. For all of Cape Girardeau's ties to adventurers and pioneers in its history, the Cape of Rusty's formative years sustained no currents of dissent and offered little evidence of individualism to challenge the beliefs imprinted on him by Rush Junior. The son would head off into the world imbued with a conservative creed that was stiffened by the near absence of differing opinions.

The city exhibited dramatic growth when Rusty was growing up during the 1960s; a population surge of more than 8,000 people brought the total to around 34,000. But the political climate remained conservative. When Lyndon B. Johnson overwhelmed Barry Goldwater in the 1964 presidential election by winning an additional 22 percent of the popular vote, his margin of victory over the right-wing Republican in Cape Girardeau was only 14 percent.

The turbulence of the sixties, with its radical changes in fashion, sexuality, music, and politics triggered in large measure by youthful outrage over United States involvement in the Vietnam War, bypassed Cape Girardeau and its Norman Rockwell sense of reality. The outside world did not intrude. Indeed, even physically, southeast Missouri remained somewhat isolated; the interstate highway connecting the city to St. Louis was not completed until 1972.

In 1968, a year when the Democratic National Convention was rocked by widespread anti-Vietnam demonstrations that turned bloody in the Chicago streets, Cape Central High School students worried about the back-to-school dance, Safety Week, the talent show, a canned food drive, and Beautify Central Week. At Southeast Missouri State University, eight freethinking instructors were let go by the administration, which helped counter a resulting protest outside the president's house by using the school's burly football players as sentries, First Amendment rights be damned. In the November election, when Nixon squeaked to victory over Hubert H. Humphrey by around a half-million votes, the Republican swamped his opponent in Cape Girardeau County. Nixon received 10,298 votes to Humphrey's 6,656—and George Wallace, the third-party "law and order" candidate, collected a respectable 2,351.

In 1969, Rusty's senior year, the high school's Student Council "led the way to greater achievement through student involvement," the yearbook reported. "The new Tiger Den was furnished with a record player, lounge chairs and pictures." Graduation photographs in the university's yearbook depicted a strikingly fiftieslike collection of finely coiffed young ladies and well-groomed young men in jackets and ties. A few members of the Association of Black Collegians raised their fists in Black Power salutes—and smiled benignly for the camera. And the war, which elsewhere fostered a sense of fatalism among so many men who feared having to fight in remote jungles, continued with little, if any, argument in Cape Girardeau. Here, United States involvement was considered right and just.

After graduation, Rusty reluctantly enrolled at Southeast Missouri State, known by the locals as "Cape State" because many of its 6,700 students lived in town. His father, whose firm handled the school's legal affairs, preached that a college degree would do him good and enhance job prospects later on. But to Rusty, the college grind only delayed the full-blown radio career that he craved. His parents eventually came to see that, too, as periodic grade reports showed him stumbling in almost all the courses that he bothered to attend. Yet in the beginning, the frustrated Rush Junior was so committed to his son's advancement that he went so far as to intrude in his academic life in a manner that would have turned most college students green with embarrassment.

Rusty failed Speech 101, for example, and repeated the course. He simply stayed away from ballroom dancing, which would have fulfilled his physical-education requirement. He snapped out of his malaise only during a course in American government, taught by Peter Bergerson, a liberal instructor from Chicago who has since become chairman of SEMO's political science department.

"His father called me at home and asked how Rusty was doing in my class," Bergerson recalls. "I thought it was strange that a parent would phone, and it could even have been mortifying for Rusty. But his father was very gregarious, very self-driven, and he almost always thought he was right. It was the first month of school and he was concerned about Rusty, who was having a difficult time in his life. It was very trying for him to exert his independence and difficult to do so under his father. He had an urge for independence, but he still held his father in awe.

"I told him to have Rusty come see me. I wasn't much older than Rusty at the time. I was twenty-five. But he did come in and I got to know him well."

As Bergerson remembers it, "the lights went on" when Rusty was in the American government course, which analyzed contemporary politics and the role of the Constitution and required students to make oral representations and participate in class discussions. "This Socratic method was a natural for Rusty," he says. "He liked to talk about issues. I wasn't really aware that he was doing so poorly in his other courses because he was doing so well in mine." In the end, he earned an A.

Rusty's ease in speaking out was also apparent when he repeated Speech 101, only this time with results different from what Bergerson applauded. Again, Rush Junior intervened, approaching a teacher in the department, Bill W. Stacy, and asking him to help warm Rusty to college life. As Stacy recalls, "He said to me, 'Bill, I've got the smartest kid in the world, he's fascinated by radio and communications. I'm trying to get him excited about intellectual pursuits, but he's turned off by school. Could you get him excited by tapping into his feeling for communications?' "

Stacy took a special interest in Rusty as a favor to the family and watched with awkwardness as the student displayed his gifts, but not in compliance with instructions. One assignment was to give a speech explaining a position, but to first lay out what the point was, the explanatory devices to be used, and the organizational approach.

Stacy intended to have the students prepare their sources in advance of the presentation. When the day came, however, Rusty said he forgot about the assignment. Nevertheless, he got up from his desk, walked to the front of the classroom and began speaking, "about what, I can't recall, but he did it beautifully and cogently. All eyes were open and on him. The students were just agog at how good he was."

But Stacy hit him with a D for the effort, to the class's astonishment. Why? "Because he didn't have an outline. He made it up as he went along. Here you had the class taking in his language flow, his poise, and I'm saying that he's talented but he can't get by on his confidence, that he's got to do it my way, that he's got to have data and citations."

He adds: "He got a D but he was damn good. And he didn't need the D. Here I was saying, 'You're good, but you have more to learn,' and he's thinking, 'The heck with you, pal.' The audience was enraptured. He saw it in the looks on their faces. They liked every bit of it. And that was good enough for him."

Stacy recognized the contradiction and its likely impact on the reluctant student. "I felt I struck out," the teacher says. "Rusty was talented, but he was already marching to his own drummer. I felt a smugness, that he was not ready to listen to a teacher."

In retrospect, it appears that the evocative young speaker simply was unwilling to apply classic rhetorical skills to what he had to say. There was something entrepreneurial and inventive in his approach—call it an instinct for instant analysis, learned from a father who also told it as he saw it—that clashed with the ground rules of academe.

He moped along at SEMO through the summer session of 1970. By that time, he had had enough and dropped out. He hated being force-fed a lot of stuff that he didn't care about. He hated the whole teacher-to-student, formalized classroom setup. He thought he already knew everything that school could teach him. More important to him, his love for the KGMO job that he had held for four years now—a job that filled his needs more than adequately— underscored a belief that everything would turn out fine.

In the God-fearing, conservative city, a model of conformity, he finally rebelled against the father-knows-best, be-a-lawyer line while adhering to the political views at its core. He convinced himself as a college freshman that he had something to say—and that, too, was unusual in Cape Girardeau. Years later, he would conclude that he actually knew very little back then and realize that he would have to demonstrate his intelligence in lieu of a college diploma.

But for now, he had but one other encumbrance to his future.

Chapter 2

BEATING THE DRAFT

In the 1992 presidential campaign, Limbaugh discussed with a radio caller the lingering questions over Bill Clinton's and Vice President Dan Quayle's draft status during the Vietnam War. Quayle's peaceful service in the Indiana National Guard and Clinton's dogged and effective maneuvers to stay out of the military continued to come under media scrutiny.

Limbaugh argued that Clinton's evasiveness on his draft history represented yet another character flaw. A like-minded President Bush visited the radio show and used the forum to needle Clinton for a "total failure to come clean with the American people" on the draft issue.

As for Limbaugh himself, the broadcaster stated that he was not drafted during the Vietnam War because he had been classified 4-F after a physical found that he had an "inoperable pilonidal cyst" and "a football knee from high school." He added: "I made no effort to evade it or avoid it."

But Limbaugh held up the 4-F classification—which he did not get until the war was winding down and which suggested a debilitating incapacity—as a more persuasive defense against would-be detractors than was supported by the facts. Limbaugh's version of his own situation was a highly condensed version of a detailed chronology. There was much more to the story.

When Limbaugh left Southeast Missouri State University in 1970, after two semesters and a summer semester, he stood to lose his 2-S college deferment at a time of continued risk for a young man of draft age. For on July 1, 1970, he and all other nineteen-year-olds faced the draft lottery that was to determine their order of military call-up in 1971.

Although Limbaugh's January 12 birthdate was assigned number 152 in the lottery, it was hard that summer to figure with certainty whether 152 would be high enough to legally escape induction. After all, there was no standard to go by; 1970 was only the first year in the Vietnam era in which the draft was being governed to some degree by the lottery, which had been reinstituted late in 1969. And adding to Limbaugh's uncertainty, there had yet to be implemented a uniform order of call-up. Despite the issuance of lottery numbers, some local draft boards were summoning men with higher numbers than other boards, and boards were still operating on a quota system.

In Cape Girardeau County, for example, Selective Service Board No. 16 responded in 1970 to manpower orders handed down from the state office in Jefferson City by drafting three men in February, six in March, nine in April, nine in July, and so on before all boards throughout the country were limited as of September to lottery numbers no higher than 195 for the balance of 1970. Even so, all those with numbers through 215 also were called for physicals.

For Limbaugh and other nineteen-year-olds, their 1971 year of prime eligibility would not necessarily be a mirror image of 1970. Still, the ceiling of 195 set in 1970 was a sign to go by, and stories in the local newspaper were less than encouraging. American involvement in the Vietnam War had begun to ebb, with 50,000 troops expected to leave Southeast Asia by mid-October, 1970, but 417,000 remained and a bloody, two-month-long incursion against enemy forces in Cambodia had ended only recently. The Paris peace talks were stalled at the time Limbaugh drew the three digits that seemed to position him only midway between a sure summons to the military and a sure escape from its grasp.

But four months after the lottery, Board No. 16 effectively spared Limbaugh. Records indicate that the panel acted on medical information obtained at his own initiative, most likely from his physician, and classified him 1-Y on November 24, 1970. In the parlance of the Selective Service System, 1-Y meant that Limbaugh was "conditionally acceptable" for military duty but would be called up only in the event of a declared war or national emergency, neither of which applied to Vietnam.

Selective Service System records stored in Washington show that Limbaugh's 1-Y classification was made not on the basis of mental or moral considerations, as the law allowed, but as a result of a physical factor—possibly the cyst or the knee problem that he later referred to on the air. According to the Military Entrance Processing Command, a pilonidal cyst was then and is today a so-called "disqualifying condition" for induction. It's a congenital incomplete closure of the neural groove at the base of the spinal cord in which excess tissue and hair may collect and cause discomfort and discharge. The malady can be corrected by surgery, but short of that it is viewed by the military as a needless risk amid unsanitary conditions in the field.

The 1-Y protected Limbaugh against having to join the military. But Limbaugh did not mention the 1-Y classification to his radio caller amid reports of Clinton's own evasiveness. The broadcaster also omitted reference to his 1-Y during a subsequent public appearance, even though he had held 1-Y for more than a year—until all 1-Ys were changed to 4-F as American involvement in the war waned.

Why the selective explanation? It may well have been because 1-Y sounded, and indeed was, far less grave than 4-F, an outright disqualification that originally denoted more severe medical concerns.

Clearly, after Limbaugh had repeatedly pounded Clinton on his draft history and called the candidate's character into question, the broadcaster appeared sensitive to any suggestion of murkiness in his own draft picture. His playful boast much earlier that his father may have bribed the local draft board to get him a 4-F had backfired when listeners, including Dad himself, called his radio show in anger. And the matter did not go away, at least not entirely.

On October 5, 1992, shortly after President Bush went on Limbaugh's program and ripped Clinton on the draft, *The New York Observer*, a feisty weekly newspaper whose influence far exceeds its modest circulation, ran a revealing front-page story. It told how records "contradict Mr. Limbaugh's own explanation for his failure to serve in the military." The piece, written by freelancer Peter Donald, noted that a pilonidal cyst is not bothersome unless it becomes infected, and it quoted David Limbaugh as saying that their father had had the same thing and "lied to get *into* the service." The inference that could be drawn by the *Observer*'s readers was that Limbaugh, fearing that number 152 might not be high enough to avoid Vietnam, latched on to the pilonidal cyst—after the lottery was held—with confidence that the condition would sideline him from the draft, as indeed it did.

In any event, the Vietnam-era draft records retained by the Selective Service System and examined for the purposes of this book make it appear that Board No. 16 accepted the word of Limbaugh's own doctor. For there is no notation showing that the panel ordered its own examination, nor do the records indicate that one was administered by a physician in the Armed Forces Entrance Examining Stations, the forerunner of today's Military Entrance Processing Command.

In other words, it seems that Limbaugh presented a medical report obtained on his own before the draft board might have reclassified him 1-A or, at the very least, ordered him to undergo an Armed Forces examination as a preparatory step toward a possible draft. The records reveal that in 1971 Board No. 16 routinely directed men in Limbaugh's age pool who held lottery numbers similar to and higher than his 152 to get an Armed Forces physical. Local men holding the numbers 145, 151, 166, 168, and 172 submitted to these examinations. Only later in 1971 did the Selective Service System impose a draft ceiling of number 125 for that year.

The documentation presented by Limbaugh for the board's consideration most likely is gone forever. Records on individuals, including medical files, were ordered destroyed after the draft ended in 1973. File folders maintained by Board No. 16 were forwarded to the region's federal records center for destruction in April 1974.

Lolla Gilbert, who was executive secretary of the board until 1974, said in early 1993 that she could not remember Limbaugh's case, "but not everybody went to St. Louis for physical examinations. If someone submitted a letter from a doctor, the board had its own medical advisers who would review the case. If the medical advisers passed on it, then the board passed on it."

It has been suggested that Limbaugh's physician at the time of the 1-Y classification was Dr. John T. Crowe, who died in 1988 at age sixty-nine. He is remembered in Cape Girardeau as a tireless surgeon who also delivered three thousand babies before retiring in 1985. In addition, Crowe was an active aviator who worked with Limbaugh's father to push for development of the municipal airport following World War II.

Limbaugh's mother said in 1993 that she did not know if her son had a physical or not, but she added that he did have a pilonidal cyst like his father.

Asked about Limbaugh's "football knee from high school," Meyr, the coach during his lone year of play, said he did not remember any injury.

David Limbaugh, who underwent an army physical and served in the Missouri National Guard after drawing a low number in his own draft lottery, laughs at the idea that his brother might have schemed in any way to avoid military service because their father "would have turned him in." The father's view was that the United States should be fighting to win in Vietnam.

Limbaugh's draft status arose during a 1992 appearance at the 92nd Street YM-YWHA in Manhattan. ABC newsman Jeff Greenfield, acting as moderator, said he had found Limbaugh's on-air explanation of his draft history "completely convincing." Still, he posed to Limbaugh a written question from the audience about whether he had ever served in the military.

In response, Limbaugh chose his words slowly and cautiously. He seemed to be saying that he had not known ahead of time that whatever physical condition he had in 1970 would free him from draft consideration.

"I had student deferments in college," he began, using the plural "deferments," as if he had been in college longer than three semesters, "and, upon taking a physical, was discovered to have a physical—uh, by virtue of what the military says, I didn't even know it existed—a physical deferment and then the lottery system came along, when they chose your lot by your birthdate, and mine was high. And I did not want to go—just as Governor Clinton didn't."

"Fine," Greenfield said, moving on.

But the lottery had come first, putting Limbaugh in draft limbo, and his "physical deferment" was formalized afterward, when he faced the prospect of being classified 1-A. Limbaugh also did not explain that whatever "physical" he had undergone differed markedly from the image that an audience probably would hold of men in their underwear being examined by an impassive military man. Whoever looked him over probably was an acquaintance, such as his personal physician. (My attempt via David Limbaugh to have Rush clarify the particulars of his physical was unsuccessful.)

Nevertheless, the 1-Y that the board assigned Limbaugh in 1970 made him a free man, so that 1971 would not be a nail-biter after all. The draft classification also served as a kind of ticket to ride into the future.

Soon afterward, Limbaugh got a call from Tim Daniels, who had worked on a local station and knew "Rusty Sharpe." Daniels was offering him a job on WIXZ-AM in McKeesport, Pennsylvania. "Well, he didn't say McKeesport, he said Pittsburgh," Limbaugh later told the city's *Post-Gazette*.

At first, the small-town Rush didn't know if he was ready for the Big Time. But he did know that he had given up on college. It was February 1971. He had just turned twenty. "When he was getting ready to leave, I told him, 'Whatever you do, be humble and respect your bosses,' " Millie remembers. "Of course, he was the wrong guy for that advice."

"I got in my blue Pontiac Le Mans, 1969, that I purchased with the meager earnings that I made and I headed here [to Pennsylvania] in the middle of winter . . . not knowing where I was going and having all kinds of car trouble. My whole experience in Pittsburgh was typified by that trip. Things happened to me that never happened to me before and I didn't know how to deal with them and I had to learn how. I'd never rented an apartment, I didn't know what a security deposit was, I didn't know what joining a union was, I didn't really know what program directors did at radio stations."

What he did know for sure was that he had left home and stepped out of his father's overarching shadow. At least for a while. No more worrying about whether the others liked him. No more satisfying his father's wish that he finish college.

"The last three years I lived here were probably the most agonizing years of my life, for a lot of personal reasons," he later told his hometown's *Southeast Missourian*. "After leaving Cape Girardeau, for the next ten years of my life, everything I did was framed by, 'I'll show them.' "

Chapter 3

THE BIG TIME

For Limbaugh, McKeesport was the Big Time. Its six and a half square miles totaled less than half the size of Cape Girardeau, but the population of 38,000 was slightly larger, and the smoke of production rose from the steel mills in plumes of industrial might.

The station was WIXZ-AM, a tiny Top 40 operation whose daytime signal was strong enough to reach most of the Pittsburgh market, one of the nation's largest.

At the time, the hits ruled AM radio. Air personalities were expected to ruffle the airwaves with patter between the platters. And Limbaugh was a personality—and a creative one at that.

Working on the air as Jeff Christie, an easy-to-remember name he would use through the 1970s, Limbaugh embraced the job and the business. He first had an afternoon show and later did mornings. Between shifts, he would spend hours and hours at the station, even when he didn't have to. A radio junkie to the core. A character who would bend the rules. If the format called for ten songs an hour, he would never quite get to that tenth record. If the newsman was out sick, he would take much longer on his own to read through the copy.

In Christiespeak, the Chicago Cubs were the "Chubbies," the

Pittsburgh Civic Arena was the "Septic Arena," Bryant Gumbel was "Bryant Gumball," and Tom Jones was "Tommy Tight Pants."

Doing a bubbly morning show in 1972, he would get to the station well before the 6:00 A.M. sign-on and spend time with a bunch of newspapers and magazines, to the amazement of his colleagues. He is remembered off the air at WIXZ as a voraciously well-read student of current events who was quick to share his conservative worldview. But on the air, he was as goofy as the format called for.

"I was like everybody else who is twenty and quits college," he later told the *Pittsburgh Press*. "I wanted to be a personality DJ. I was always possessed with the desire to be the reason people listen to the radio."

To lighten the show's commuter advisories, for example, he invented the infamous "Pitt Talk Tube" and cast Rick Toretti, a Penn State student who wrote the show's half-hourly newscasts, in the equally fictitious role of a helicopter pilot surveying Pittsburgh's chronic crunch of traffic. "One car is backed up five feet," Toretti announced one morning over the sound of a whirring propeller, not long before Limbaugh canned the bit by having the copter "crash" on the air into radio oblivion.

Another time, Limbaugh tried to reach Queen Elizabeth, failed to get through, but ended up interviewing the head of the monarch's household. "It was so easy to recognize his talent," said Raymond Gardella, who was then WIXZ's general manager. "He had a lot of drive and ambition." Gardella likened his performance to that of "the early Imus." Don Imus, a wildly inventive morning man, was then taking hold on the New York dial at WNBC-AM.

Limbaugh recalled years later how he would visit a local department store before doing an afternoon show and then call one of the salesclerks during his program to say that he was speaking on one of those new "picture phones." He said this amazing phone could actually show the party being called. Unconvinced, naturally, the clerk would then hear Limbaugh describe in all too convincing detail what she was wearing at that very moment.

"My strongest memory is that he loved to have his back scratched," said Mary Jane Wolf, who supervised commercial production at the station. "Even during his morning show, he would say to me, 'Please scratch my back,' and then when he was talking on the air he would say, 'Ahh, one of the secretaries is scratching my back right now and it feels so good.' "

And there was plenty of back to scratch. Limbaugh had yet to balloon into a 300-plus giant; he would let that happen after reaching New York more than a decade later. But he was pressing the scale at about 250 when a concerned Gardella bet him a new wardrobe that he could not lose sixty pounds. Accepting the challenge, Limbaugh cut back, and over time he had to bring his belt in notch after notch to hold up his pants on a shrinking waistline. In the end, he got the new clothes, though he would put back the weight again and again. It was always a problem.

WIXZ was a revolving door of talent, but Limbaugh hung on longer than most, even though his brash and youthful manner came to put him at odds with Gardella.

During this period, he also had an eye for women. One woman shared his first sexual experience—for Limbaugh was finally away from home, after all. He took another date to a restaurant in Pittsburgh and tried to impress her with his knowledge of wines. After asking the sommelier which year was good for the wine he wanted, he was told: "For you, sir, the year you drink it."

Limbaugh was working at WIXZ a short time when another twenty-year-old disc jockey joined the station from Harrisburg, Pennsylvania. Bill Figenshu, who would go on to a lofty position as head of Viacom Broadcasting's radio division, took up Limbaugh's invitation to split the $200-a-month rent on his basement apartment in the nearby town of Irwin—the apartment where Rush had notched his first sexual conquest.

Their bachelor digs had green shag carpeting, a kitchenette, rented furniture, and "hot and cold running cockroaches," recalls Figenshu, who was known during his evening show as Bill Steele. "The guy was a slob. Every six months we would clean the bathroom and collect the pizza boxes. Our lives were total radio. Cleanliness was not a high priority. We would do the laundry together on a Saturday and suck down the pizza burgers as the clothes spun around.

"We had our dreams at that point. We just weren't sure where we were going."

In time, however, Figenshu peeled off to work in the bold new world of FM radio, moving to a progressive-rock station in Nashville. He took a cut in the $150-a-week pay that the roommates were earning under the AFTRA contract at WIXZ to flee the nitwit tunes that passed for hits in the early 1970s. The Osmonds were big ("One Bad Apple"), as were the Bee Gees ("How Can You Mend a Broken Heart") and the Partridge Family ("Doesn't Somebody Want to Be Wanted"). But Limbaugh was a personality and personalities worked in Top 40. The idea that FM would someday surge in popularity was inconceivable.

Among those enjoying Limbaugh's on-air routine was Bob Harper, the program director at Pittsburgh's KQV, the number-two station in the market behind KDKA and one of the country's leading Top 40 outlets. "I would listen to him in my car and he would crack me up," he says.

"We were looking for guys to move the format, to move the music along. The master at this sort of thing was Dan Ingram at WABC in New York. He would talk over records and be funny in these short bursts. And Rush was incredible that way, too."

"I think we fired him," Gardella remembered hazily in 1992. Indeed, Limbaugh's version had it that he was dismissed by WIXZ after eighteen months over a "personality conflict" with the program director. Limbaugh later said he had played too loose with the playlist, airing the Rolling Stones' "Under My Thumb" too often. "I loved the song . . . and I violated the music rotation by playing it every day. . . . I was having a personality spat with the PD [program director] at the time and you know how these things are. I mean, they look for the nearest convenient excuse they can."

Harper hired him in 1973 to succeed KQV's evening disc jockey, Jim Quinn, who had made it to New York. Limbaugh, who by this time was sporting a mustache that swept off jauntily at each end and hair that covered his ears, would report to work early and circulate around the station to greet people in the various departments. Then when it was time to go on the air, he settled into a studio that put the disc jockey on display to pedestrians passing by

Seventh and Smithfield—"the corner of Walk and Don't Walk" in KQV parlance—who cared to stop at the railing outside and peer through the showcase window.

Still, for all the visibility that KQV gave him, Limbaugh understood that people tuned in mainly for the music and so it was silly to take himself too seriously. He recognized the artificial nature of being the man at the mike and hyped the setup with laughs while pretending to be a superheavy rock jock. "You put these fellows in a banal setting, and ask them to perform in a structured, artificial environment, but every once in a while you get someone who puts a certain spin on the assignment," Harper says.

Within the tight constraints of KQV's format, Limbaugh began to forge the bombastic, on-air persona that would prove so popular in national syndication more than a decade later. He spoofed being a disc jockey in the way that Steve Martin would come to parody a standup comedian during his own standup routine: "Now, I'm going to play two commercials, a public service announcement, and a record, with one hand behind my back, and I will do it all flawlessly in eight minutes and ten seconds."

Listeners may have been none the wiser, but other broadcasters got his joke on KQV ("14-K") and loved it. "The really good guys know that the broadcast has to happen on more than one level," says Harper, who has since formed his own radio consulting firm. "Rush instinctively got that very early on."

The seamless pacing of his evening show among the jingles, bells, gongs, songs, weather forecasts, and snippets of banter bore the mark of a Top 40 pro. Always speak over the opening notes of a record and always cut out at the precise second that the first lyric is sung.

Some chatter from his show as preserved on a rare recording made April 12, 1974:

"Fourteen-K. You are just minutes away from fourteen hits in a row. About fifteen minutes from now. David Chastity [Cassidy] and the Partridge Family in love." Fade up: "I Think I Love You."

Spoken in a nasal ringmaster's bark over the calliope circus music that opens Three Dog Night's "The Show Must Go On": "Fourteen-K! Hurry, hurry. Step right up, ladies and gentlemen, yes, step right up for a choice front-row seat, for the award-winning Jeff Christie rock-and-roll radio show. And we now direct your attention to the center ring, where the Terrific Trampolinis will perform their death-defying act of walking a tightrope seventy-five feet above a pit of hungry Australian rabbit bats, all the while balancing Tommy the Tiger on a unicycle. In the event of an early supper, fear not. The show will go on, for as we all know, the show must go on."

"Music radio, Fourteen-K. You little crumb crunchers are just about five minutes away from fourteen hits in a row. Right now, McCartney and Wings and 'Jet.' "

Over the eerie beginning to Mike Oldfield's "Tubular Bells," the theme of "The Exorcist": "Musicradio Fourteen-K, with The Great Fourteen-K Giveaway, where you and your family can win one of thousands of prizes. Be listening starting Monday on Fourteen-K. Jeff Christie, a Friday night, kicking off fourteen hits in a row. This is gonna add up, you people, ah, let's see, to at least forty-seven and a half uninterrupted minutes of music this hour."

"Eight-sixteen at Fourteen-K. The award-winning Jeff Christie rock-and-roll radio show, with fourteen hits in a row, the sound-track to Christie training film number nine . . ." And then he brought up "Pillow Talk," a sexy tune by Sylvia.

". . . Stick that thumb up in the air, Vanity Fair": Fade up: "A thumb goes up . . . ride, ride, ride, hitchin' a ride."

"Good evening to you, music lovers, all across the fruited plain, it's eight twenty-nine at Fourteen-KQV . . . You are smack el-dabbo in the middle of fourteen uninterrupted hits in a row with song number one": Elton John's "Benny and the Jets."

"Eight thirty-four at Fourteen-K, Jeff Christie rock-and-roll radio show with fun and frolic for all, forging onward into the pitch of black on a Friday night. David Essex rocking on in the middle of fourteen in a row." Fade up: "Rock On."

Limbaugh was already using one of his current signature phrases, "across the fruited plain." And this next song intro reveals an early use of "excellence in broadcasting," the nickname he would later give the network of stations that carry his national show.

"Nine oh-three at Fourteen-K on the award-winning Jeff Christie rock-and-roll radio show, with fun and frolic for all, some of you no doubt still wondering what award I have won. I'll tell you: none other than the Marconi Award for excellence in broadcasting." Fade up: Elton John's "Crocodile Rock."

This rapid-fire disc jockeying helped prepare Limbaugh for his current labors more solidly than it might at first seem. "Being a deejay teaches you the elements of broadcasting that are crucial, no matter what kind of show you're doing—timing, brevity, quickness, get in, get it, and get out," Limbaugh said. "It just gives you the basic fundamentals of broadcasting that you need."

At the same time, even a cursory listen to Jeff Christie on KQV— "often imitated, often mimicked, often copied, but never equaled"—reveals how much he himself copied his idol, longtime Chicago disc jockey Larry Lujack. Mainly, it was from Lujack, who called himself "Superjock," that Limbaugh took the seeds for his own boastful persona.

But there was more to the Lujack worship than a young fan's borrowing from the Chicago jock's on-air shtick. Limbaugh's suggestion that his early appropriations were the only ones overlooks his striking use later on—in the 1990s—of Lujack's actual lines and audible mannerisms. At KQV, however, the fist-tight format allowed Limbaugh only so much license to show off his or anybody else's stuff.

To work in Pittsburgh radio was to feel poised for the really big markets. After all, Jim Quinn, whom Limbaugh followed at KQV, had graduated to WPLJ-FM in New York and disc jockeys Fred Winston and Gary Gears had moved on to Chicago. KQV further enhanced such promise because it was owned by the mighty ABC, whose flagship station was the one and only WABC in New York, the Top 40 powerhouse of Dan Ingram and Cousin Brucie. Its chimes and sounders echoed in KQV's own presentation.

In short, KQV was the right place and the right company. But as Limbaugh would learn time and again, good fortune in the radio business lasts only so long as the ownership, the management, and the format favor what you do. Any one of these elements could change overnight and often did, thereby upsetting the whole. As it turned out, KQV became a ticket to nowhere.

Toward the end of 1974, ABC prepared to sell KQV to Taft Broadcasting. Meanwhile, lame-duck management pressed Jim Carnegie, the new program director, to fire Limbaugh. "For about ninety days, they kept telling me to fire him, saying he was a no-talent bum," Carnegie says. "But I was very pleased with the guy. Finally, I either had to fire him or get fired along with him. I called him in and gave him the bad news. He was hurt because he knew he was doing a good job."

To add insult to the pain, general manager John Gibbs reportedly told Limbaugh that he would never make it as an air talent and that he should seriously consider going into the sales end of the radio business. Gibbs was so unimpressed with Christie's skills that in 1992 he claimed to have no recollection of employing the disc jockey, even when told that the broadcaster was the one and only Rush Limbaugh. "I can't recall hiring him or being responsible for his severance," he said.

"I told Jeff, 'Look, we'll meet again,' " Carnegie says. "Then, on New Year's Eve, the new owner fired me, too."

Limbaugh phoned Harper, who had become program director at WKBW in Buffalo, in search of a job. But his admirer had nothing for him.

Three years after leaving home for the big time, he was heading home. Back to Mom and Dad in Cape Girardeau.

"I spent seven months doing nothing," he said. "I was bummed out. I loved the city of Pittsburgh."

Chapter 4

KANSAS CITY BLUES

Jim Carnegie says he felt Limbaugh—that is, "Jeff Christie"—had the talent and the glibness to become one of the great jocks in Top 40. And Carnegie retained that appreciation after rebounding in 1975 as operations manager of Kansas City's KUDL-AM and KUDL-FM.

"The first person I called to do the afternoon show on the AM was Jeff, in Cape Girardeau," Carnegie, who later became the editor and publisher of *Radio Business Report*, recalls. "His mother answered the phone, and when I said I wanted to speak to Jeff, she put the phone down and yelled out, 'Hey Rusty!' He was so excited. I could hear him say, 'Mom, it's about a job.' "

Crossing the state to Kansas City, Limbaugh spent the first few months playing the rock of the moment and oldies on KUDL-AM, as well as slamming into listeners who phoned the on-air line. He incited the audience between records and then abused those who dialed him up to talk back. "People were cracking up at gas stations at some of the things he said," Carnegie remembers. "He didn't want to do mornings, he wanted to do afternoon-drive. He just wanted to be himself."

Limbaugh considered it a challenge to get all the lines to light up on the studio telephone. "They said I was rude," he confessed years later. "I'd hang up and insult people. Everything was flavored with humor."

But when the AM station became KCNW-AM, an affiliate of NBC's ambitious News and Information Service, a round-the-clock feed out of New York, he shifted to the FM station and its much more subdued presentation. He helped mellow KUDL-FM's rock format and hung on to the job even after Carnegie was fired, again, early in 1976, and the station endured another of the ownership changes that plague the disc jockey's trade.

Ross Reagan, the general manager brought in to implement the AM-format switch, remembers that "Jeff Christie" was never even considered for one of the local positions created to provide local news inserts as part of the News and Information Service programming.

"He was on the FM station watching over a semiautomated, soft-rock sound," Reagan says. "His one opportunity at creativity was a brief, public-service talk show that was buried somewhere early in the morning on the weekend. It wasn't supposed to be controversial, but he would attempt to bend the rules and make it controversial. Not only did he lack the experience for a talk position, but his one attempt at public affairs was not memorable.

"He was a nice guy, with a good sense of humor and also with very definite right-leaning ideas which were evident to everyone around him. I had no real indication at that point that he had a terrific amount of ambition, although he was certainly a very confident guy.

"But you could tell he had the kind of personality that could get you into trouble."

There's the word again. Personality. It was an asset or a liability in radio, depending on the format. An asset to Limbaugh these days, but a liability back in Kansas City.

Unfortunately for Limbaugh, he brimmed with personality at a time when FM radio was beginning to take great and somewhat unexpected strides in popularity. Coming out of nowhere in the late 1960s, FM stations by the middle 1970s were claiming around

40 percent of the listening audience (and would eclipse AM stations as they nearly doubled their share over the next fifteen years). And as the FM outlets gained in acceptance, they also reconsidered some of the more carefree elements that had long marked their sound. Driven by market ambitions, FM station managers placed a greater value on conformity in their presentations. And AM radio, whose utter predictability had made FM a cherished alternative only a few years earlier, now also became an unexpected source of guidance in the development of tighter formats and least-offensive broadcasting.

One of the monsters that emerged out of FM's wish for safe and sure programming was automation. FM stations wishing to present a kind of cost-effective, audio wallpaper would equip their studios with a system of long music tapes—some setups even offered prerecorded time checks by a disembodied voice—that could be programmed to broadcast for hours on end with little operator assistance. As a result, the staff announcer on duty often had to be more like a computer programmer than a broadcaster. And those who prided themselves on being broadcasters first and foremost quickly learned that they mainly had to serve the automation system and make sure that it functioned smoothly.

And here was Limbaugh—a playful, pudgy disciple of Top 40's high-octane presentation—now enslaved and shackled by KUDL-FM's soft-rock automation dragon. Minding it, worrying about it. As Reagan put it, "He watched the automation system. He was the voice of the station much of the day." It must have been deadly for him.

Nevertheless, the easygoing George Benson tunes that the station played were Bryan Burns's favorite listening. And Burns knew Limbaugh. Working in the marketing department of the Kansas City Royals, the city's major league baseball team, Burns kept in close touch with radio personalities for miles around, sending them souvenirs and inviting them to games, in hopes that they would talk up the club and its various giveaways at Royals Stadium while on the air. These intermittent contacts turned into a friendship after the two bachelors discovered they were from the same general corner of Missouri—Burns came from Flat River—and had Cape Girardeau acquaintances in common by virtue of a year Burns had spent in the town at Southeast Missouri State University.

They had a few meals together. Then, pooling their modest incomes, they moved up a few notches in life-style by renting a more-than-spacious three-bedroom apartment in Overland Park, a suburb of Kansas City located in Johnson County, Kansas. For them, this was living, with room enough to spread out the gadgets they both loved, including the multiple TVs they used to watch at one time.

"Even back then, in the late seventies, Rush was doing the same thing off the air that he does now on the air—talking about politics and conservatism," Burns recollects. "The difference is that I was the only listener. It was the longest free preview in the history of broadcasting. And today, Rush hasn't changed from the fellow he was then, except that now his forum is a whole lot bigger."

Around this time, Limbaugh went on a blind date with Roxy Maxine McNeely, an outgoing woman with long, reddish-brown hair who was working as a sales secretary at WHB, another local station. It was her first job in town since a concern for her mother's poor health had prompted her to return from a seven-year stay in New York City. The Hertz rental car agency had lured her east after she graduated from the Weaver Airline and Personnel Training School in Kansas City. Not that she wanted to go, but her mother urged her; the job offer was too good to pass up and she would be expected to send some of her paycheck home.

However, the experience helped make her, like the gypsy jock Limbaugh, independent-minded. Like him, she had toughed it out, sharing a two-bedroom, one-bathroom apartment in Queens with seven other women on arriving in New York. Like him, she switched jobs, going from Hertz to other positions with a foreign diplomat, a publishing company, and a second car-rental agency, and finally moving up to an apartment of her own near Lincoln Center, just a few blocks from where Limbaugh would live after moving to New York in 1988.

"He was a lot of fun," Roxy recalls of their first get-together. "He could talk the entire evening away. He would draw you out, find out what your interests were and then start arguing with you. Because I was just back from New York City, there were a lot of New York jokes from him. 'How could you live there?' Or he would say to other people, 'She has no opinions, she lived in New York.' It certainly was ironic when you think that he ended up there himself.

"At the time, my station did Top Forty and Rush was doing a lot of talk on the air at KUDL. I hated radio. It all seemed very phony to me, but of course Rush loved it."

In the summer, about three months into the lease with Burns, Limbaugh announced that he and Roxy were getting married and would be moving into their own place. However, sooner than stick Burns with a crushing expense, Limbaugh insisted on paying his agreed-upon share of the lease for the balance of the year.

The wedding took place on September 24, 1977, at the Centenary United Methodist Church in Cape Girardeau, with a reception afterward in the church social hall. The two of them, both twenty-six years old, looked ever the traditional couple; he in a tux, floppy bow tie, and carnation on the lapel, and Roxy's bright face framed by an ivory picture hat trimmed with organza and lace. Her white gown was made of satin and organza, with lace and pearls encircling a high neckline and fitted bodice before dropping to the skirt and long train. She followed two bridesmaids and a flower girl to the altar, holding her own bouquet of pink roses and small white gladiolas. David Limbaugh served as his brother's best man, with Burns and another friend as ushers and four other pals helping to seat the guests. An organist filled the church with pomp and joyful noise.

"It was huge," Roxy remembers. "All his family were there, plus about half of Cape Girardeau and the other towns around. My mother had taken sick on her way to the wedding and ended up in a hospital in St. Louis, so I can remember me in my gown and Rush in his tux going up there afterward and bringing her a piece of the wedding cake."

The newlyweds bought a house in Overland Park. "It was small and quaint in a very established, tree-lined neighborhood," Roxy says. "Rush was not a fix-it person, so we had to have someone in anytime something went wrong. But we had a lot of stereo equipment all over the living room. And magazines everywhere. And newspapers from various states. Newspapers and magazines on the tables and onto the floors.

"It was real interesting for me. Rush read everything. A lot of it was about politics, which he always talked about, especially when he was around his dad."

Roxy girded herself for the debates between her father-in-law and husband when she and Rush made the six-hour drive in her Nova across Missouri to spend the weekend in Cape Girardeau. On one visit, a deep snow fell and kept everyone housebound. The hot chocolate flowed as the Limbaugh men hashed and thrashed over political issues and shadings of those issues. "It was always very loud—and usually ended up with a lot of laughter," she says. "But it was basically a guy thing. I would visit with his mom in the kitchen. She'd tell me about her social club and what was going on around Cape. Or she and I would go see Rush's grandparents."

Except for get-togethers with Limbaugh's old friend Craig Valle and his wife, there were few other contacts to recall a childhood spent there. The weekends were devoted mostly to family time. But the love from his family provided no hedge against the cruel vagaries of the career he had chosen.

Back in Kansas City, he was fired again, making KUDL the third station to broom him away in his short career.

Meanwhile, Joe Abernathy came back to town. He had been the general manager of KMBZ-AM and sister station KMBR-FM, but was now fresh from three years at the helm of WIOD in Miami, where he had installed a format known as the "Great Entertainers." They included Larry King, whom Abernathy brought back to radio after the interviewer spent three years out of the business following an arrest for grand larceny and a bout with gambling debts. (The charges were later dropped because the statute of limitations had run out.) King was joined on WIOD by Mike Reineri, out of

Cleveland; Big Wilson, an institution from New York's WNBC; afternoon personality Bill Calder; and Bob Cole, who did an all-night show of talk and country music aimed at truckers on the move. Heavy on the conversation and gags and light on the music, Abernathy's WIOD format was in many ways ahead of its time, a hybrid long before Howard Stern would do a raunchy morning talk show on New York rock station WXRK-FM.

Abernathy returned to Missouri in 1978 to join in the purchase of an AM station and a new FM outlet licensed to the community of Liberty. He moved the FM operation to Kansas City—KFIX-FM—and located the studios on Country Club Plaza. His plan once again was to mix talk and music.

"He pitched me for a job," said Walt Bodine, one of the market's best-known radio hosts. "I made a point of meeting him for lunch in a place where all the stations' time salesmen used to eat. So word got back to KMBZ, where I was working at the time, and they came through with a nice raise to keep me."

As Bodine remembers the period, Abernathy wanted him to do an evening talk show and KMBZ's popular Mike Murphy to host a morning talk program between which the new station would play pop. The boss's original idea was to say "The FIX is in" though the station was eventually nicknamed "The FIX" and said "The FIX is on."

Murphy signed up, but first had to sit out a six-month, no-compete period dictated by his contract with KMBZ. His brother Pat was hired to do mornings in the interim. When Bodine declined the job offer, it opened the way for Rush Limbaugh, still "Jeff Christie," to come do the evening show. He submitted a tape of his work on KUDL, which included his talkative public-affairs segments on the station, and won over program director Jim Gallant.

"He was the first guy we found to do the evening show, taking calls and talking to guests," Gallant remembers. "There was something about the tape that I really liked. He had a good, bright, attention-getting sound. There was just something about him that made you want to listen to him. I talked Joe into giving him a shot."

For a few heady weeks, Limbaugh had big hopes of becoming a talk-radio somebody and putting the Donny Osmond records behind him forever. But KFIX would be yet another disappointment.

Although Abernathy recalls that "revenues were great," despite a suburban-based transmitter that did not reach into the southern part of the city, "The FIX" took its place in the annals of Kansas City radio either as an ill-conceived disaster or a noble experiment. After Larry King had gone national from Miami, on January 30, 1978, with a late-night show on the Mutual Broadcasting System, KFIX became one of his affiliates and the host went to do his program from the station as a favor to his old boss Abernathy. A party for advertisers was held to mark the occasion. But shortly before King was to start broadcasting, bad weather cut power to the transmitter so that Mutual's newest star was never heard in Kansas City that night.

Murphy appealed to listeners thirty-five and older who were used to enjoying him on AM radio. His fans could not find him on the FM dial and KFIX's transmitter served the city so unevenly that listening became an exercise in frustration. Murphy later became a midday talk host on Kansas City's KCMO-AM. "Limbaugh was on at night," he recalls. "He did a little flying-saucer stuff, that sort of thing. He didn't sound like the same guy he is today."

But Ray Dunaway, who had returned to his hometown the year before to host the morning show on KMBZ-AM, remembers an effective Limbaugh on KFIX. "One night, he had on a woman from the Kansas City chapter of NOW when Congress was deciding whether to extend the deadline for passage of the Equal Rights Amendment," he says. "And Rush told her, 'Well, it's like playing football, and the game is almost over and you women want another quarter so you can win.' He was very good at getting his point across. Excellent, in fact."

"I think he was a little bit ahead of what people were ready for," Gallant says. "I thought he was really good. But if he was there a month, that was a lot . . . I remember him being temperamental."

And personalities clashed. "I remember getting flak over Jeff

Christie and letting him go," says Abernathy, who brought in Bill Calder from Miami to take over the evening shift.

After only a few weeks of career promise, Limbaugh was out of work again. The fourth time. Once more, his particular radio talents and on-air style had impressed some of his colleagues, but fallen short in the eyes of the station's top man. It was as inevitable a hazard of the business as changes in format and ownership, but no less painful and frustrating for one as ambitious as Limbaugh.

"But I looked at it and said, well, hell," Limbaugh told an interviewer years later. "I wanted to be taken seriously. I had been a moderate failure in radio as a deejay. I had not distinguished myself at all, other than I was the guy with a lot of potential, if he'd just learn when to shut up. So I said, 'Well, hell, I want to be taken seriously in life, and I've failed. Just let me move on and do something else.' "

He told the *Sacramento Bee:* "I was disillusioned with radio. It isn't the real world if that's all you do. Most radio stations are toilets. Some have flushers, some don't. Radio people are a little weird. You're in a little world with a microphone and you have to tell yourself that thousands of people are reacting to you. You go to lunch and nobody knows you. You live a lie in that little room."

The loss of the KFIX job also brought family pressures to bear as he considered his next move. "His dad was a big influence," Roxy says. "He was always somewhat disappointed that Rush didn't pursue a more recognizable career—not that it had to be law—but a more acceptable career. Rush was made to feel like the black sheep of the family.

"His father and he battled a lot about what he was doing with his life. 'When are you going to grow up?' 'You can't make a career out of this.' That sort of thing. I think it was his father who was hurt more by his losing the job. And Rush really wanted to please his father."

After twelve years on the radio, Limbaugh finally became a listener. He laid aside his headset and his dreams of radio glory.

Burns, his former roommate, persuaded him to take a part-time position in the Royals' office of group sales in 1979. "He took the job, but he took it under pressure," Roxy remembers.

If it wasn't the big time, as McKeesport had been eight years earlier, it was, at least, the big leagues.

Chapter 5

PLAY BALL

For a young man wanting to make a fresh start, the Kansas City Royals in 1979 was a good organization to hook up with. The team had debuted only ten years earlier as part of the American League expansion, and it rose to challenge the New York Yankees for the pennant in each of the three seasons before Limbaugh arrived.

Royals Stadium, where he worked, was only six years old. Baseball was sound and prosperous. The American Pastime. And Limbaugh was a fan. The new guy in the front office considered it such a glamorous position that he was willing at first to overlook his meager salary, which would not exceed $18,000.

Unlike New York, Chicago, and Los Angeles, Kansas City was not so glutted with professional sports teams that the public's loyalties were diffused and scattered. The Royals and Kansas City Chiefs were it. Even if his new position was many steps removed from radio, he was at least able to stand proud as a representative of a beloved major league team after years of being anonymous when not on the air.

"Rush had outspoken views, but he didn't blend in real well, so it was difficult for him to go to the Royals," Roxy recalls. "Rush was not a real people person, which is why he went into radio. You can be comfortable with people when you're behind the microphone. On the radio, you're the one in control. The Royals helped him to get out there. Still, he resisted somewhat because it was hard for him to develop relationships with people. They thought he was either off-the-wall or arrogant."

Parties and other socializing came with his new terrain, and Limbaugh would later remember the period as "a hoot" before he had to grow up. At one gathering, disc jockey Randy Raley, who had come to Kansas City in 1978 to work at KYYS and knew Limbaugh as Jeff Christie from radio circles, encountered him off in a room smoking marijuana with another fellow. Raley would recall the episode in striking detail during the 1992 presidential campaign, when Limbaugh was hammering Bill ("I didn't inhale") Clinton on the issue of character. Raley, by then the morning man on KSHE-FM in St. Louis, said that he asked Limbaugh at the party why he had left radio for the Royals. "And I also remember it because at the time I had a picture of [Royals third baseman] George Brett that I carried around in my car, and as the three of us were standing in the room I kept wondering how I could get this Jeff Christie to have it autographed for me."

If the party was one of the two times when Limbaugh himself said he smoked pot, he did not say. He conceded only that he had toked up once on the campus at Southeast Missouri State and again with a friend in Kansas City, adding that it made him nauseous. "If that was sick, gimme some of that!" Raley scoffed. The disc jockey didn't buy the idea that Limbaugh could ever have been sickened by the smoke. "He looked like he knew what he was doing."

Limbaugh's part-time job in group sales eventually became a full-time position as director of group sales and special events when his pal Bryan Burns shed the latter responsibilities to oversee the team's marketing effort. Limbaugh's post required him to publish pocket schedules, organize community nights at the Royals' games, and persuade local employers to sponsor days at the ballpark for their workers. Follow-through involved myriad details, such as arranging for a firm's president to throw out the first ball and setting up photos with Brett and other star players.

"I was willing to sublimate my ego for some security," he told an interviewer. "Being around the Royals allowed me to meet people I wouldn't have, like the president of Coors." It impressed him to have entrée with credibility—to get practically anyone on the phone simply by identifying himself as "Rush Limbaugh from the Kansas City Royals."

His job also put him in frequent contact with local radio stations as he organized various promotions designed to sell tickets and fill the stadium's forty thousand seats. After years of yabbering inside a glass booth, he developed a business perspective by seeing how people used radio. "You know, it's weird when you spend all of your life [in] a glass-encased room, at a microphone, and you have to imagine what people are doing," he said later. "And you tell yourself, everybody's listening to me, everybody's listening to every syllable I say. You have to say that in order to affect this attitude. Then you go out and you're introduced to people, and they've never heard of you. That's what makes people in radio head cases." Working in an office environment made him see the paranoid stresses of the radio life all too clearly, even if he was not entirely free of the medium's personal allure.

Special events—days when souvenirs were given away at the ballpark—were another of his chores to bring in fans; it was partly up to him to rope corporations into paying for the bats, hats, and other handouts offered at home games. For example, among the special events of the 1983 season were Getty Poster Schedule Weekend, Coca-Cola Sports Wallet Day, Shrine Parade Night, Yago Ladies Shoulder Bag Day, Kodak Camera Day, Hostess Cake Helmet Night, and Coors Seat Cushion Day.

As he told a gathering of radio salespeople years later, he got a good piece of advice with the Royals that applied to the marketing of his radio show: Forget about those who don't like baseball. Concentrate on the many others who love the game.

Limbaugh did not travel with the team when it played on the road, but he had to attend all home games. He directed the commercials that flashed on the scoreboard and saw to it that VIPs and visiting groups were comfortable. As one associate put it, "If the company president on hand for a game wanted to talk about Ringo Starr or George Brett or drought in Africa, Rush could do that, too."

He brought his disc-jockeying ear to bear on the selection of hit songs played at key moments during the games. At the heart of his responsibilities was a fair amount of showmanship.

Personally, however, he was hurting. Under self-imposed pressure and the influence of his father to make something of himself, he worked at a job far removed from his first love, radio. "He would joke a lot about the mentality of ballplayers," Roxy says. "There was no growth for him there."

Or at home either. "We just sat down one day and decided our marriage was over," she remembers. "It was mutual, nothing ugly." Although the excitement and the love had faded, Limbaugh clearly was the one being dumped. "There was some pain and a sense of failure, but I think we realized that this was not working out and we needed to move on," Roxy says.

They had been married only a year and a half when she filed for divorce, in March of 1980, and moved in with a girlfriend. Her petition to the District Court of Johnson County, Kansas, said that she and her husband were incompatible.

Rush put up no fight, and agreed to let the court hear his wife's case without further notice to himself. David Limbaugh reviewed his brother's side of the legal work.

The case moved swiftly. On July 10, 1980, Roxy appeared with her attorney in an Olathe courtroom to bring things to a close. Limbaugh stayed away. The judge granted the divorce.

"Rush and I just took each thing that we owned in the house and whoever had it originally took it," she says.

She kept her 1975 Nova and various furnishings. She also retained ownership of the refrigerator, allowing him to use the appliance until she might want it for herself. She obtained the restoration of her maiden name, McNeely.

Limbaugh kept stock in a family corporation, as well as his gas-guzzling 1971 Buick Riviera. He paid $35 toward court costs.

Although no alimony was involved, Roxy received a lien in the amount of $1,650 on the Overland Park house in exchange for her interest in the property. Limbaugh would pay the lien four years later when he sold the place. Meanwhile, the house was his alone and he ambled about in it, his wife gone so soon.

"I think we left as friends," Roxy says. "We talked several different times afterward, but then no more. I missed his family."

"I don't see him married with kids," adds Roxy, who eventually remarried and has two sons. "He devotes so much time and energy to what he does that there's nothing left for anyone else. Hindsight is always clearer, but I just don't think he has the energy for a relationship. We were just getting started, two people that ended up together. Now, looking back, I think he was happier on his own. Relationships are hard for Rush. People are hard."

"I was doing what I thought I had to do," Limbaugh later said of the marriage in an interview with *Time*. "There was romance in the idea of *being* married. It was just the wrong reasons."

Writing in his first book, *The Way Things Ought to Be*, he noted that he reached beyond his means to buy the Overland Park home in the misguided belief that everyone had to own one, but then he had to juggle his paycheck to cover mortgage payments and other bills. Roxy says she remembers no such difficulties. Nevertheless, Limbaugh wrote that he had to satisfy his appetite for snacks by buying them at convenience stores that accepted credit cards. And it is remembered that he was a lonely guy who did his laundry at a friend's house to save on quarters. He picked up a few extra bucks every now and then by voicing a commercial. Apparently, it was never enough.

In addition, there was no disguising the subservient, "sideline" nature of his work, which slowly came to gnaw at him and drill home the realization that job security fell far short of expectations. The Royals did not even list him with the rest of the front-office personnel in their annual media guide until 1981, as director of group sales/special events. His sonorous radio voice did not ring out on the stadium's public-address system. He received no additional stipend to go to New York to narrate a videotape of a season's highlights that made the rounds of Boy Scout troops and chambers of commerce. "You just knew Rush wasn't using the talent he had," recalls Louise Adams, his secretary at the time.

In 1982, he drooled over a $35,000-a-year job selling potato chips in Liberty, Missouri. But he did not get the position.

"And you know, the enthusiasm for the game I didn't find among front-office types in baseball," he would lament to Bob Costas on NBC-TV's "Later." "I found, 'It's the business.' It's a matter-of-fact approach to it. And there were some people that I ran into during my five years in baseball who thought fans got in the way of the purity of the game. 'Get the fans outta here! They don't even know what they're booing at,' said one famous, notable PR director I won't name. 'Get 'em outta here! This is absolutely crazy. They don't even know what they're talking about!' And I found that just incredible, the cynicism that exists in some front offices about the customers."

Surely there was something more challenging he could do with his life. "I will be very honest," he once said on his radio show. "I was in a position of absolutely no consequence." After all, the team was supposed to win games and advance to the World Series, whereas Limbaugh had nothing to do with that manly objective. He went so far as to say that his main jobs were to line up somebody to throw out the ceremonial first pitch before each home game and to make sure that the singer of the National Anthem was sober. Oh yes, he also had to enter the clubhouse and get players to autograph baseballs for visiting VIPs, sometimes putting up with their guff in the process. "And I don't know, frankly," he added, "how the Royals are getting along without me in these massively important positions."

However, he spent five years with the team and this enabled him to make lifelong friends. Some were players whom he had first admired from afar, such as Jamie Quirk, John Wathan, Dave Chalk, Amos Otis, Hal McRae, Ken Brett and his All-Star brother, George.

Limbaugh became particularly close to George Brett when the slugger was at the height of his popularity and powers, batting over .300 in each season that Limbaugh was with the team. On the surface, the two seemed to have little in common, but Limbaugh was impressed by Brett's willingness to help him in his job most of the times he was asked, and Brett found Limbaugh understanding on those occasions when he preferred to decline a goodwill appearance. As he put it, "Rush made you feel comfortable saying no."

It could be that each saw in the other a measure of the easygoing calm which was so sorely challenged in their respective positions. In the 1980 season, for example, Brett was chasing after a goal he almost reached—to finish the season with an all-but-impossible .400 batting average—and the press was chasing him during that pursuit. It impressed Limbaugh that Brett bore up under the pressure and remained grounded despite the momentous fame. For Limbaugh, who had always aspired to such renown, to witness this drama up close was a rare privilege.

At the same time, Brett relished the opportunity in Limbaugh's company to escape from the spotlight. "I enjoyed being around him," Brett says. "He would pull up a chair at your locker and just bullshit with you—about life, about the Pittsburgh Steelers. I always knew he was bright, but I never knew he was that bright, because we used to talk about personal things."

Brett invited him to his birthday parties and they had dinner together. Though Limbaugh was no home repairman, he did know gadgets. "Whenever I would buy something, like an answering machine or a VCR, I didn't know how to hook it up—I still don't, as a matter of fact—and so I would call Rush to come over and do it," Brett recalls. "With the first answering machine I ever had, Rush, who's great with voices, did the taped message like Howard Cosell. It was something like, 'Hello, Lou (that's my nickname) isn't here at this time, and chances are that even Lou is wondering where he is at this time.' When I'd call people back, they'd say, 'How did you get Cosell to do that for you?' Yeah, Rush was my handyman. He was like Tom Poston on the 'Newhart' show."

Brett once returned the favors when it mattered. To help generate a big turnout on "Olathe Night" at Royals Stadium, the team organized a barbecue luncheon in the Kansas community featuring the manager and a few players, each of whom earned about two hundred dollars to go sign autographs and pose for snapshots. This one year, an advertised player told Limbaugh at the last minute that he wasn't going to attend and would be playing golf instead.

To avert a letdown in Olathe, Limbaugh sheepishly approached Brett, who was considered too big to be asked to do this sort of thing. Yet halfway through the explanation, Brett cut him off and asked what time he should be there. In fact, he got his pal Jamie Quirk to go along as well. The day was not only saved, it was a bigger-than-expected hit.

After Limbaugh was long gone from the team and working on KFBK in Sacramento, he went to Oakland whenever Brett and the Royals were in town to play the A's. When Limbaugh moved to New York in 1988, the Royals' visits to Yankee Stadium allowed the two friends to rendezvous for dinner, with Brett sometimes bringing along a contingent of Limbaugh "dittoheads," such as catcher Mike Macfarlane.

When Brett married his wife, Leslie, in February 1992, Limbaugh rose at the reception and sang a special song for the couple that had been written by a mutual friend. "His voice wasn't bad," Brett says. "I've heard worse." For a present, he offered to pay their airfare to anyplace they wanted to go in the world. "But it wasn't the present," Brett adds. "It was the letter he wrote. It was the most professional letter I'd ever seen. It talked about friendship and loyalty. I mean, it brought tears to my eyes."

Limbaugh impressed his pal further at the end of the 1992 season, when Brett finally succeeded in becoming only the eighteenth player in major league history to get three thousand career hits. Naturally, Limbaugh flew back to Kansas City for a weekend of parties marking the occasion, including a late Saturday dinner with Brett and about forty other people at Stroud's, a popular fried-chicken restaurant. After the meal, the guests all started putting money on the table until the waitress came over and told Brett that the tab had been paid by Limbaugh.

"Why are you doing that?" Brett asked him.

"Because I can," Limbaugh said.

It was also late in Limbaugh's stay with the Royals that he caught the attention of Michelle Sixta, who was helping to pay her way through Central Missouri State University in Warrensburg by working as a stadium usherette. "I thought Rush was arrogant when I introduced myself to him," she later told the *Sacramento Bee*. "He says he was talking to someone, but I got him right as he got off an elevator. Anyway, he heard I thought that and later came over to apologize. I think I liked the pregame music tape he put together. It was different and professional. He'd clown around in the press box. You knew who he was."

The feeling was mutual. Before going off to give a talk about the team one night in Sedalia, Missouri, Limbaugh asked his secretary, Louise Adams, if her daughter Suzy, another usherette and a college suitemate of Michelle, would like to drive over from Warrensburg to see him in action. She said yes. Then, on second thought, Limbaugh called back wondering if Suzy would bring Michelle. She did.

With Michelle occupying the center seat next to Limbaugh, Suzy felt like the odd woman out on the passenger side to her friend's right. Indeed, the courtship began that evening.

Michelle, a graphic-arts major who came from a large South Kansas City family, dated Limbaugh on weekends, and they also saw each other when she drove in from campus to usher at games. She was ten years younger, born in 1961, but mature for her age—a tall and dignified woman with big, light eyes who would fall in love with the quietly suffering Limbaugh.

At times the college dropout expressed to her a belief that there was more to life than higher education and that who one knew mattered just as much in the rat race ahead. Listening to his earnest opinions, Michelle was struck by his intelligence, while he had enough of the kid in him to be attracted by her youthful exuberance. A mutual friend surmised that, despite the age difference, they met halfway.

They married in 1983 at the Stadium Club in front of about fifty friends and relatives—a much smaller affair than the wedding with Roxy six years before. Afterward, Michelle moved into the Overland Park home in which Limbaugh had been rattling about alone. For a few more months, she had to commute to the Warrensburg campus before graduating in the spring. But for all of his newfound domestic bliss, Limbaugh's battle at work continued unabated.

"He developed and he made very good friends in the organization and he was well liked," recalls Dean Vogelaar, the Royals' longtime director of public relations. "At the same time, we felt like he was a duck out of water. You always felt that Rush was not doing what his talents called for, although he did his job well."

In addition, even if Limbaugh aspired to a higher position with the club, promotions were rare. "In a company as small as ours, to move ahead means that people have to move on, and there was little movement of that sort," says Spencer (Herk) Robinson, one of Limbaugh's superiors at the time and now the executive vice president and general manager. "And it's not in the nature of the baseball business to expand. You don't change the structure of your organization from year to year."

Limbaugh came to loathe working in the background and he saw that he was ill suited to the corporate life. The players were the stars and made the big money. He also recognized that the lack of turnover in the Royals' front office had stymied whatever career he might be building in Major League Baseball. In fact, the long, 162-game seasons that dragged through the hot summers soured him on baseball itself.

He told the radio-industry newsletter *Talkers* in 1990 that his last two years with the Royals "were not very pleasant in terms of just enjoying it and enjoying my life. No fault of people at the Royals. I was just doing the wrong thing. I considered myself already a failure at radio so I stuck with it because I didn't know what else I was going to do. And this was corporate America, a great organization, and I figured, 'Hell, if I can't make it with this bunch, I'm gonna have trouble everywhere.' Well, you have to be there every game, five years in a row. You have to. It's your job. It takes all the ingredients of being a fan away. I found myself, toward the last two years, 'Lose, lose, lose. Don't make the playoffs so the season will end.' "

The Royals unwittingly obliged him. They were shut out of postseason play all but one of Limbaugh's five years with the team. That was in 1980, when they defeated the Yankees for the American League pennant—losing to the Philadelphia Phillies in a six-game

World Series—and earned Limbaugh a giant league championship ring that he wore for years afterward.

Professionally, Limbaugh was no better off than he had been as a failed deejay five years earlier. It was all too clear: He had joined the Royals in order to be taken seriously. And now, in 1983, he completed a circle to where he started from, still wanting to be taken seriously.

He was thirty-two years old, depressed and hating the routine that was paying him only around $18,000 a year—less than he had earned a decade earlier as Jeff Christie, the Pittsburgh deejay spinning Partridge Family hits.

As it turned out, Limbaugh's days with the Royals hastened to an end when Bryan Burns, who brought him to the team, left to work in the New York corporate offices of Major League Baseball. His good friend was succeeded as director of marketing in August 1983 by Dennis Cryder. In other words, Limbaugh now had a new boss.

"It became apparent to me about a month after I got here that Rush's expertise was in the audio end of things, the radio commercials we did, the music we used, that sort of thing," Cryder, now the team's vice president for administration, remembers. "I can hear that even now during his radio show with the music he plays going in and out of commercials. He had a natural talent for that. He knew, for example, how to play mind games with the music when the other team was at bat and the game was close."

But Cryder had a broader agenda to serve and it was unclear to him whether Limbaugh wanted to dig in for the effort. "I was new and I sat down with Rush and told him that I wanted to make this thing go, that I wanted to grow in the organization," he says. "I told him, 'Look, you know the pitfalls around this place. Do you want to do this with me?' "

Not really. Limbaugh was burned out, royally, and lacked the energy to march behind a new commander. He was fired.

Limbaugh would look back years later and say that he wouldn't have traded his time with the Royals for anything. All in all, he concluded that they were five of the best years of his life and helped prepare him for the success that was to follow.

Chapter 6

BACK ON THE AIR

In five years with the Royals, Rush Limbaugh had built a bridge to cross back into radio. Working in sales and public relations for the team, he maintained special contact with its Kansas City radio outlet, KMBZ-AM. He set up baseball promotions with the station, voiced the introductions to the game broadcasts, and spoke on the air with Curt (Mother) Merz, the afternoon host, during pregame shows.

As he told an interviewer: "I had a conversation with a friend who said, 'Well, what are you going to do if you're going to leave the Royals?' I said, 'I don't have any idea. I'm so depressed. . . .' He said, 'What do you think you're best at?' 'Well, there's no question I'm best at being on the radio.' He said, 'Well, go back to that.' I said, 'Oh no, I've already failed.' He said, 'No, no, no, no. Do what you're best at, because regardless of how well you do it, that's what's going to make you happy.' "

So one day in 1983 Limbaugh went to see KMBZ news director Phil Mueller and asked him for a job. "He brought along tapes of his earlier work in Kansas City radio and, of course, a lot of people were still around who remembered him from back then," Mueller recalls. "He suggested doing an airshift, as well as perhaps some commentary. First, I tried him out on a weekend, doing an airshift, handling the phones, to see how he might fit in. And when I came in that Monday morning, there were messages waiting for me from higher-ups in the Jackson County Democratic Party. There were calls of concern and others from people saying, 'Right on, Rush.' I knew something was working."

Limbaugh was hired under his own name in November as KMBZ was undergoing a gradual, though no less radical, transformation from a longtime format of music and personalities to "news you can use." At first, Limbaugh read the news during the afternoon show hosted by Merz, a station veteran whose celebrity had originated during his football days with the Kansas City Chiefs. The problem was, Limbaugh would slip in his own conservative opinions during the newscasts, irritating station management. Yassir Arafat of the Palestine Liberation Organization was reported to have left Beirut "with his tail between his legs." And on one winter afternoon, he paused during the headlines to warn Merz never to mention Eleanor Roosevelt lest the remark prompt him to erupt in rage.

Bill McMahon, a consultant to KMBZ, sat down with the broadcaster to hear him out. "When management wants to fire someone, it usually means that the person has talent," he says. "I spoke with Rush for about an hour, and during that time he basically did his monologue, the whole bit. I was enthralled. He was provocative and entertaining.

"I told him, 'Look, I think I can save your job, but you have to promise me, that if I can get the proper platform for your opinions, you will keep your opinions to yourself when reading the news.' He agreed. And that's how his commentaries were launched."

Certainly this was a good way to separate Limbaugh's personal views from the news and to label his ideas as one man's viewpoint, take it or leave it. But KMBZ was owned by Bonneville International Corp., a broadcasting company belonging to the Church of Jesus Christ of Latter-day Saints—the Mormons—a denomination not known for bringing controversy to the airwaves. Limbaugh had license to expound, but that license would be reviewed often by management. From time to time, listener complaints apparently reached all the way to Temple Square in Salt Lake City.

Limbaugh, for example, claimed to envy the attention given the Reverend Jesse Jackson for his inflammatory remarks about Jews. He said that Sen. Edward Kennedy would make a fine ruler for the Soviet Union. Also: "More people have died at Chappaquiddick than have died in nuclear-power accidents."

After Michael Jackson's Victory Tour passed through Kansas City, a local visit by Jesse Jackson inspired Limbaugh to do a parody of the "Rainbow Tour." Another time, he illustrated the new ideas of presidential candidate Gary Hart by offering thirty seconds of silence.

Tame stuff by today's standards, especially for Limbaugh. "But this was the wrong company," McMahon says. "They couldn't handle it."

One zinger laughingly recalled around Kansas City a decade later was prompted by plans of the Country Club Plaza to go upscale, to replace traditional Middle America shops such as Woolworth's with tonier establishments. Taking note of this swipe at average folks, Limbaugh suggested that management simply ban all ugly people from the Plaza. Some listeners protested, and Limbaugh was chastised by management for going too far.

"Folks were talking about that one for weeks!" says Tom Schulte, an account executive with KMBZ who now owns KMOQ in Joplin, Missouri. Another time, Limbaugh singled out the nearby blue-collar community of Raytown, Missouri, and announced that all those in the area who liked to bowl lived there.

"We all knew that it was just a piece of programming, but he got everyone talking about the station," Schulte adds. "As an account executive, every call I made would begin with the other person speaking about Rush. He created a brand-new awareness for us."

Even if that awareness was not always respectful. In the *Kansas City Star*, TV and radio critic Barry Garron wrote an open letter to Limbaugh: "The problem is that you are being paid to offer intelligent commentary and your listeners are being sadly short-changed. They're not getting any great insight from your political prognostications, either. . . . I sure wouldn't mind stopping you from listing so far to the right that you keep falling overboard."

But Limbaugh was rolling. The college dropout who had failed as a record spinner and corporate factotum now reveled in the attention he was getting. His friend George Brett filled seats with the force of his ballplaying; Limbaugh was now cocking ears as a result of his gifts of bombast and troublemaking. He knew he had something going, if only he could win the higher-ups to his side.

In May of 1984, Merz was unexpectedly fired after ten years with the station, and Limbaugh inherited the afternoon show. And in time, as Schulte put it, "things got a little hot in the kitchen."

"I remember getting one call from a listener who was upset about something he said that had to do with politics and government," recalls Russ Wood, who was KMBZ's general manager. "The fellow said, 'You leave that guy on the air and I'm coming down there with my gun.'

"He became too provocative, so we wanted him to back off a little. There were several conversations and Rush would say, 'I have talent. Let me do my thing.' He felt he needed more rope. He had a very forceful personality and an agenda to say something in the industry, and he was bent on making that statement on that station."

Limbaugh told the *Sacramento Bee* years later that because KMBZ's talk format was new, he had to tease the audience "and make them mad—violate every rule in the book—just to get them to call." He knew they were out there because the phone lines lit up right away whenever he played a political version of Trivial Pursuit. But it was hard to generate calls of opinion. Teasing didn't always work.

He had teasing in mind at the 1984 Democratic National Convention. "I remember he was happy as hell to be there," says Ray Dunaway, the KMBZ morning man, who did broadcasts with him from San Francisco that summer. "He watched the thing endlessly in his hotel room when he wasn't working and inside the hall he would walk around to see Peter Jennings, David Brinkley, and all the rest of the network stars in action. I remember, too, that he had a notion that one of the hotels may have been a gay hotel. The hotel bar had pictures of Judy Garland and Marilyn Monroe on the walls. So Rush went in there and tried to tape an interview with one of the patrons, thinking the guy might say it was a gay bar, and that way Rush could then say that homosexuals were supporting Walter Mondale."

It never happened. But while in San Francisco, Dunaway was able to see that among fellow Missourians at least, the struggling radio broadcaster was a somebody. "We went to the hotel where the Missouri delegation was staying and the state chairman made a big fuss over Rush," Dunaway says.

Back at KMBZ afterward, the fun started to drain out of Limbaugh's job despite his best efforts to stay afloat and in good graces. In late August, after the Republican National Convention, there was what Mueller calls "the Saturday morning massacre." The news director and sales manager were fired. Sure, Mueller, now co-owner of KUTA in Blanding, Utah, had received a few memos urging him to rein Limbaugh in, "but I was unaware that we were both heading for the cliff."

With Mueller gone, Limbaugh's situation recalled the time when Bryan Burns had left the Royals for New York. Rush began to hear footsteps, especially after Wood left for Bonneville's KSL in Salt Lake City and was succeeded at KMBZ by a new management team brought in from KIRO, Bonneville's news/talk pride in Seattle. The Kansas City AM-FM operation was losing money, and Bonneville was bent on changing KMBZ from its freewheeling style to a more structured news/talk format. As a result, it seemed more than clear that Limbaugh's from-the-hip remarks would be incompatible.

"He used to call me every night around nine o'clock and say, 'Are they gonna fire me?'" Dunaway says. "I was on the executive programming committee and he knew that Andy Ludlum, the new news director, was not real happy with him."

Noel Heckerson, then a KMBZ newscaster and now the news director, says that Limbaugh would squeeze into the announcer's booth with him and ask: "What do you think? What do you hear?" Heckerson told him: "I'm hearing the same things you're hearing, Rush."

Limbaugh's insecurity ran deeper still, according to Patty Schulte, the station's executive assistant and personnel director. "Rush was a nice person, a real friendly sort, but he was careful in that he didn't trust all those around him," she says. "We would have lunch together and I wanted to tell him to loosen up. Kansas City was not ready for him. It was not the right market for him. He wanted to know if people liked him. He was unsure of himself and that was partly because he got little positive reinforcement. Then again, those who are better at what they do than a lot of other people often are doubly concerned about what people think of them.

"He didn't enjoy his own sense of humor as much as he should have. He tended to lean more toward worry. 'What did they think of this bit?' He used to call me and Ray Dunaway at home and ask us what we thought."

Lucille Pickett, who was a saleswoman at KMBZ, recalls: "Rush had a typical deejay's personality—kinda paranoid. He wasn't as confident as he appears to be on the air. He was just developing his so-called act, but he got a lot of heat. They were really riding his butt. They worried because they all thought he was swear-to-God serious all the time. So Rush needed to be reassured."

Five minutes before one broadcast, Limbaugh was handed a memo from Ludlum saying his job performance had become a concern. Certainly not the sort of communication that underscores job security. Specifically, the memo told him to refrain from political opinions and personal attacks, to stop sounding so formal, and not to speak with his colleagues while on the air. Limbaugh says that Ludlum remarked: "You either shape up or you're out."

Limbaugh says he was also ordered to quit using "therefore" and "so forth"—a dubious claim that even his own brother never believed. Then, in mid-September, he received his final memo: "Unfortunately, I cannot share your enthusiasm for your performance."

Limbaugh's ouster after ten often outrageous months on KMBZ, prompted a retrospective by Barry Garron in the *Kansas City Star*.

The broadcaster told the writer that he had been caught off-guard by the new management. "I did what I was told to do. They wanted a rabble-rouser. When they [later] said to bring it in, tone it down, I did." Each memo prompted him to seek coaching and advice, he said, but the decision to fire him probably originated higher up in the corporation.

Dunaway agrees: "I think Bonneville realized that it was a risk to have him on in afternoon-drive. They messed his head around pretty good. For Rush, it was a question of finding a place that could use him. KMBZ needed his talent, but didn't use his talent."

In fact, his firing had as much to do with corporate intrigue as it did with Limbaugh's ability to stir controversy. Although the circumstances were unknown to him at the time, he had to go because his talent for slinging shots risked damage to a secret business strategy being conducted on a management level.

Bonneville executives were trying to get back the local rights to carry the Royals' baseball games. The radio affiliation, which the station dropped after many years in 1983 following a dispute with the team, was now held by KCMO. The affiliation was not up for grabs again until the 1986 season, but Bonneville figured that it could prevent KCMO from winning the Royals a second time by competing with the rival station for the rights to the Chiefs' games in the meantime and thereby drive up the price that KCMO would have to pay for football. As Bonneville sized things up, KCMO would then be left financially unable to win the more desirable baseball franchise when it became available.

As a result, while Limbaugh was broadcasting on KMBZ in 1984, Bill Steding, a Bonneville executive whose responsibilities included the Kansas City station, aggressively went after the Chiefs. In the middle of this courtship, however, Limbaugh made caustic remarks on the air about Jack Steadman, the football team's president. Limbaugh complained about an increase in the Chiefs' ticket prices, about the amenities at Arrowhead Stadium, about the need to attract better players, and about Steadman himself. Familiar gripes in any sports town. However, Steadman became enraged and called KMBZ to complain.

Naturally, given the stakes involved, station manager Paul Leonard heard him out. Leonard then looked at Steadman's grievance as the last straw in the employment of Limbaugh. He phoned Steding and got him to agree that Limbaugh should be fired. The broadcaster's days at the station may have been dwindling, but his skewering of Steadman was a case of messing with the wrong man at the wrong time. Limbaugh's time to go had come. Certainly, Steadman had to be appeased if the company's own game plan was to succeed.

So Limbaugh was let go, not knowing the full reason why. In 1985, KCMO obtained local rights to the Chiefs' games but paid dearly to win them. And in 1986, after promising to give the Royals showcase treatment on the air, KMBZ wrested the baseball team away from KCMO.

"I think Rush did what Rush did—he said what he wanted to say," Leonard recalled in 1993. "He was not interested in fitting into any kind of corporate structure. So you can build a franchise *around* a guy like that, or you can hammer the guy and get him to march in step with everyone else."

But considering that Leonard was too preoccupied with the overall picture to have any sense that Limbaugh might develop into a superstar, and had no time "to get inside Rush's head," it was far easier simply to axe him and be done with it. In radio, it happens all the time.

Meanwhile, out in Sacramento at news/talk station KFBK, the controversial Morton Downey, Jr., was having trouble on the air that would prove advantageous to Limbaugh. He told a joke during his morning program involving a Swede, a Norwegian, and "a Chinaman," which sat poorly with City Councilman Tom Chinn. He found it degrading and insulting. To worsen matters, Downey was dismissive when Chinn called KFBK to complain.

The station suspended Downey without pay after only four months on the job. His absence was to run a few days. "We think it's a regrettable incident and have taken steps to make sure everyone understands that is not basic radio policy," KFBK general manager Paul Aaron told a reporter. However, a suspension seemed like child's punishment to station owner C. K. McClatchy, a reserved gentleman whose politics were left of Downey's and who was also a good friend of Chinn. When McClatchy phoned Aaron to question the penalty, the general manager explained that he didn't believe the Chinaman joke should be fatal considering that Downey was willing to apologize. As Aaron tells the story, McClatchy then said: "Paul, I don't think you understand me. At five o'clock today there's going to be either one opening at KFBK or two. You decide which it's going to be."

Downey never returned. His "suspension" eventually became a "resignation" and he moved on to WERE in Cleveland, four years away from the brawlfest of a TV show that would introduce him to a national audience.

As a result, Limbaugh's return to radio after a five-year absence was not derailed by his firing from KMBZ. For in a rare stroke of luck and timing, McMahon's partner on the KMBZ consult, Norm Woodruff, was also acting program director of KFBK. He recommended Limbaugh to Aaron, who brought him out to Sacramento. "Rush had an incredible desire to succeed and he was willing to do almost anything to get the job and do what needed to be done," Aaron says. "He was well-read and up-to-date."

Aaron had him do an audition broadcast during a weekend. "He connected with the audience," the executive says. "He brought interesting topics to the table, he was obviously intelligent, and he drew people into the conversation." He also would be able to carry the conservative banner unfurled by Downey.

Bruce Marr, a former program director of Los Angeles talk powerhouse KABC who started consulting KFBK after Downey's departure, also suggested that the slot be offered to Limbaugh. "There was just something in him," Marr said. "He just jumped out of the radio. He was not permitted to do in Kansas City what we wanted him to do at KFBK."

Limbaugh accepted the job, returned to pack up his life in Kansas City, and then headed west again with Michelle. Only weeks after losing out at KMBZ, he went on the air October 15, 1984, a far less confrontational host than Downey.

"Later on, someone in our newsroom got a letter from Rush saying he was doing well," Heckerson recalled. "And it was clear he was doing real well because he sent along a photo of a highway billboard that said, 'LISTEN TO OUR RUSH HOUR.'"

Chapter 7

SACRAMENTO

KFBK-AM was a sleepy old station of little importance to its owner, the McClatchy newspaper chain, until a new chief executive officer hired Paul Aaron as general manager in 1982 to give it new life. At the time, KFBK and sister station KAER-FM were losing around $1 million a year, but CEO Irwin Potts authorized outlays for research, promotion, and talent to try to turn them into winners. It irked McClatchy that the company's hometown radio station was being beaten by KGNR-AM, a news/talk rival that belonged to an out-of-town newspaper outfit, the Tribune Company of Chicago.

One of Aaron's first moves before signing Limbaugh had been to undermine KGNR by bidding for its all-stars. Unable to lure away morning host Dave Williams, Aaron tried a different tactic. He went after newsman partner Bob Nathan, as well as the morning show's producer, Betsy Brazeil, thereby showing Williams that he would have the same comfort zone if he joined KFBK. And so they defected, all three of them.

When Limbaugh arrived months later, he found the talk climate uninspiring. Here it was, only two weeks before a presidential election involving Ronald Reagan—a former governor of the state, a former resident of Sacramento itself—and the hosts were interviewing a local sewerage director or sounding out a cook for a new spin on carrot cake. Two San Francisco stations, KGO and KCBS, also reached the state capital, but they offered little local flavor for the appreciable audience they had there.

Not that Limbaugh represented a higher degree of civic responsibility. In the twelve years that he had been eligible to vote, the son of a Republican party bulwark had never registered. Not in the Pittsburgh area and not during the stretch he lived in Overland Park, Kansas. And he made no move to register after relocating to the Sacramento area in 1984, thereby staying away from the polls for the second time that Reagan, his hero *Ronaldus Magnus* (Ronald the Great in Rushspeak), was on the ballot for president.

In fact, Limbaugh might have let the registration slide indefinitely had a local newspaper columnist not called him on the matter. As the broadcaster later maintained during a public appearance, the writer had been tipped off by "the Democratic apparatus" and then phoned to ask if it was true that he was unregistered. "And I said, 'I don't know, I'm on my way to the registrar's office.' I've no excuse for it. It was just pure and simple laziness. . . . Candidates didn't need me either back then."

Still, he was puzzled by the local shortage of radio discussion about national issues and the campaign. What's more, he thought, who needs guests on a radio talk show? His highly unconventional idea was to establish himself as The Expert, so that he alone would be the impetus for people to tune in between nine and noon each morning.

In fact, Limbaugh had little respect for anyone else on the station. Although he had achieved no lasting success before coming to town, his ego was as oversized as his waistline. But this was an asset to him in picking up where the headstrong Downey had left off, even if he offered a more altruistic view later on.

"I used to think radio was for me to become a star and get my ego thrills," he told an interviewer. "I wasn't listener-oriented, I was me-oriented. As I got a little older, I realized the key to my success was making the audience want to listen to me."

The novel concept of presiding over a show of one worked. More specifically, KFBK management left him alone to be himself.

"When I got that freedom, the responsibility hit me," he later told *Radio & Records*. "You can't blame a lack of success on the record rotation or the spot load—it's all on you. That responsibility perks you up and puts you more in touch with what you have to do to succeed."

Unlike in Kansas City, where he suffered an unwillingness on the part of listeners to phone in their opinions unless some game or gimmick was in play, in Sacramento the audience wanted to share their views. Limbaugh said he believed that living in the capital of a populous state familiarized people with the ways of government and spurred them to discussion. As a result, he found hosting a talk show to be a pleasure.

"He was different from the start," recalls Kitty O'Neal, who became the show's producer soon after Limbaugh arrived and was greeted with a big, overwhelming hug on her first meeting. "He was outgoing, playful, and impish. I sensed immediately that he was much more intelligent than Downey."

O'Neal tried to convince Limbaugh that he needed guests on the air, but he disagreed, and none came to the Sacramento studios except for a liberal professor from a local college who did an occasional point-counterpoint exchange with him every few weeks.

Even more significant in Limbaugh's development was that he railed against "failed liberalism" and its poster boy, Sen. Edward M. Kennedy, while distancing himself from the kind of hurtful venom that fellow conservative Downey used to spew at his callers. Limbaugh was eager to put space between himself and his predecessor, saying at one point that Downey was profane, as well as an insubstantial conservative. By offering a gentlemanly approach, even to those who challenged his views, the newcomer was also, perhaps naively at the time, laying deeper roots of job security than if he had set himself up as another of the fire-breathing talk jocks loose across the land. In fact, he stressed that his was a kinder, gentler style. "I want controversy because of the issues, not because of rudeness or abruptness with a caller," he told the *Sacramento Bee* a month after he started at KFBK. "I don't want people saying, 'Did you hear how he hung up on that caller?' I'm a very argumentative person, but I do it with responsibility."

Clearly, in Sacramento, Limbaugh was trying to find and claim his niche in the radio business. During the four years he would spend at KFBK, his on-air shtick would evolve even more closely into the mischievous, often outrageous amusement that would later claim a large national audience. He explored the use of sound effects and summoned hallway passersby into the studio for discussions at whim. If he spilled his cup of coffee, or the brew was too hot, he told his listeners. As matter-of-fact as this banter was, it was all the more innovative for being put on the airwaves, long considered off-limits to the mundane vagaries of everyday living.

At the same time, the spontaneity—which continued long after-ward—was driven by his keen awareness of what worked on the air and by the approval that he received from his closest associates. In other words, Limbaugh's carefree inventions were more calculat-ing than they sounded. "If I ever said anything about the show, he'd say, 'What do you mean exactly?' " O'Neal recalls. "I had to look at him in the studio through the glass and I had to listen to what he was saying. I felt he needed feedback and support. I felt he doubted himself."

Limbaugh's insecurity also became apparent to Aaron when the broadcaster tangled with him over the flimsiest issues simply to assert his own importance. Early in his stay, when KFBK was satisfied that its lineup of Dave and Bob, Limbaugh, and weather and traffic features matched the market-researched expectations of Sacramento, Aaron mailed a four-color promotional brochure to every home in the city. Naturally, it highlighted Dave and Bob, who were shown in a photograph because morning-drive is when a station makes its money and baits the hook for the day. Limbaugh, however, erupted in rage when he saw that he was not pictured in the mailing. That he had yet to develop in the market did not offset his anger.

"The man is the most talented personality in radio," says Aaron, who later became general manager of KFAB in Omaha. "He does what no one has been able to do before. He's able to build the morning audience into a bigger share at midday. But he's basically an insecure guy."

Another time, Limbaugh insisted on being allowed to decide which sponsors could advertise on his show, a preposterous demand that would be like a rookie reporter telling his editor which stories he would cover. Specifically, Limbaugh was objecting to a car dealer that was paying to have him read its commercials live during the broadcast. "I told him that life was free, that he did not have to read the spot," Aaron recalls, "but I also told him that if this was his decision, he would not be doing the show.

"He came in without a whole lot of success, but from time to time he would try to reassert his value, at least to himself."

When KFBK's Mary Jane Popp was preparing to lead a cruise jointly sponsored by a travel agency and the station, bookings turned sluggish, so Aaron decided to team her in a radio spot with Limbaugh. But he refused to do the commercial. He did not want to bail her out and help save the cruise—until Aaron made it clear that the station was committed to the success of the venture and he had to do it. Grudgingly, he complied, though it grated on him enough to come up in conversation even years later. As Aaron put it, "He was never a team player."

Unless he was captain of the team. "Looking through the pane of glass, I'd give him thumbs up or thumbs down in reaction to things he said," O'Neal remembers. "If it was thumbs down, then he'd call me into the studio and I'd go on the air with him and say, 'You're out of your mind.' He didn't do the show in a vacuum. It was a very social show."

Another difference from Kansas City was that Limbaugh could see his quirky strokes register favorably in the all-important ratings compiled throughout the year by The Arbitron Company. A decade earlier, at KQV in Pittsburgh, he had pushed the envelope of disc-jockeying by actually telling his listeners what he was going to do next and how long it would take him to do it; his show presented mindless hit music while also serving as a kind of inside entertainment for those who were hip enough to appreciate his sly, ulterior motives. But the music was king and Limbaugh's creativity less apparent to those who paid his salary, whereas in Sacramento he recognized that his own talk could make for an entertaining program and become the main reason to tune in.

And listeners did just that. In Downey's brief tenure, he had helped lift KFBK into the black and multiplied negligible ratings during the nine-to-noon slot into a hefty 5 share. Limbaugh took over a broadcast that was already gathering steam and grew the numbers over time to a 14.4 share, meaning that 14.4 percent of all those tuned to radio during a so-called average quarter-hour listened to Limbaugh. With most radio markets so fragmented that each station claims little more than a thin sliver of the total audience, a double-digit helping of the pie was impressive indeed. It offered irrefutable evidence that Limbaugh and his style had found their mark. What's more, his popularity tripled the ad rate so that KFBK could charge around $150 a minute.

He had finally become a success in a notoriously iffy business. The response in Sacramento rejuvenated and vindicated him. It felt so sweet that he wanted his father to know about it and to realize the role he had played. "I'm basically doing the same thing we did at the dinner table," Limbaugh told the Cape Girardeau newspaper. "Throwing ideas out, talking about them, arguing about them. It's maybe just not quite as civilized."

"Rush had been at KFBK six months when I came in as news director and head of programming," says Tyler Cox. "One of the smartest things I've ever done in my career was to listen to Rush's show for a few weeks and then tell him, 'Just go back and do your show.' He had it nailed, and the reaction was phenomenal. There was no reason to meddle or try to change it. Between the phone response and the street talk about the show, the numbers skyrocketed. I would go to chamber of commerce meetings, the Lions Club, and people wanted to talk about Rush. It was one of those magic times."

In the summer of 1986, Cox and Limbaugh took his show to

Washington and, in a radical departure, hooked him up with guests such as George Will, Sam Donaldson, David Brinkley, Robert Bork, and various congressmen.

On KFBK, he proclaimed his broadcast "an excursion into excellence in broadcasting," another use of the phrase that he would use to name his national network a few years later. He also defined for the first time a "Gorbasm," an orgasmic response he saw in those who viewed the *glasnost* initiatives of Soviet leader Mikhail Gorbachev all too approvingly. Dripping with sarcasm, he read a news story about Russian citizens being allowed to buy their own homes and remarked: "Isn't that big of Gorbachev?"

He also got miles of notoriety from savaging the feminist movement, a favorite target for years to come. He said it was designed to assist unattractive women and that a typical speaker was a "frumpy-looking woman who has been discriminated against because she is unattractive and hasn't found a decent guy to marry."

In addition, he brushed off and reused an outrageous bit that had worked so well in Kansas City—calling for a ban on ugly people so that they would not be allowed to walk the streets during daylight hours. Here again, it was another of the calculated controversies that talk hosts have practiced for years in a shameless bid to seize attention. Limbaugh, however, had his intimates believe that it was a Swiftian gesture designed to make light of California's body-worshiping narcissism. In any event, the calls poured in; comparisons to Hitler were made. Limbaugh had to confess that he was joking. But not before realizing that his listeners were following his banter intently, perhaps too intently, considering the rage he was able to provoke.

Was it all an act? Yes, much of it. As conservative as Limbaugh basically was, some of his opinions were too outrageous even for him to believe. But in Sacramento, he grew into the act. The absence of serious radio competition was no reason to avoid the bold and daring polemics that would etch the act in people's minds. After speaking particularly outlandish lines on the air, he would look through the glass at O'Neal and give her a wink. "He didn't vote, he didn't care," she recalled in 1992. "I don't think it was his intention at all to become this big, conservative icon for so many people. A lot of it was just shtick—still is shtick." Yet Limbaugh knew that good shtick could take him far.

A ridiculous bit in which he guiltily maintained that the devil could be heard when he played backward a Slim Whitman record, "Una Paloma Blanca," not only had some listeners believe him, but had others go so far as to see his contrition as a true act of exorcism. Limbaugh and his employers discovered that listeners responded not only to his views, but also to his commercials. He said that he finally came to realize in Sacramento that the only role for people in radio was to sell advertising. The realization spread when Filco, a local electronics retailer that did little radio advertising, was persuaded to let Limbaugh try to sell its cameras. The response was so favorable that Filco ended up signing him as spokesman—a relationship that continued in a TV campaign and lasted even after Limbaugh left for New York.

Another early score was on behalf of the local Nutri/System weight-loss franchise. He did its commercials on the radio and lost a lot of pounds through the regimen before he agreed to appear in a TV spot holding out the waistline of a grossly oversized pair of pants: "Hi, I'm world-famous radio talk show host Rush Limbaugh." On top of the egotistical bravado that was his stock in trade, the sight of him standing inside monstrous trousers prompted people to ask: Who is this guy? Which was his intention all along.

Limbaugh wanted to escape the ups and downs of ratings by giving himself what he called "ratings insurance." That is, instead of being judged solely on the basis of Arbitron numbers, he also wanted to demonstrate his ability to move product. In the process, he thought, he would also get to show off his ringmaster's knack for grandstanding effectively.

And that led to a dilemma. Limbaugh was such an effective commercial pitchman that he eventually had to resist doing practically every spot in his program "because I wanted to hold on to my credibility and my believability," he told an audience later. "And I didn't want any of that to be watered down, nor did I want to be perceived as a huckster, nor did I want the audience to believe that I perceived them as customers."

Nevertheless, he also wanted to maximize his salesmanship, and so arose the idea of charging premiums for the commercials he touted himself. According to Aaron, a fifty-two-week commitment from such an advertiser cost about $60,000 and another $10,000 went to Limbaugh. With a half-dozen or so arrangements like this, he well exceeded his salary in premiums. Personal appearances added still more. To his amazement, farflung groups such as the California Pear Growers Association were willing to pay him up to $500 a speech. A phone company and a bedding distributor were among the sponsors that retained him as spokesman.

By 1986, the onetime nickel-pincher's annual income approached $100,000 a year. Local organizations roasted him; others invited him to talk. He was grand marshal of the St. Patrick's Day parade, even though he wasn't the least bit Irish. He helped a travel agency sell seats on a two-week tour of Hong Kong and Hawaii and naturally went along for the ride.

"I went to visit my brother when he was working in Pittsburgh, and I could see that he had it all together, even though I, too, thought, he should have finished college," David Limbaugh recalls. "But it wasn't until I visited him in Sacramento, and went to see him give a speech out there, that I realized what a star he was. The people just worshiped him. There was so much fan loyalty. I had no idea how this would ever translate to any kind of national audience, but I knew back then that it would work for him sooner or later."

Two years after Limbaugh hit town, the volume of business he was personally endorsing and voicing began to trouble him. At a time when even the shoes he wore were obtained through a contract with a sponsor, he feared that listeners were unable to tell the difference between his own remarks about a product and the prepared text that he read. Although he wondered if he was developing a credibility problem, others with influence seemed to have no such concerns.

He started writing an opinion column for the *Senior Spectrum Weekly* newspaper and doing commentary on local television. Even government authorities were buying in. When Regional Transit opened the second leg of its light-rail system, which Limbaugh had derided on the air as "late rail," the broadcaster agreed to serve as master of ceremonies at the unveiling.

The clamor for Limbaugh's attention, in addition to the piles of fan mail he received, prompted Michelle to leave her job as a saleswoman with a printing company and become an assistant to her husband. She knew firsthand that he had become a bona fide celebrity because people were now stopping her in grocery stores to ask about his views. She took home a bunch of KFBK stationery in order to tackle his correspondence.

Home was the former model unit in a development located in the suburb of South Natomas—a two-story structure with white carpeting and a backyard patio with gazebo and barbecue. Endorsements for local stores helped supply the bed and lamps; spots Limbaugh did for Filco earned him the washer, dryer, and twenty-five-inch TV set on which he and Michelle enjoyed "Dallas" and nightly playbacks on the VCR of the soap "All My Children."

Life appeared to be sweet indeed. After feeling a financial squeeze in Kansas City, he was earning six figures from a job that he enjoyed, so that he could save money and still meet the payments on a house that he loved. "I even love being able to buy eight rolls of toilet paper because now we have the room to put them away," he told a visiting reporter from the *Sacramento Bee*. "I can buy two six-packs of diet soda. I take a certain amount of pride that in this vagabond business I can own a house. A new house."

Michelle described him as sensitive and serious, while he quipped that she was the right woman for him because she knew not to take him too seriously. However, behind the rosy picture that they presented to local reporters and admirers was a marriage starting to splinter. In 1986, two years into their stay, Michelle confessed that the couple was having problems, partly because she wanted to forge her own career outside her husband's widening shadow of fame and importance. His egocentricity and housebound ways also took their toll. Here they were in sunny California, and much of the time he preferred to head home to the air conditioning and the computer diversions. On a day when he did take to the outdoors, going along on a boat ride with KCRA-TV anchorman Stan Atkinson and other friends, he wore a navy blue blazer in the bright sunshine and looked as if he was being poisoned by the fresh air. "Michelle was a very attractive, energetic woman who preferred to be out," an associate recalls. "She totally subordinated her interests to his. Her role in life was to say, 'Yes, Rush.' "

Not that Limbaugh's own affection started to ebb along with hers. One day at KFBK, O'Neal drew his attention to a magazine ad showing a model with long, beautiful legs and commented that it was impossible for anyone to look so fine. But Limbaugh disagreed, saying, "Michelle looks just like that." Although he was almost completely self-absorbed, it was obvious that, in his own way, he worshiped her.

Limbaugh occasionally voiced an ambition to do a talk show from Washington, but basically he was content simply to cruise along in Sacramento as a local hero. "Right now, I want to be happy for once in my life," he told an interviewer. "I'm an infant for talk radio. In a way, I'm just being born."

Ah, but Bruce Marr, the talk consultant who had encouraged KFBK to hire Limbaugh in the first place, had other ideas. Around this same time, Marr was under contract to recommend candidates for an afternoon opening at WOR, New York's leading talk station. He made the suggestions, but he also told Bob Bruno, the program director who later became general manager, that there was one fellow whom he was saving for himself. Which was fine by Bruno, who may have missed out on an early opportunity to claim Limbaugh for WOR, but would get the chance again to bring him into the fold.

The fellow Marr was saving for himself also remained nameless to Edward F. McLaughlin, a former president of the ABC Radio Networks who had recently gone into the syndication business. Marr visited New York several times a year and over drinks would tell his old friend Ed, "I've got the next big star." The syndicator would ask who it was, but Marr teased him by refusing to supply a name. The consultant wanted the time to be right and he also wanted an agreement that would bring himself along on the ride to riches that he was certain would follow.

Early in 1988, as McLaughlin was nearing the end of a two-year, noncompete period with ABC, Marr was ready. He told McLaughlin: Rush Limbaugh, KFBK, Sacramento. Although McLaughlin knew that Limbaugh was posting handsome ratings out west, he had never heard the program that Marr was so keen on. In fact, his main interest in KFBK at the time was as the target of a buyout; he saw himself running the station and its FM sister after acquiring the properties in partnership with his friend Paul Harvey, ABC Radio's veteran news commentator. That deal was never consummated, and KFBK was purchased by Westinghouse Broadcasting Corp. from McClatchy Newspapers, but during a visit to Sacramento McLaughlin finally got to sample Marr's find. Listening to the radio in his hotel room, he was unimpressed with Limbaugh. Too pompous, he thought. A blowhard. Certainly no one who would ever score with a national audience.

But McLaughlin liked Limbaugh personally when Marr later got the three of them together for dinner that February in the syndicator's native San Francisco. Limbaugh was at ease through the meal, even though he was unsure what would develop from their meeting. McLaughlin, his curiosity revived, returned to Sacramento for another listen. This time, he decided to tune in not as a broadcast executive, but as a member of the audience. He rented a car and drove around the city as Limbaugh boomed out from the dashboard. Instead of losing the voice amid the distractions of the road, McLaughlin was drawn into the show. He felt a direct connection between Limbaugh and the listener. He liked the topical ideas, strong viewpoints, and show-biz elements.

"Rush and I did a lot of talking after that initial dinner with Ed," Marr recalled. "I knew a deal would be worked out."

Chapter 8

ENTER THE DEALMAKER

For a writer of short stories, *The New Yorker*'s interest in publishing a tale would be as good a launch to prominence as he might hope for. For a curveballer facing another dog summer in minor-league anonymity, the call-up to the majors is reason to rejoice. For a local talk-radio host wanting to reach a national audience, the approval of Ed McLaughlin was one of the best possible stepping-stones.

Like Bruce Marr, McLaughlin became a believer in Rush Limbaugh. A big believer. For McLaughlin was a player. Not a particularly active player at the time Marr brought him to the dinner table in San Francisco, but one whose drive and managerial strokes during the fourteen years he ran the ABC Radio Networks ideally qualified him to market "Rush Who" to a string of stations around the country. He was, as a colleague put it, "one of the all-time schmoozers," a man who liked his cocktail and belied his executive pedigree by once trading songs with the bartender when the night and the mood were right.

He was a native of San Francisco, where his paternal great-grandfather, a former Dublin cop, had gone by way of New Orleans to police the roughneck forty-niners drawn by the discovery of gold. In the generations that followed, the McLaughlins put an abundance of policemen and other civil servants on the local payroll.

Born in 1926, Ed had other ideas when he returned home from military service late in the Second World War. He became part owner of a nightclub at twenty-one and also made money in real estate. But these entrepreneurial ventures were curtailed by his call back to duty during the Korean War. Serving in the air force, he was stationed in England, where American bomber crews were restricted to base most of the time and where he satisfied their need for amusement by presenting live shows of traveling entertainers.

Home again, he got a degree from San Francisco State University and then plunged into the radio business. He was a salesman with an Oakland rock station (KEWB) and then became a sales rep for a national time buyer before ABC hired him in 1964 as general sales manager for the company-owned KGO in San Francisco. He rose to the top job of general manager two years later.

KGO was new to news/talk programming just as the format was beginning to take flight around the country. As a result, while ABC's profitable rock-and-roll stations, including New York's WABC, viewed the larger ABC Radio Network as an albatross and balked at having to interrupt their music shows with the network's newscasts, Don McNeill's hour-long "Breakfast Club" and ABC's even longer dinnertime news program, McLaughlin came to value the network because it helped him fill hours of airtime with information programming.

Nevertheless, in 1966, ABC Radio president Ralph Beaudin hatched the innovative—and FCC-approved—idea of customizing the network to fit the disparate formats of the stations that ABC owned, as well as its many affiliates. In place of one monolithic network clumsily serving rock, talk, and so-called beautiful-music outlets, four different networks were set up beginning in 1968 under the same ABC marquee. For example, the Contemporary Network tailored its news and features to WABC and the other rock stations, and the American Information Network fed Paul Harvey and similar news/talk segments to KGO and the rest of the talk outlets. In this age before the commonplace use of communications satellites, the newly multiplied networks were able to transmit their broadcasts to stations via ABC's long-distance phone lines at no additional expense because they were simply filling those minutes of each hour that the lines had been idle when one network served all takers.

Privately, the operators of the larger radio stations hoped that the multinetwork concept would prove so unwieldy as to do what they knew ABC founder and chief executive officer Leonard H. Goldenson was loath to do—kill off the network. However, the expansion into four specialized networks, coupled with built-in economies, helped reverse annual losses that were said to go as high as $3 million, and the new setup even started to make money. But previously unaffiliated stations were not forming long lines to get a piece of ABC for themselves. Goldenson called on McLaughlin to improve the situation, knowing that he was a top manager and that KGO was a loyal customer of the Information Network.

In 1972, McLaughlin left San Francisco to become president of the ABC Radio Networks. He had always wanted to go to New York, but he was disappointed that it would not be as head of the ABC-owned stations. After all, he considered himself a station operator; he had turned around KGO and made money, sending its first profit to New York in dollar bills, 118 of them.

As network president, he increased the number of ABC affiliates by enticing newcomers with offers of annual compensation and he headed off a potentially embarrassing problem of accountability to advertisers by working to ensure that the affidavits on which stations reported the commercials they aired would be closely weighed by the FCC at license renewal.

Besides managerial acumen, McLaughlin had an ear for talent and product during the fourteen years he ran the network, and it would serve him—and ABC—well. Among his smartest moves was to buy a radio-syndication company called Watermark in 1982 and thereby bring its two highly successful countdown shows into the ABC fold. The bigger catch was "American Top 40," launched twelve years earlier by disc jockey and host Casey Kasem and his partner, Don Bustany. It was being carried on weekends by about three hundred stations; the earnest Kasem ticked off the hottest pop hits of the week and stitched together the songs with listener dedications and artist trivia. In a refinement of the so-called barter arrangement that Watermark had with its affiliates, McLaughlin continued to offer them the show free of charge, but he cut the number of commercial minutes available for local spots and claimed the time for ABC so that the network would see a greater return on its investment.

"Ed bought 'American Top 40,' along with 'American Country Countdown,' and he used the shows to open the door to ABC News," Kasem recalls. "A station now couldn't get 'American Top 40' without also taking something like eighteen newscasts a day from ABC. Now, ABC had a wedge. We lost one or two key affiliates, including KIIS-FM in Los Angeles, but by and large most stations stayed put.

"Ed kept up on what was going on. He knew radio inside and out—and he also knew that personalities were very important. I remember they went out of their way to welcome us. They threw a big party. They really did it romantically."

"Radio is personality-driven," McLaughlin says. "Listening is personality-driven by the consumers. It's a lot of personalities connecting with the audience. Casey Kasem, counting down, connected with the audience. It was dramatic. Radio has always been a personality business. Radio lost it when they decided that music was more important than other aspects of it."

McLaughlin also had been the main reason that commentator Paul Harvey stayed firmly in place with ABC. "Harvey needed a feeling of importance and he got that from Ed," a friend says. "Ed would write him a note when he heard something he liked on the air. Something like that can save you a million dollars at contract time."

And McLaughlin, though a friend of Harvey and his wife, Angel, had to consider the financial importance of the Chicago-based broadcaster. As network president in 1978, McLaughlin persuaded an initially reluctant ABC board of directors to approve a seven-year contract for Harvey at a time when the broadcaster had 770 stations carrying his two daily programs and was rumored to be considering a jump to the Mutual Broadcasting System, then recently purchased by Amway Corp., a longtime sponsor of his.

During the next six years, Harvey's fortress of affiliates grew to number 1,300. With such unsurpassed clearance for a radio show, Harvey's happiness was obviously vital to ABC, and McLaughlin's involvement with ABC was known to be vital to Harvey.

So much so that Harvey almost left ABC, his outlet for more than three decades, in the mid-1980s when the ramifications of the media company's $3.5-billion merger with Capital Cities Communications Inc. were unclear. When it was announced in 1985 that the smaller Cap Cities planned to swallow up the behemoth ABC, Harvey felt concern for McLaughlin's future and for his own negotiations toward a new contract. Uncharacteristically for Harvey, a fussy man with little public profile off the air, he began making loud noises to the press. In April, he told the New York *Daily News* that his negotiations were "in limbo. I'm waiting to see what happens when Capital Cities Communications takes over. . . . Leonard Goldenson and the network have been like family to me. I don't know what the new company has in mind for radio. Until the smoke clears, I have to make my plans accordingly."

Although few were aware at the time, Harvey's plans included a serious flirtation with the CBS Radio Network. At an NCAA basketball final that spring, a mutual friend pulled aside Dick Brescia, the senior vice president of CBS Radio, and conveyed a message that Harvey wanted to speak with him. A startled—and delighted—Brescia learned that Harvey was uncertain about the pending merger and wanted to explore his options.

In the phone call that followed, Harvey explained to Brescia that he was loyal to ABC, it had given him an exciting life, but he still believed he deserved more. Would CBS be interested in his services?

What a question. The possibility of the popular Harvey leaving ABC for CBS was seismic.

"In broad terms, the salary figures he gave me were modest numbers," Brescia recalls. "I told him right away that we would do better. I was smelling some blood, certainly vulnerability on ABC's part. We could have doubled his salary and still made money. He was making around $3 million a year and we could have gone to $6 million."

However, Brescia faced one high hurdle and he told Harvey that it would take a while to clear. As it then appeared, before Harvey could broadcast news at CBS, network policy required that he become an employee of CBS News and accept its editorial strictures, including a church-state separation from commercials. But Harvey's earnest delivery of the spots that punctuated his newscasts and commentaries had long endeared him to advertisers. Even if this practice now stood to grate on the CBS News of Walter Cronkite and Dan Rather, both of whom had had to pass up lucrative commercial endorsements, surely there was a way to bring Harvey aboard as an independent contractor, Brescia argued. After all, another veteran broadcaster, Lowell Thomas, had had his own special arrangement with the network (and commentator Charles Osgood would switch from CBS News to the CBS Radio Network in 1992 in order to be free to voice commercials).

As it turned out, CBS's news and radio divisions reacted nervously when asked by Brescia to sort through the red tape. The in-house discussions dragged on. Meanwhile, over at ABC, the merger with Cap Cities took effect in January of 1986, after which Ben Hoberman retired as president of ABC Radio, a lofty position that held sway over both McLaughlin's networks and the stations owned by ABC. But McLaughlin, long regarded as Hoberman's heir apparent, did not get the job. It went to James P. Arcara, a longtime Cap Cities soldier who was president of that company's radio stations.

Shut out of the number-one job after a decade and a half atop the networks, McLaughlin saw that his growth within the newly enlarged company was over, so he resigned and left the store to the newcomers. His vacated post with the networks was handed over months later to another Cap Cities veteran, Aaron Daniels, who had known Arcara since 1971, when the two of them started working together at the helm of company-owned radio station WPAT.

Although McLaughlin was depressed and lacked a clear idea of what he wanted to do next, he cashed in valuable stock and accepted an office at ABC as part of an exit package. In addition, he agreed to perform a vital service, something that he alone was able to pull off in those uncertain weeks after the merger. He would try to make

Harvey happy. On behalf of the newly formed Capital Cities/ABC, whose principals had had no previous dealings with Harvey, he agreed to act as a consultant in the tense contract negotiations.

McLaughlin convinced the newly arrived rulers of Cap Cities/ABC, especially president Daniel Burke and chairman Thomas Murphy, that Harvey was worth an enormous salary. And he convinced Harvey, then sixty-eight, that it was foolish to climb the mountain all over again, that he should stick with ABC even though his old friend would no longer be running things.

In October, Harvey signed another seven-year deal that would pay him up to around $7 million annually, the largest pile in radio, and give him the right to veto any advertisers that he did not want on his broadcasts. (In 1991, he signed a new contract that extended into the twenty-first century, at a sum of about $10 million a year, which proved that McLaughlin's stubborn belief in the broadcaster was now shared by those on high.)

Despite Harvey's advancing age, his continued presence on 1,200-plus ABC affiliates allowed the network to exercise considerable leverage over the stations. His enduring popularity helped ABC Radio place additional network programming on the stations' airwaves, while his own shows earned an estimated $5 million to $6 million in advertising annually above and beyond the salary.

Harvey reportedly represented as much as one-quarter of the ABC Radio Network's profits. Meanwhile, CBS, the network that let him get away, was to finish 1986 with a distant $9 million in earnings.

"ABC can get an affiliation because of Harvey," McLaughlin said later. "Paul is now the strength of the Information Network. Paul is more important now than he was twenty or thirty years ago. I learned so goddamn much working with him. In some ways, I think that I owe Paul."

The premier lesson, as McLaughlin saw it, was that radio is show business, too, no less than movies and television. As a result, it needed stars to thrive.

The lords of Cap Cities saw things differently. In 1988, Kasem's negotiations toward a new contract collapsed over money. The disc jockey, brought into the fold by McLaughlin, reportedly was earning more than $1 million a year at the time, but wanted $3 million to renew. Despite an estimated $5 million a year in profit from "American Top 40," the network expressed fears of a downturn in the popularity of radio's Top 40 sound, as did happen within the next few years, and offered Kasem only slightly more than $2 million to stay on.

Nothing doing. In a major development within the industry, Kasem was then snatched up by the syndicator Westwood One in a five-year deal said to be worth $20 million. Although ABC continued "American Top 40" with Shadoe Stevens as the new host, at a fraction of Kasem's salary, Westwood created a competing weekend countdown, "Casey's Top 40." It quickly parlayed Kasem's considerable fame into an equal, if not superior, lineup of stations, beginning with 420 to Stevens's 475.

Industry savants questioned how ABC could have let Kasem get away; after all, "American Top 40" was considered a gusher. The answer, however, was that McLaughlin didn't run the store anymore. (Kasem went on to develop two other shows with Westwood One, and was being heard on more than one thousand stations, before signing another multiyear contract with the syndicator in 1993.)

Limbaugh was not McLaughlin's first entrepreneurial venture after leaving ABC. In 1987, the executive formed his own company, EFM Media Management Inc., in order to syndicate the daily radio broadcasts of Dr. Dean Edell. The physician was based at McLaughlin's alma mater, KGO in San Francisco, and offered medical advice for an hour each afternoon as part of ABC Talk-radio's lineup. But ABC, now in the hands of thrifty Cap Cities, was planning to drop him so that it could hire a replacement for less than the $90,000 he was earning.

McLaughlin offered to keep the show going without interruption, at no cost to ABC, in return for the right to sell all of the commercial time. In effect, EFM Media would own the show and pay Edell. And ABC, which was souring on its daytime talk programming because of minimal success, would maintain continuity with Edell's affiliates while not having to pay his salary or find a successor. The arrangement sounded so good to ABC that it agreed to allow an exception to the two-year noncompete clause that McLaughlin had accepted when he resigned the year before.

From all indications, McLaughlin got the far better deal. Not only did ABC put him in business, but he took an established radio property and expanded its affiliate base by tapping many of the contacts he had made during his years with the network. In addition, McLaughlin spun off the "Dr. Dean Edell Medical Minute" at minimal extra cost and syndicated the informational segment to hundreds of stations, reaping mid-six-figure revenues from the additional advertising paired with the feature. McLaughlin scored, courtesy of his former employer, which seemed none the wiser. He also saw how he might do it again.

"I made money for ABC, then I just changed the venue," he said later. "I did it for them and now I was doing it for me. Very simple."

But the Limbaugh launch was much more complicated than the takeover of the Edell program. The get-together over dinner in San Francisco turned into weeks of conversations between Limbaugh, Marr, and McLaughlin. And even after all the talk, they talked some more when Limbaugh called in his brother, David, from Cape Girardeau to represent him as they sorted out the details. Finally, at the end of March in 1988, five men gathered in a large suite at the Sacramento Hilton: Marr, the Limbaugh brothers, McLaughlin, and his own attorney, Howard Abrahams. For two days, they discussed and haggled toward the finish line.

Limbaugh had agreed on a guaranteed starting salary of $150,000 a year before David flew west to join the talks—the lawyer was unhappy that the dollar figure already was off the table—so this major concession left the attorney to address a number of ancillary areas that would affect earnings over the long haul. Marr's role, for example, was still undecided, and McLaughlin and company were pressing Limbaugh to accept a long-term deal.

Eventually, the Limbaughs accepted a six-year arrangement and language that gave McLaughlin the right to match any other offer that the broadcaster might receive at the end of the contract. In exchange for this latter point, however, the brothers won McLaughlin's willingness to match not only a competing salary that might be offered down the road, but also the terms and work location spelled out in the offer. This gave Limbaugh freedom later on if, say, he wished to relocate to Los Angeles.

For two days, the men talked and fenced. They also continued talking when Limbaugh broke off to do his daily radio show at KFBK. Loosening their ties, they moved from the living room to a nearby conference table, then back to the couches when in need of a seventh-inning stretch. David had negotiated a lot of contracts in his young career and further prepared himself for the Sacramento sessions by asking clients who owned Cape Girardeau's KZIM-AM about the fine points of radio syndication. At the Hilton, he ran numbers through his personal computer. McLaughlin referred to spreadsheets showing commercial revenues based on his own anticipated ratings for the show. McLaughlin's projections, which turned out to be strikingly accurate as the years passed, were crucial to the negotiations early on because Limbaugh's initial salary was to be guaranteed for the first two years against these earnings to come.

The salary was to be secured by the new venture they were setting in motion, as well as by McLaughlin himself, with the provision that the syndicator could recoup any personal losses he might incur in paying Limbaugh by tapping future profits from the endeavor. Affiliate stations were to get the show free of charge, but they would have to air four minutes of commercials an hour supplied by the producers; they could retain nine per hour for themselves. The parties also agreed that Limbaugh would work as an independent contractor, responsible for paying his own taxes, and they concurred on a detailed list of "reasonable" expenses, including telephone charges, installation of an 800 line, the salary for an affiliate-relations staffer, liability premiums, and promotional costs.

In the end, they put together a new entity to be incorporated in New York State, PAM Inc., an acronym formed by the initials of McLaughlin's wife, Pat. PAM would own Limbaugh's national show and split the profits among the host, Marr, and McLaughlin, whose EFM Media Management would act as general manager of the franchise and de facto bookkeeper. Specifically, it was reported that Limbaugh was to get 30 percent of the show's profits, prompting him to boast to the *Sacramento Bee* that he expected to take in $250,000 the first year, or about two and a half times his local earnings. As it turned out, Limbaugh's total earnings from the national show did not exceed his $150,000 salary the first year, when the program was slowly being rolled out. Rapid growth began in year number two.

Nevertheless, for a talk jockey who had been unsuccessful outside the nation's thirty-second-largest radio market, one who was known nowhere else except maybe Kansas City, the deal with McLaughlin was more than favorable. In effect, it gave Limbaugh an ownership stake in his own show in return for his on-air services. McLaughlin described him as a "partner under contract to my company." Marr planned to continue his own involvement as a consultant to the broadcast.

By the end of April, as word circulated in Sacramento that Limbaugh had given a fellow named Ed McLaughlin the right to deliver his show to a national audience, it was not immediately believed that he would have to leave the state capital. McLaughlin pointed out that satellite technology made it possible for Limbaugh to base his show just about anywhere. After all, Edell was broadcasting coast to coast from San Francisco. Limbaugh, on the other hand, sounded as if he was preparing to pack his bags in full view. He cockily told the *Bee:* "Look, nobody stays here who has ambition and confidence. I've always wanted to live in a big, thriving city." Privately, however, the insecure Limbaugh was shaking. What was he doing? He feared that he would jeopardize all the comforts and friendships he had amassed in Sacramento to cast off into unknown waters. "He would have preferred to do the national show from Sacramento," O'Neal recalls. "He had a lot of trepidation."

He called his buddy Bryan Burns, now working for Major League Baseball in Manhattan, at home one Saturday night and told him, "I may be coming to New York." There was uneasiness in his voice because of uncertainty about the step up to his own major league and the myriad headaches that would await a small-town guy plopped in the middle of Sodom. He wanted Burns and his wife to help him and Michelle navigate their move, rent an apartment, and make sense of the forbidding subway system.

Limbaugh also fretted that it would be difficult to extricate himself from his KFBK contract, which extended another year, because his only legal window of escape was to find a position with a station in one of the country's top five markets. In other words, a big leap from number thirty-two Sacramento. McLaughlin hoped to find a big-city stage, but he had nothing firm in hand when Limbaugh notified KFBK management that he was planning to leave and that he would give them the required month's notice in due time.

As a result, the onus was on McLaughlin not only to construct a chain of affiliate stations for the new show—and no syndicated venture was complete without an outlet in New York City—but also to finesse Limbaugh's way clear of the Sacramento station that he now so clearly had outgrown. KFBK general manager Rick Eytcheson would not concede that the popular host might be moving on. He dismissed the talk of a national show as rumor.

But McLaughlin would secure his reputation as a radio genius by turning this rumor into Technicolor fact. From the insider's position he continued to hold at ABC, coming and going from an office that the radio network provided him, he knew a few things of enormous strategic value. To begin with, his friend Owen Spann, an interviewer he had brought to ABC Talkradio from KGO in San Francisco, was nearing the end of a contract and having health problems in New York. He would not be staying on, thereby creating an opening in the ABC talk lineup from noon to 2:00 P.M., Eastern Time.

Filling this hole would have freed Limbaugh from KFBK if any of the stations carrying Spann's show was located in one of the top five markets. But none was, a clear reflection of ABC Talkradio's anemic performance and the long-established trend among talk stations toward locally originated programming during the more lucrative daytime hours. Talkradio's tombstone was ready, but the date of death had yet to be inscribed. As a result, while Spann's small-town affiliates presented McLaughlin with a possible start-up constituency for Limbaugh's show, the syndicator still had to obtain a home for the host in one of the big cities if they were to go into business at all.

This is where the crafty McLaughlin combined his insider's knowledge with one of the many contacts he had developed during his tenure at the network helm. In New York, the leading radio market, ABC flagship WABC was foundering in red ink. Six years into the talk format, the onetime king of Top 40 was losing more than $2 million a year, much of that because of dismal returns on the equally dismal New York Yankees' broadcasts. Its hodgepodge of local and network talk shows trailed the rival WOR in the ratings. WABC hungered for programming ideas and cost savings.

Enter Frederick D. Weinhaus, a gruff Cap Cities bottom-liner installed as WABC's general manager in January 1988. In Weinhaus, McLaughlin had someone who had paid little attention to talk radio before joining WABC. Weinhaus was a numbers cruncher, numb to the subtleties of on-air dialogue, who would be far more impressed by the chance to save a few bucks, and who wanted to salvage WABC but do it on the cheap.

Enter also John Mainelli, a well-traveled news/talk specialist brought in as the station's program director in March, partly as a result of McLaughlin's intervention.

In the forty-year-old Mainelli, McLaughlin had a friend of several years whose talents and intelligence he had often extolled to others in the ABC organization. "I thought he was bright," McLaughlin says. "And I helped him get jobs. He and I talked a lot. It had nothing to do with Rush. I was impressed by him."

So when the pressure mounted to nail down a major-market home for Limbaugh, the first vital step in syndication, McLaughlin called on Mainelli. "We had a dialogue," McLaughlin says. "I also know he has a good ear. The people who ran WABC before him were total assholes. So I was happy to have John."

McLaughlin loaded up Mainelli with tapes of Limbaugh's show on KFBK. The program director knew the California radio markets, especially San Diego, San Francisco, and Los Angeles, but he considered Sacramento small-time and by no means cosmopolitan. "Sacramento, in and of itself, you wouldn't want to risk too much on," Mainelli says. "But I listened to the tapes and I started to make a list of why I didn't like him. I listed that he was bombastic and I didn't know if he could back up the bombast with credibility. There were a lot of tapes, but I owed Ed a favor so I kept listening. And I kept listening because the guy definitely had something, and I found myself listing almost all positives. That he had a great command of the language. That he was bombastic but self-effacing. That he was up on current events. That he was entertaining."

The hard-nosed Weinhaus didn't care one way or another; it was Mainelli's decision to hire Limbaugh or not. McLaughlin had to have a Los Angeles outlet and he had to have New York. Mainelli was willing to give him New York, but he told the syndicator it would be awkward for the station to get rid of network programming from ABC, only to turn around and air another national show with still more calls from Keokuk, Iowa. He proposed to McLaughlin that Limbaugh instead do a local show for WABC that would stand apart from the new syndicated venture. McLaughlin and Limbaugh agreed.

The idea was fine with Weinhaus, but he wanted to meet Limbaugh just the same. The get-together was arranged at the annual radio convention of the National Association of Broadcasters, held in Las Vegas. Mainelli collected Limbaugh at the latter's hotel room, warned him about Weinhaus's intimidating manner, and then accompanied him to the general manager's suite. Weinhaus was persuaded, as Limbaugh later wrote, that he "was not some hick off a pumpkin truck."

As a result, it was decided that Limbaugh's program for WABC would supplant psychologist Joy Browne's call-in show, which came to the station from ABC Talkradio. He would be heard locally from 10:00 A.M. to noon, when he would sign off on WABC and then go do his syndicated show for the rest of the country until 2:00 P.M.

The parties then started putting the other pieces of the puzzle together. In a deal worked out with Weinhaus and Arcara, the ABC Radio president who had beat out McLaughlin for the top job two years earlier, Limbaugh would do the two morning hours on WABC in exchange for the use of a studio and station engineers made available to produce the syndicated show. In addition, WABC agreed to air the commercials placed on Limbaugh's national program during his two New York hours, a generous concession that would satisfy advertisers that their spots were reaching the number-one market.

The marriage between WABC and Limbaugh triggered his divorce from KFBK and would introduce him to a big-time, Big Apple audience. To sweeten matters for McLaughlin, ABC came through and decided to accept Limbaugh as Spann's successor, even though the newcomer's show, like Edell's a year earlier, would be owned by McLaughlin. Happily for McLaughlin, a confident man, the combative Limbaugh now would also serve as a dandy lead-in to Edell's hour-long program.

ABC Radio was complacent and lacked vision. To the network, the availability of Limbaugh simply solved a scheduling problem, just as McLaughlin's takeover of the Edell show had saved ABC a few bucks and kept everyone happy. As one network principal recalled, "No one at ABC knew that Limbaugh would be an oil well." In handing over a lineup of Spann affiliates now willing to carry Limbaugh's show, as well as an efficient sales organization that would help bring in sponsors, ABC asked for no piece of the action, no advance against future earnings, nothing from McLaughlin except about $1,500 a week to pay for satellite time. Even the satellite was up and ready for McLaughlin's use. ABC, now run by Cap Cities executives known for their thrift, appeared satisfied with the standard 15 percent that its sales department would earn for selling McLaughlin's commercial inventory. Crumbs would do just fine, thank you.

"We figured that if we utilized our sales force and sold the time on the show, it could be a good deal for us," Aaron Daniels recalled after leaving ABC in 1990. "As for the affiliates, most of them were small stations and would have to get their programming to replace Spann from somewhere." In other words, why not from Limbaugh via ABC?

New York usually was the hardest market to crack but McLaughlin had managed to crack it first. It was dealmaking so cunningly smooth and successful that Limbaugh's eventual popularity on stations around the country would prompt radio's movers and shakers to look back at McLaughlin's sleight of hand and view him as one of the masters of the game. Four years later, McLaughlin was asked whether he actually got ABC to pay in some measure for the launch of Limbaugh's show out of New York.

"Not in some measure, in every measure," he said. "If I told you how I started my company, it's the greatest story of all time. ABC did it for me. And they didn't know it."

ABC was blind to the idea that this was being done to them?

"They had every opportunity to evaluate my company. I even offered part of it to them."

In the infancy of EFM Media, McLaughlin invited ABC to buy a partnership interest so that he could jump-start the company with the added access to the network's stations and other resources. But nothing ever came of his offer.

After Limbaugh went on the air, ABC Radio recognized his show's value to WABC and other stations around the country, and this time it made an overture to buy EFM Media. But as McLaughlin tells the story, Arcara was vetoed by higher-ups in Cap Cities/ABC.

And because of this shortsightedness, ABC lost the chance to obtain the next big moneymaker, its own successor to Paul Harvey. Asked in 1993 whether Limbaugh was the big fish that got away from ABC, Arcara declined to discuss his company's dealings with EFM Media. "If there was some kind of nebulous feeling [of regret], I would not know how to measure it," he said. But as Daniels reflected after leaving ABC, "It was too bad we didn't make the purchase, but at the time no one ever assumed that Limbaugh's show would become so big so fast."

"We were not aware of Rush Limbaugh," recalls David J. Rimmer, who was the ABC network's program director for talk programming. "We let him get away. Sacramento was not a place where we would ordinarily go looking for talent. We used to look in places like Miami, Tampa, Boston, San Francisco, and Los Angeles. Limbaugh was not a name that came up at ABC and he was not pitching himself to us. We tended to hear from the same people over and over again; we called them 'the usual suspects.'" And because ABC Radio had long since decided to maintain the sleepy

Talkradio, instead of planning for its future growth, Rimmer and others traveled hardly at all to do as McLaughlin had done—find talent.

In 1988, ABC simply wanted those two afternoon hours filled. Nothing more. McLaughlin's guy would do just fine. "They just didn't see," McLaughlin says.

"Ed had something to prove," says New York disc jockey Jim Kerr, who had known McLaughlin since the early 1970s and fills in on the radio during Limbaugh's vacations. "Ed didn't want to feel like an old fart being put out to pasture after he left ABC. I remember him telling me that he found this star in Sacramento and he was going to move the guy to New York and do great things and the guy was going to be great. Everyone snickered behind his back. He wanted to step up to the plate again—and he ended up hitting a home run."

Chapter 9

NEW YORK, NEW YORK

Goodbye, Sacramento.

On June 16, 1988, WABC announced that Limbaugh would join the station, fittingly enough, on July 4. The two-page notice offered a sampling of his views on feminism ("The feminist movement was created to allow ugly women access to the mainstream of society"), Mikhail Gorbachev ("The only difference between Gorbachev and other Soviet leaders is that Gorbachev is alive"), and nuclear arms ("There's only one way to get rid of nuclear weapons—use 'em. All of 'em. Then there won't be anyone left to build more"). The station assured the press that there were many more where those came from. Which was scant recommendation, considering that talk radio in New York had chewed up and swallowed countless conservative wannabes through the years.

Meanwhile, Limbaugh's trepidation about crossing the country unsettled him so much that he wanted to strangle those who came up to him and voiced horrors about living in New York. The day after a farewell party thrown by his loyal sponsors from Filco electronics stores, Limbaugh was feted again, this time by his colleagues at KFBK. He received an elegant money clip as a sendoff gift and in return he told them how much he hated to leave. He said he agonized over his decision "because New York is not my ideal place to live. I really regret the fact that this business is such that, for me to maximize my potential, I have to go there."

He said that Sacramento was as good an environment as he would ever have, that nothing else would touch it in terms of life-style, friends, and freedom on the air. "For example," he added with a smirk in his voice, "I have a meeting Sunday with John Mainelli, who runs WABC, who wants to tell me what he's expecting of me the first day. I've never had a meeting here with anybody telling me what they expected of me any day. Now I have to go there and bite the bullet and yes sir, yes sir, three bags full and let them think they're running the show."

The prospect that he might now come under the thumb of WABC management cut into the satisfaction that the step up was giving him, because at KFBK he had finally encountered superiors who appreciated his skill while they pretty much left him alone. Limbaugh offered living proof that a radio talent could rise to his potential and use his instincts wisely when management showed confidence in him and eased off the controls.

He did his last broadcast from KFBK on July 1 and then flew to New York over the weekend for the Fourth of July premiere on WABC. The downing of an Iranian civilian airliner by a U.S. Navy warship in the Persian Gulf gave him an issue to lay on the New York audience. Still, KFBK had not heard the last of him. The station planned to carry the two-hour syndicated program that he was to host each day after his two hours on WABC, but that national show was not scheduled to start until August 1. Limbaugh bridged the gap by doing a second, Sacramento-only broadcast for three weeks beginning July 11.

He moved into a suite with kitchen at the Parker Meridien Hotel, located near the radio station, before renting a $2,700-a-month unit high up in the South Park Tower on West 60th Street. Without naming the street where he lived, he would repeatedly say on the air that he lived on the Upper West Side, a neighborhood of youthful sophistication. But most seasoned New Yorkers considered West 60th little more than Midtown, or Hell's Kitchen even, never the

Upper West Side. It was within a short walk of Lincoln Center and its Metropolitan Opera House, as well as Central Park.

"No sane person would look forward to living in this city," he told the *Sacramento Bee* when a reporter came to check on his progress in August. "The climate, lack of open space, lack of service unless you bribe someone . . . All of it makes me look forward to when I can work from wherever I want. To live here, you have to forget everything you ever knew about decency."

But hindsight cast a gentler light, for in his book four years later he said that he warmed to New York right away and loved the ease of getting around without having to worry about his own car and where to park it. Not that he walked the relatively short distance between his apartment and the WABC studios, or availed himself of his day-to-day proximity to Central Park by meandering along its walkways in the summer sunshine. Hardly. Flaccid and lazy at more than 250 pounds, and ballooning by the week, he simply let taxicabs take the place of his own car. Michelle said she wanted him to walk to WABC, but he would go a few blocks and then flag a cab. One afternoon early on, he planned to look at a friend's apartment with an eye toward taking over the lease. Although the residence was only about a fifteen-minute walk from WABC, Limbaugh sized up the distance and said, "I can't make it," putting off the inspection until another day. Michelle said that he didn't like to exercise or sweat.

And Michelle suffered as a result of his preference for couch-potato living. Or she finally decided to suffer no more. She appeared embarrassed by his grossly overfed size. During an early visit to WABC, colleagues did double-takes on seeing his slim and attractive wife. Apparently sensing the reaction, she said to one of them, "Everyone wonders how he got someone as beautiful as me."

Indeed, their marriage, which had been stressed by Limbaugh's eclipsing fame and sedentary ways in Sacramento, deteriorated further in New York. Although Michelle sat in on some of his early broadcasts, not everyone realized that she was, in fact, his wife. The conversation between them was so stiff, or so centered on the topics being discussed on the air, that she appeared to be his consultant or his publicist.

Michelle sometimes went out at night while he stayed home. Except for McLaughlin, with whom Limbaugh spent a lot of time off the air, his friends were few. Being by themselves in the city underscored that they "just didn't have a whole lot in common," Michelle told *Vanity Fair* later. She wanted to shop and drink deeply of the plays, exhibits, and other cultural riches of the great city. He preferred to spend his free time watching TV and noodling on his computer. "You know," Michelle said, "Rush was never one to go to museums."

It became apparent soon after their arrival that the marriage was crashing. He didn't talk about Michelle; he talked about Rush. As Roxy had observed during his marriage to her, "Relationships are hard for Rush. People are hard."

The gulf that grew between Limbaugh and Michelle prompted him to conclude that she had been happy amid the distractions and the social network that they shared in Sacramento but that she did not love him when it was just the two of them acclimating to New York. This analysis of the problem may have overlooked his own inability to invest in the relationship. Nevertheless, the breakdown cut deeply into his self-esteem and made him excessively wary and often intimidated in his dealings with women afterward. It hurt him more when Michelle started seeing another man after they separated. Limbaugh referred to him derisively as "Mr. Wonderful," though friends saw that he remained fond of Michelle, even after their divorce was finalized in 1990 and she remarried the following year.

"I think he was very, very happy with Michelle," says Louise Adams, his former secretary. "I think he would be married today. But she wanted to do her thing; she wanted her career. In New York, she found her own job and they went their separate ways. But I still think Rush loved her very much."

Without Michelle, Limbaugh continued to indulge in the vegetative sports that suited him but troubled her. On one Monday morning, he described a perfect weekend he had had—not getting dressed, not leaving his cluttered apartment, ordering takeout for all his meals, listening to music and reading.

At the same time, he became temperamental and sometimes threw things across the room in anger. His moods swung high and low. Besides aching deep down over a love gone sour, a second time no less, he was depressed by the lack of attention being paid him as a broadcaster in New York. And this was no minor regret considering that the radio work, which had been his major interest all along, was now pretty much all that he had. To be ignored while trying on the radio to play "everybody's favorite songs," as it were, seemed a fate worse than abandonment by his wife. For it was the career that he talked about.

He often bemoaned to his colleagues that he feared failure in New York and wondered if he shouldn't return to Sacramento and the security it offered. Limbaugh liked to be liked. Weinhaus, his general manager at WABC, certainly was no help in that regard. He came up to Limbaugh and told him bluntly that he would never make it in New York—a reverse pep talk that sank his spirits even lower.

To help him offset such lows and achieve some highs, McLaughlin spent hours at WABC before, during, and after Limbaugh's broadcasts to show support and to advise on matters of content. McLaughlin served as a kind of surrogate father and best friend. Meanwhile, Limbaugh did what he always did and immersed himself in the priority pursuit of advancing Rush Limbaugh, radio luminary. As his work consumed his life, his real life, the one not reflected in the thick glass that enclosed the studio, receded and got lost in the clutter as he set about constructing the giant, mythic personality whose talent was "on loan from God." His marriage to the image of fame and importance remained unbroken. He would show his real father, back home in Cape Girardeau, that all the failures were behind him.

On August 1, 1988, as the noon newscast marked the end of his WABC broadcast, Limbaugh left one studio and entered another more secluded room to finally launch the syndicated show conceived during months of conversation. The host and McLaughlin said time and again that the original audience consisted of only fifty-seven stations, a modest total that would stand in striking contrast to the hundreds added in the years afterward. However, it could be that the initial constituency included as many as eighty-seven stations, as one ABC Radio official of the period has since maintained, having remembered that Owen Spann held about one hundred outlets and only a few of them defected rather than carry the untested Limbaugh as his replacement.

In any event, when ABC's noon newscast ended, a flip of the switch activated Limbaugh's microphone and the network relayed his voice to a ground-based "earth station" operated by GE American Communications across the Hudson River in Vernon Valley, New Jersey. This so-called uplink then beamed the signal to an earth-orbiting satellite, Satcom I-R, one of the high-flying birds that helped do away with the costlier land-line distribution of network radio shows beginning in the late 1970s and 1980s. Shot into space years earlier, Satcom I-R, which would be replaced by the newer Satcom C-5 three years later, received the Limbaugh transmission and redirected it over the continent, where affiliate stations, equipped with satellite-dish antennas, plucked the signal from thousands of miles above the earth and transmitted it to their listeners. Earth to space and earth again.

Among the takers in those early days of Limbaugh's national show, besides KFBK, were small outlets such as WHKY, in the furniture-making region of Hickory, North Carolina; WNZT in Columbia, Pennsylvania, part of the Harrisburg market; KUTA, in the economically depressed region of Blanding, Utah; and more important affiliates in Minneapolis, San Diego, and Miami on which McLaughlin hoped to build his way into the biggest cities.

At first, WNZT was barraged with calls and letters. By December, the volume had lightened and was running fifty-fifty. Predictably, those who loved Limbaugh loved him madly, and those who hated him did so with an equal passion. But that didn't mean that these critics stopped listening to him. Oh no. After all, this was talk radio. Anger came with the territory.

So did hero worship. Weeks into the program, a woman wanted to echo the praise heaped on Limbaugh by the previous caller. Rush, she remarked, "ditto" what that fellow just said. Which henceforth made "ditto" the phone caller's timesaving shorthand for "go to it" or "love ya" or "with you all the way."

The first "ditto" begat other "dittos" and eventually "mega-dittos," to become the most commonly used idiom in Limbaugh-speak.

Chapter 10

GOING NATIONAL

To fully appreciate how crazy it seemed for McLaughlin to place Limbaugh's show in coast-to-coast syndication during the daylight hours—in midday, instead of during the profitable morning-drive slot—one only had to survey the historical landscape. Television had long since delivered the knockout blow to radio as America's leading entertainment medium. TV had reduced the surviving radio networks in more recent years to hourly newscasts, play-by-play coverage of big games, assorted daily features, such as Paul Harvey's popular commentaries over ABC, and nighttime talk programs, including Mutual's "Larry King Show."

Outside of the newscasts and short segments, network radio pretty much had been closed for business during the daytime since soap operas and variety shows last aired coast to coast in the 1950s. Locally oriented programming, thousands of disc jockeys spinning the hits, had long since become the norm. The dial was now fragmented by specially targeted formats of music and talk as the number of stations had more than doubled since 1970, exceeding 10,000.

If radio had receded to a supplementary role in the postwar TV era, daytime radio on weekdays was little more than a runway for the networks' evening flights, such as NBC Talknet's "Bruce

Williams Show," and their weekend staples, including Casey Kasem's countdown show and "American Country Countdown" with
Bob Kingsley. Audiences were smaller at night, so stations were
less concerned about yielding some of that airtime to network programming. The syndicated weekend offerings presented another
cost-efficient way to save on personnel costs.

McLaughlin knew firsthand that syndicated talk worked poorly
during the day because he himself had been unable to succeed with
ABC Talkradio's daytime lineup when it was among the networks
under his authority. Begun in 1982 by ABC Radio Enterprises,
a kind of research-and-development department that was out of
McLaughlin's purview within the company, Talkradio was eventually made one of his ABC radio networks and allowed to stumble
along with unimpressive affiliates and meager financial returns (after
several years of big losses). Talkradio was a prime candidate for
extinction, but industry watchers believed that ABC feared serious
credibility damage if it scuttled yet another hour-upon-hour format.
Painful memories of Superadio, one of the great debacles in media
history, ran deep within the company.

Superadio was envisioned as a round-the-clock, Top 40 sound
that local stations could take by satellite from ABC in New York
without having to hire their own personalities. Major disc jockeys
of the format such as Dan Ingram, the wisecracking great of WABC;
Larry Lujack, Limbaugh's boyhood hero from the Chicago dial;
Robert W. Morgan, a veteran of Los Angeles's KHJ and elsewhere;
and Jay Thomas, a New York radio personality who later moved
to KPWR in Los Angeles (and a starring role on NBC-TV's "Love
and War") were signed to do airshifts and state-of-the-art studios
were constructed for their use. Rick Sklar, the programming genius
behind WABC's unprecedented success with Top 40 in the 1960s
and 1970s, was hired to work similar magic at Superadio. The
problem, however, was that only a few stations agreed to become
ground-floor affiliates, and losses were projected into the millions
of dollars even into the fifth year of operation. As a result, an
embarrassed ABC junked Superadio at the eleventh hour before the
scheduled sign-on in 1982.

"The only thing I ever did for Superadio was fly to New York for this big press conference," Lujack remembers. "I ended up getting paid for a year. It was the greatest gig of my career."

Although Talkradio continued to muddle along through the 1980s, with affiliates now allowed to fill slots in their schedules by cherry-picking from a sequence of shows featuring Joy Browne, financial adviser Bob Brinker, conservative Ray Briem, and others, the network was still only slightly better off than it had been during McLaughlin's tenure at ABC. The core problem was that Talkradio had started out essentially as a syndicator of programs originating from KABC in Los Angeles, where British-born interviewer Michael Jackson was a popular institution and psychologist Toni Grant drew a sizable audience of women with her pointed advice to aggrieved callers. But what appealed to Los Angeles did not necessarily excite listeners out of town. While the newfound availability of KABC's all-stars to cities and suburbs around the country helped trigger the seismic transformation of WABC from Top 40 to talk on May 10, 1982, by 1987 the New York station and other key affiliates chafed at having to air network shows beamed in by satellite from Los Angeles in lieu of homegrown, local talents who related more closely to the audience.

The time had come for WABC to do what it was reluctant to do since launching the talk format—drop the network fare and install a local ratings-getter in the afternoon. As a result, WABC's decision to put conservative agitator Bob Grant in afternoon-drive in lieu of the network's Michael Jackson prepared the way for Limbaugh's local show in 1988. In other words, even ABC's own flagship station, which was vital to the profitability of network programming, dismissed the Talkradio offerings or consigned them on a tape delay to the netherworld of late evenings and overnights. ABC couldn't win with its own people.

Yes, McLaughlin knew all the pitfalls tied to daytime talk, he knew that stations basically preferred to put their own people on the air in the belief that local issues would then take precedence. But it was clear to him, as it was to a few within ABC, that filling time differed greatly from placing talent. Maurice Tunick, who was hired by McLaughlin as ABC Radio's vice president/talk in 1985, argued to his superiors that Talkradio had the wrong air personalities. The brass disagreed and asked, defensively, who out there was better than Michael Jackson? "We went ahead with the mindset that Talkradio was not working, and couldn't work, even though it was an innovative concept," Rimmer, the former ABC talk programmer, recalls.

Tunick wanted the fiery Bob Grant to occupy a slot in the Talkradio lineup, but WABC prevented the conservative from going national. Management rejected the idea mainly because it feared that his local orientation would be diluted by an influx of calls from the heartland. McLaughlin offset those same reservations when he sought to place Limbaugh on WABC by allowing him to do a separate two-hour show for the station. All the while, McLaughlin believed that his Sacramento discovery could break through stations' longstanding resistance to network programming because Limbaugh was exciting, different, and competitive—all the things that ABC Talkradio was not. "You don't try to create another Paul Harvey," he said. "You try to create another personality that maybe will have the same kind of impact and success as Paul Harvey."

After observing the listlessness of ABC Talkradio up close, and faulting himself for having given the problem network less of his time than it required, McLaughlin became convinced that talk stations were looking for a Rush Limbaugh and not necessarily another interview show that listeners would dial out when the guest of the hour started to bore. Indeed, looking back in 1992, Tunick tended to agree with his former boss, saying, "Rush should have been ours. We should have found a Rush Limbaugh. Rush demonstrated that good programming and a dynamic personality worked during the daytime. He established the first national show to clear good stations in top markets."

But that was far from apparent to New York listeners, who had drifted away from WABC in large numbers long before the station made it a three-talk-station town. At first, they were hearing only the local show that Limbaugh was doing. And how much buzz could come of a program airing from ten to noon, when most of the city was at work? "Rush came in like a whirlwind and he had the same sort of manner off the air," says Pat Ryan Garcia, WABC's director of public relations at the time. "He came in each morning with all his newspapers and clippings. But he felt underwelcomed in New York. The studio for his syndicated show was off in a corner and you really had to make an effort to go by it. There was no hoopla or fanfare. I don't think he ever got over that he was not so big in New York as he was around the country."

Not long after he joined WABC, Limbaugh went to a party hosted by a station sponsor aboard a yacht berthed in the East River. Although some of the men were already fans of his show, most of the women had no idea who he was. This did not deter him from getting into a heated discussion about feminism with an advertising executive from *Ms.* magazine, all the while sounding as if he were on the radio. On this and many other occasions, it was hard for colleagues to tell where his on-air persona ended and the real Rush Limbaugh began—or whether they were one and the same.

He also sought redress from signs that he had second-class status on the New York station. When WABC management printed up T-shirts to promote morning man Dave Dawson and Bob Grant, Limbaugh felt bruised and wanted to know why there were no Rush shirts. The cold truth was that his ten-to-noon program mattered far less to WABC's fortunes than the drive-time efforts of Dawson and Grant. Nevertheless, the promotion director felt sorry enough for him to get authorization to produce Limbaugh T-shirts after all. First, however, he suggested an artist to prepare the design, which only complicated an otherwise simple printing matter.

And then there was Weinhaus, who managed WABC in large measure by instilling enough fear to keep his people ever wary of him and their job security. When a small-town newspaper published a large feature about Limbaugh and his national show four months into the broadcast, Weinhaus scoffed at the idea that a New York personality would be impressed by coverage from the sticks. Still, Limbaugh had to be careful with Weinhaus. Although he was not on the general manager's payroll, a dissatisfied or vengeful

Weinhaus had a number of ways to undermine the setup whereby WABC headquartered and staffed the national show and, just as important, aired its national advertising in New York. It was doubly ticklish because McLaughlin and Limbaugh had no contractual protections; their deal with WABC was sealed with nothing more than a handshake.

Limbaugh was no longer accustomed to having superiors advise him on his broadcast technique. He had come this far because the people he worked for had finally recognized that his act was unique and that he knew what he was doing. However, when Mainelli cautioned him in the beginning not to repeat bits too often and suggested that some listeners might be offended by the sucking-sound "abortions" that he performed on annoying callers, Limbaugh listened without complaint because he sensed that the program director was also speaking for Weinhaus.

On the caller abortions, Mainelli wasn't the only one expressing concerns. In Limbaugh's wish to illustrate the absurd by being absurd himself, the vocal opponent of abortion mischievously believed that he had devised a way out of annoying phone calls while still holding to his vow never to hang up on people. Sound effects of a vacuum cleaner whirring on, with a faint scream then heard in the background, followed by the sound of the vacuum going off, simulated the suctioning of an actual abortion. Crude and tasteless as it was, some callers were so amused that they volunteered to be "aborted" on the air.

But there was no winning over a great many others who became horrified at Limbaugh's latest prank. They called their local stations and complained. And the station managers then called Limbaugh and pleaded with him to halt what had become a public-relations nightmare. He told them it was only the "prochoice crowd" raising hell and urged them to hold firm. Or, as he explained to an interviewer, "The shit that hit the fan over that feature was unlike anything I've ever done."

But after about three weeks of the stunt, he decided to get out of the caller-abortion business when it seemed clear that he had made a loud and effective point. He asked why it was that fake abortions were considered insensitive compared to the real thing, performed thousands of times a day across the country. Moreover, he suggested that his critics recoiled at the squeamish nature of the gimmick because deep down they, too, disapproved of abortion. On the radio, that limitless theater of the mind, Limbaugh had unwittingly staged a drama as provocative as anything by David Mamet. Once more, he had shown that people did not just listen, they responded.

Despite the WABC promotion director's polite arm-twisting, the few reporters covering the New York radio industry were slow to take Limbaugh seriously. His name, real as it was, seemed ridiculously contrived; his egomania and minor-league background suggested to the savvy that he would raise hell for a few weeks and then be flushed like so many other New York wannabes before him. Jonathan Schwartz, a novelist and sophisticated disc jockey then with New York's WNEW-AM, would write an "At Large" column about talk radio for the magazine *GQ* in which he decried WABC as "a violent and witless outlet in the New York market with an attack mentality and a mediocrity of spirit" and laid aside Limbaugh as "a bottom-of-the-barrel if ever you heard one."

Yet this dismissive view of the newcomer could not have been at greater odds with McLaughlin's pride and confidence. In the fall of 1988, when I finally agreed to meet Limbaugh and write something about him for *Newsday*'s "AM/FM" column, McLaughlin had only ninety stations in the Limbaugh network. Nevertheless, he said: "He could be the next Paul Harvey. . . . He will be the most-listened-to radio personality in the country—bigger than Larry King, Sally Jessy Raphael, and Tom Snyder. I will do it."

The next Paul Harvey? Yeah, right.

Limbaugh, on the other hand, conveyed an earnestness off the air that was hard to dislike: "Half of the people who call WABC expect to get beaten up. I don't have a high-brow attitude. . . . I have always as a broadcaster felt that a cheap and easy way to get an audience's attention is to say 'fuck.' I've desired a long-term career, one that is cycle-proof. Now, we're seeing the combative cycle in talk radio, while I strive for a good, entertaining program that has controversy without spitting on people."

At WABC, where Bob Grant often snarled at callers and hung up on them with abusive exasperation, Limbaugh was struck by listeners' desire to phone in regardless of the topic at hand. "I want to expand my audience and get people to call, but I want them to call because of what they're hearing from me, not because the phones happen to be open."

However, in the land of hot talk, a city where a two-hour radio show was competing for attention with five daily newspapers, dozens of other broadcasts, and myriad cultural diversions, Limbaugh found it difficult to stick with his purist intentions, particularly in the early going. He tore into a caller who pressed him relentlessly one morning, telling him to "shut up" before ending the conversation. It was something he had sworn never to do, but he thought for a moment that maybe "this is what it takes" to establish his franchise. On reflection, he disagreed and later on the air he apologized to the caller for being rude, even though it certainly appeared that "you have to be rude and crude to make it on talk radio in this town."

"To stand out in radio, I have to be outrageous, I have to be 'on,' but I have to do it my way," he said. "It's a psych job every day. A lot of people don't put the kind of work into it that I do. It's easy to get phone calls, but getting calls because of what you're saying— getting good ones—is a challenge. I don't have a high-brow attitude. I'm not an intellectual. I'm just trying to have fun."

As Limbaugh tried to do just that, he also got to share his act with the folks in Cape Girardeau when KZIM-AM signed on as an affiliate. The local station put up a high billboard in the middle of the city (that now says, "THE RUSH HOUR BEGINS AT 11 A.M."). His parents, who had received tapes of his broadcasts through the years, were able to hear him live in action for the first time since he left hometown outlet KGMO-AM nearly two decades earlier. His mother phoned him in New York time and again to show her happiness, except for the day that she chastised him for taking a shot at Amy Carter and saying that the former president's daughter was ugly.

Although his father's health was failing from diabetes, he listened closely and questioned why Rush had to use so much comic material. He failed to grasp that it was the humorous coating of conservative views that had placed his son before a national audience in the first place. He didn't get it. He was too serious a man to see immediately that his own closely held opinions and the insights shared night after night across the kitchen table were now echoed loudly and more widely by a far-from-serious, conservative wise guy.

Even David, who knew that his performer of a brother could be reserved and much less talkative off the air, had his own surprise on discovering that Rush had developed an amusing act. "I always thought of him as being more serious-minded, like my dad," David says. "Growing up, I didn't know what a funny guy he was.

"My father was always distressed that Rush didn't go into law. He was disappointed that he dropped out of school. He felt that radio was a dead-end career. He saw Rush as floundering, being in an insecure job. But Sacramento had let Rush be himself—and it turns out that he was right all those years."

On the heels of the KZIM affiliation, Limbaugh returned home to Cape Girardeau in March as an exalted son. Mayor Gene Rhodes proclaimed Rush H. Limbaugh III Day. In the evening the broadcaster was guest speaker at the annual Lincoln Day dinner, an annual GOP flag-waving event sponsored by the county Republican Women's Club. It was fifty years since his revered grandfather had been similarly asked to rally the faithful. With his grandson on the dais, the crowd of 1,300 was the largest ever to attend; it included county officials, state representatives, and the local congressman.

Eighteen years after the college dropout left town in a balky Pontiac Le Mans, he was back by request, a sought-after speaker where once he felt the odd man out. "It's a rare occasion for a person to be invited back to his hometown . . . as a guest speaker before a large crowd after becoming a success in doing something that he really likes to do," he said. Three months later, he returned a second time, to address the graduating seniors of Cape Central High School, where his own classmates twenty years earlier had considered him, as he put it, "a dry ball."

He was, at last, a hero in his hometown.

* * *

Meanwhile, McLaughlin forged ahead in his quest for more radio affiliates. His goals were to have one hundred by the end of February 1989, which he achieved, and two hundred by 1990. At first, one of the biggest problems was convincing stations that they didn't have to be local to get listeners. Few expected that leading radio stations would give up choice parts of their daytime and allow McLaughlin's EFM Media to claim several commercial minutes during each hour in exchange for the broadcast itself—that is, in the kind of barter arrangement common to radio syndication.

"There were targets," McLaughlin recalled. "I knew exactly how to run my little store. It all comes down to very simple planning. Put up your targets on a board. I needed New York, I needed L.A. Had to have them. Or the show doesn't fly. It never fucking flies. You can have a great talent, but if certain things don't happen, that talent goes *pffttt*. I'm the one guy in the world who could get those two markets. And I did. Did I kiss ass? You bet your sweet life I did. But that never bothers me, to get my point across."

His Los Angeles target was KFI, a struggling station that had switched to talk in June. Howard Neal was the general manager and George Oliva came in as program director with less of an aversion to network programming than his predecessor. "I knew they weren't going to kiss my ass, but I needed them more than they needed me. When you know that, you sell." McLaughlin flew into town. "I kissed a lot of ass to get Rush on KFI—more than I would ever do again." But he succeeded.

In March, talk personality Geoff Edwards resigned from KFI, which then fired a newsman and two producers who worked with him to make way for Limbaugh's broadcast in late morning. So much for the homegrown lineup that allowed KFI to raise high the slogan, "We're talking Southern California." It was only eight months into the venture, with 109 stations in the fold, and Limbaugh was already being welcomed on a 50,000-watt station in the country's second-largest radio market, no longer confined to the 1,000-watt KWNK-AM out in Simi Valley.

"At first, people are going to be mad as hell," Limbaugh predicted to the *Los Angeles Times*. "They're going to be offended, they're going to take it all too seriously. Then, after a month, there will be unabashed love." He believed that Orange County would fall his way sooner, saying he expected to own the conservative bastion in a week.

McLaughlin believed that the venture could live without Chicago, at least for a while, so Detroit became his next big target. Chuck Fritz, who had bought WXYT-AM from Capital Cities, was an old friend. Again, McLaughlin got on a flight. It took a lot of talking, but McLaughlin eventually made Fritz a believer. The country's eighth-largest radio market was able to hear Limbaugh when WXYT cut longtime host David Newman's midday shift to make room.

This was hardly the best possible outlet; WXYT's 5,000 watts paled alongside the 50,000 of WJR, the ABC-owned powerhouse that was home to the popular J. P. McCarthy. But the decision to carry Limbaugh in Detroit represented more valuable momentum and was so appreciated by McLaughlin that in 1993 he continued to resist a reconsidered desire for the show from WJR, one of his affiliates during the ABC years. Fritz's early loyalty counted for everything. "That's the way I run the company," McLaughlin said. "The way to do business is to make a deal and go for the long term."

WJR took a further hit in 1989 when Bob Talbert, a columnist with the *Detroit Free Press*, wrote a valentine to Limbaugh in which he revealed his defection from McCarthy's "Focus" show in order to have a Rush lunch on WXYT every day. "I detest his spiteful name-calling and arch-conservative caterwauling, yet I enjoy him when he does it," Talbert said. "I can't stand his constant bragging, blowing his own horn, trumpeting his own fame, yet I nod my head in tune with his egomania. . . . He's the most entertaining radio talk show host in America with the most outrageous two hours ever on radio."

In the summer, WLS in Chicago announced that it was giving up on its struggling music format, once one of the most influential in the country and the place where Limbaugh had thrilled to Larry Lujack's antics. The station's switch to talk programming uprooted two of the most respected disc jockeys in America, John Landecker and morning man Fred Winston, and gave McLaughlin a Chicago slot for Limbaugh sooner than the syndicator had expected. (WLS also tried to simulcast an hour of Bob Grant's WABC show and get him for a second hour exclusive to Chicago, but, again, his New York bosses said no.)

McLaughlin's next big score was WGST-AM in Atlanta. The station decided to stir its schedule and bounced Tom Houck, a gravel-voiced liberal, to the seven-to-ten evening outback to make way for Limbaugh in early afternoon.

As 1989 ended, 178 stations were on board, except for a day in December when WLS nervously yanked the show for a few minutes in mid-broadcast when Limbaugh the wordsmith called for a halt to women "farding in their cars" because "farding on the highway is very dangerous, as well as offensive to others."

Fard means to paint with cosmetics, as the WLS general manager went on the air to explain before resuming Limbaugh's show. The host was trying to have some fun and refrained from offering his own explanation of the prank until the next day. Meanwhile, the incident went a long way to illustrate that his antics were beginning to penetrate below the surface—a broadcaster's dream. A wire service latched on to the incident. So did one of Limbaugh's occasional targets, the mighty Paul Harvey: "Shop talk: Chicago radio station WLS has pulled 'The Rush Limbaugh Show' off the air, objecting to his on-air language." Limbaugh insisted that it was not a publicity stunt.

In another significant development for Limbaugh around this time, CBS was having a look at him. The TV network's "Pat Sajak Show" was sagging in the late-night ratings and affiliates were rebellious. As a result, CBS hatched the idea of using guest hosts on the Friday show as a sign that it was trying out new talent and possibly even shopping for Sajak's replacement. Comedians John Mulrooney, Tom Parks, and Elayne Boosler, as well as actor Mario Van Peebles and Limbaugh, were scheduled.

Until now, Rush had been indifferent about having a side career in television partly because he was so consumed by the effort of making his radio show a solid success. Still, he played along with the tube. A year into his radio program, he taped a TV pilot with feminist Gloria Allred called "Talk Wrestling." And that's what it was, polar opposites going at each other's ideas in front of the camera. An ardent advocate of the women's movement was thus pitted against one who smirked that he, too, favored the women's movement, especially when he was walking behind one. Another favorite of Limbaugh's held that feminism was a means for unattractive women to gain easier access to the mainstream. Allred, of course, considered comments like these to be a hurtful trivialization of the women's movement. She maintained that Limbaugh was trying to make a joke of women so that they would not be taken seriously.

Lorimar Television, whose offerings included "Dallas," one of Limbaugh's favorite shows, produced the pilot with an eye toward syndicating "Talk Wrestling" on stations around the country. It was a period when Morton Downey, Jr.'s politically oriented TV show began to plummet in popularity after a stormy year of screams and fistfights. A similar one-on-one pilot, "Clashpoint," which featured the conservative Bob Grant debating liberal Democrat Mark Green, had been made by MTM Productions but did not interest enough affiliates to go into syndication. In the end, Lorimar scratched its plans for "Talk Wrestling" after viewing the initial results. Although the company then pursued Limbaugh for other TV ideas, the discussions broke down over money.

In addition, Doug Llewelyn, the host and interviewer on TV's "The People's Court," approached Limbaugh about putting together a syndication project, but that idea languished as well. And the possibility of being part of a revived "To Tell the Truth" didn't go far. Rush was not disappointed.

On the other hand, subbing for Sajak was an opportunity on the great CBS. Limbaugh had been a guest of Sajak, so heading into his March 30, 1990, appearance as a one-night host he saw nothing unusual in his being welcomed by the same network that recently had suspended Andy Rooney from "60 Minutes." The latter action was taken apparently over controversial remarks about blacks attributed to Rooney by a gay newspaper and comments about homosexuals that appeared in some of his commentaries.

Limbaugh's own conservative, often caustic views on gays were no less controversial. In one appearance, he had compared allegations of womanizing against unsuccessful cabinet nominee John Tower to Rep. Barney Frank's admission of intimacy with a male prostitute. He said that a fondness for women would cost one a role in government. Referring to Frank, he added: "But hire some pervert homosexual to run a prostitution ring out of your condo, and they'll call you a genius." He mentioned one woman and said she "looks like she could be a dyke if she wanted to be." He also referred to AIDS as a "modern-day plague on homosexuals." To those gay activists who had demonstrated inside New York's St. Patrick's Cathedral months earlier, he said: "Take your deadly, sickly behavior and keep it to yourselves."

Nevertheless, Limbaugh, who had a lot riding on the coast-to-coast TV date, gave assurances that he would stay away from controversy on the 30th. He said that the matter of gays would not even surface. But how wrong he was. CBS started receiving hate mail after Limbaugh's appearance was announced. With studio tickets distributed on a first-come basis, many of his foes were able to obtain seating.

On a scale of catastrophes, Limbaugh's night in the spotlight was a train wreck as AIDS activists in the audience disrupted the broadcast with shouts of "Go home!," "You're a Nazi!," and "We will follow you anywhere you go—we will not let you speak anywhere in America!" All this, on the air, in a time slot usually peopled by stars and singers innocently plugging their newest goods. So incessant was the protest against Limbaugh that commercial breaks merely punctuated it, as if CBS was determined to complete an embarrassing hour, and get it on the air, rather than cancel the show and televise a rerun instead.

Limbaugh chatted up one of his favorite women, Sydney Biddle Barrows, the blue-blood Manhattanite whose illegal call-girl service had earned her the nickname "Mayflower Madam." But their conversation served as a mere sideshow to the disaster brewing off-camera. Try as he did to respond civilly, and even ignore his opponents, the situation became hopeless. A man peeled off his shirt, put on a military-style uniform, and sat menacingly in the front row, arms folded across his chest. It looked like more trouble, so at that point the producer ordered the security guards to clear the house. This left Limbaugh looking foolish as he finished the show and signed off in front of an empty house.

He explained later that he had kept his cool because he believed that an eruption of his own might have prompted CBS not to air the show. Even though it did air, however, the sight of Limbaugh as a political hot potato did him no good at all. CBS said thanks, but no thanks to the conservative lightning rod.

"I still don't know what happened," he told NBC interviewer Bob Costas a year later. Limbaugh wondered why the network producers didn't stop the taping and kick out those who were disrupting the show. "That never happened at CBS," he complained. "They were encouraging them to continue with this. I think that they were hoping for a rambunctious Morton Downey–type show, which there is no way I am ever going to get near, in terms of behavior or content or whatever, 'cause it's not anywhere near what I do, anyway. . . . But they wouldn't throw them out and let us do the show that we wanted to do. Why, I don't know. I never, never inquired."

But as gloomy as the Sajak experience had been, it was only a temporary derailment.

As spring bloomed in Washington, the show continued to roll on and prepared for greater impact in the capital of power. Tyler Cox, who had been Limbaugh's head of programming at KFBK, was now concluding a stay of two years at Boston's WBZ, where management had been unwilling to carry Limbaugh or any other syndicated talk programs during the daytime. "The minute I knew that I'd be going to WWRC in Washington, I called Ed McLaughlin and asked for the show," Cox says. "But unknown to me, he was also having discussions with WMAL. It was a stronger station, a significant affiliation. We made a big offer to get the show, but we could not bring the same prestige. Ed got credibility for the show in Washington from WMAL."

McLaughlin pulled Limbaugh's broadcast from the poorly rated WNTR and placed it on the ABC-owned WMAL in June. The pickup by WMAL represented a giant step away from daytime music toward news/talk programming; indeed, the availability of the show may have hastened the transformation, which now put the station in competition with WWRC for the Washington talk audience. (WWRC also was unable to snag Limbaugh in 1992, when WMAL finally responded to McLaughlin's pressure and added a third hour of the broadcast, rather than lose the franchise to its competitor.)

WMAL reaped a quick payoff on its addition. Limbaugh's summer report card from The Arbitron Company showed that he significantly improved on the ratings of his predecessor in the 1:00 to 3:00 P.M. time slot and more than doubled the number of male listeners twenty-five to fifty-four years old. In addition, his new outlet in Washington increased his exposure to the pundits, columnists, and network news stars who worked in the capital. Among the listeners was Ted Koppel, whose respectful impression of the show ultimately would help lead to appearances by Limbaugh on ABC's "Nightline."

Indeed, 1990 became the year that his radio show sank deep roots in syndication and the host earned increasing and ever-satisfying prominence in the mainstream media as a conservative voice. Like a cranky child finally seated at the dinner table with the grown-ups, he took his place among those he loved to poke and jive. He would consort with the enemy and show that it could be fun.

Chapter 11

GROWING PAINS

Days after the Sajak fiasco, Limbaugh's growing ego received a big boost from a research report prepared by ABC Radio. The survey found that the previous year he drew slightly more than one million listeners during a so-called average quarter-hour. Of this million, more than half were fifty-five and older, falling outside the age group considered most desirable by many leading advertisers. However, another 475,000 were between twenty-five and fifty-four, thereby constituting a substantial chunk of advertisers' most-sought-after audience. "The Rush Limbaugh Show" was good for conservatism and for commerce, too.

By April, McLaughlin's once outrageous vow to clear 200 stations by 1990 was fulfilled. In fact, Limbaugh's show claimed 210 outlets, including ten of the nation's top ten markets, an amazing feat for a program less than two years in syndication, even if Philadelphia's WCAU and San Francisco's KGO were airing only rebroadcasts on Saturdays and Sundays.

McLaughlin was by now so full of himself and his success that he began to think about expanding the venture to a third hour. At the time, WABC was still carrying Limbaugh's two-hour local show and skipping the two-hour syndicated program, a few hours of which New York listeners could hear repeated on weekends. Limbaugh had yet to obtain his own office at the station. What's more, as McLaughlin understood it, WABC would never carry the national show, thereby forcing Limbaugh to continue his double life on the air.

WABC, the cornerstone of McLaughlin's franchise, might have ignored Limbaugh's syndicated effort forever had the New York station in 1990 succeeded in making the broadcaster a bigger part of its operation. What happened is that Mainelli resigned as program director in December, 1989, after Weinhaus brought in Steve Kane to be WABC's new morning man. It became clear within months that Kane, who had been famous in Miami for staging on-air bouts—pitting white supremacists against black militants, gay activists against gay bashers—was not working out in New York with his touchy-feely discussions about members of his own family. Dozens of tapes from other WABC hopefuls offered no immediate choice of a replacement.

Mainelli's successor, Valerie Geller, a news/talk broadcaster in her first job as a program director, studied the landscape and concluded that Limbaugh would work well as the morning host, especially if paired with newswoman Kathleen Maloney, who offered an appealing contrast whenever she pressed her liberal views in on-air arguments with him. In a rare departure for Limbaugh, he had bowed to Mainelli's instructions and shared much of the first hour of his WABC show with Maloney, who functioned as a de facto cohost. Nevertheless, as lively and collegial as their on-air presentation was, off the air Limbaugh spoke to Mainelli and argued that he shouldn't be sharing the microphone with anyone.

When Geller got Weinhaus to accept her idea of teaming the two in morning-drive, she presented the idea to Limbaugh over hamburgers. She proposed that he do WABC's morning shift from six to nine or ten, then use the next two hours to relax and prepare for his national show. "Sure, it would have been a long day, but the radio show was his life anyway," Geller recalls.

For Limbaugh, who commanded little of the attention in New York that he had had in Sacramento and was now getting around the country, the move to mornings on WABC held considerable appeal. It would be a way to break through to prime time—and prime Big Apple visibility—after two years in the chorus of yak-kers. For Geller, Limbaugh's switch to dawn patrol offered a way to maximize his shtick, bring some fun where it was now lacking, and perhaps, over the long haul, steal some of the growing audience of male listeners commanded by Howard Stern, the morning shock jock of WXRK-FM.

In a fascinating coincidence, the two men shared the same birth-date (January 12)—Limbaugh in 1951, Stern in 1954—and were reinventing the talk format as they went along. The major difference was that Stern's vulgar obsessions and stream-of-consciousness kvetching reached vastly more listeners in New York. They drank morning coffee while tuned to his raucous show, or crawled into Manhattan from Long Island and Westchester with long stretches of commuting time leavened by his antics on the car radio. Lim-baugh, on the other hand, got to the table at 10:00 A.M., after most people had turned off the radio and hunkered down to their jobs. For them it was still "Rush who?"

Limbaugh told Geller he would think about it, but not without bringing McLaughlin into the discussion. Of course he would think about it. Not only did the move to mornings hold several strategic pluses, but WABC was dangling a salary of around $500,000 a year. As things then stood, he expected to earn only around $300,000 in 1990 from the two-hour syndicated show (besides extra revenues from personal appearances). He took home no paycheck for his two-hour New York show because WABC staffed and accommodated the national broadcast.

"I adore Ed McLaughlin, I'm his biggest fan," Geller says. "But he was mad. He took me to lunch and said it wasn't going to happen and I should drop the subject with Rush."

McLaughlin had bigger plans for Limbaugh. The syndicator did not want him to settle for a morning show, lucrative though it would be, that would tire him and perhaps hold him back from brighter opportunities on the national stage. And anyone shrewd enough to see beyond the fat salary had to have been sobered by WABC's unstable record in morning-drive. Kane was the station's sixth morning man since it had switched from Top 40 to talk eight years earlier; he was the third person in the job in two and a half years of Weinhaus. Chances were better than even that a half-million dollars for Limbaugh would only have raised expectations for a quick surge in the morning ratings—or else. And if Limbaugh had been axed as WABC's morning man, his horse shot out from under him, he might have had to shuffle back to Sacramento instead of succeeding in syndication while based in New York. "If Rush had failed in morning-drive on WABC, it would have been all over for him," McLaughlin says.

More specifically, the syndicator was irked that the approach to Limbaugh had come directly from WABC management, as if to circumvent the existing agreement that EFM Media Management had arranged on the broadcaster's behalf with the station. "I was prepared to sue," McLaughlin says. "But, yeah, Rush was flattered by the offer. He wondered if it was possible to compromise, because he was still having little impact in New York City."

This muted impact also concerned McLaughlin, who started to sniff around in search of a better showcase for Limbaugh's show in New York. The obvious alternative was WABC's rival, WOR-AM. The latter talk station ruled the format in New York at the time, with a long-established lineup that included "Rambling with Gambling" in the morning, interviewer and consumer maven Joan Hamburg, grandfatherly adviser Bernard Meltzer, and politically minded Barry Gray, a dean of the talk game. At the National Association of Broadcasters' annual radio convention, held in Boston during the fall of 1990, McLaughlin sat down with WOR general manager Bob Bruno and program director Ed Walsh and asked them to take Limbaugh's show away from WABC.

On the one hand, McLaughlin's entreaty could be viewed as a seditious, even ungrateful swipe at WABC, which had been instrumental in launching the national show by providing a New York outlet for his services. On the other hand, WOR was also a vital affiliate of the ABC Radio Networks; it carried Paul Harvey's commentaries and the evening talk show of Sally Jessy Raphael. In other words, if WOR agreed to take Limbaugh away from WABC, McLaughlin knew that he would still be keeping his boy in the extended ABC family.

But WOR declined the offer. "At the time, the idea of taking a network show in the middle of the day—we passed on it," Bruno recalls. "We didn't want to be an affiliate."

Limbaugh continued to struggle with his lack of New York clout. When C-SPAN televised two hours of his radio show in 1990, he was miffed by a *New York Times* review of the event, but unsure whether he, Rush Limbaugh, local radio hopeful, should respond with a letter to the paper. They wouldn't print it, would they? The *Times*? Sheepishness welled within him until he was finally persuaded by Geller to fire off something—and the something was indeed printed, laying out a credo of sorts.

He argued that he didn't, as charged by *Times* critic Walter Goodman, tell his fans "what they want to hear. Rubbish. I tell them what I want them to hear. . . . Critics insist that responsible discussions of great issues be tedious and formal . . . . Enter talk radio, where people are free to participate in the dialogue by telling others what they think, rather than having to listen to the same endless parade of pointy heads and academics offered up by the morning shows, the midday shows and the late shows on television." So there.

Limbaugh's initial reluctance to address the mighty *Times* reflected his continuing lack of self-confidence in his personal affairs, a problem that had been exacerbated by Michelle's dropping him and finding another romantic interest soon after they came to New York. A friend introduced an attractive woman who was open to a romance, and she spent a few hours with Limbaugh at WABC. Rush had to have picked up her signals, but he did not follow through after she left the station that day.

On the air, he sometimes swooned over Sydney Biddle Barrows, the "Mayflower Madam." Not only had she appeared on his ill-fated Sajak stand-in, but another time they dined together with a group of other people. "But he's never called me," she told *Vanity Fair* afterward. "I haven't heard one word from the man."

Friends sensed his insecurity in conversations, especially after his many appearances out of town. "Every Monday, he would say, 'I met this woman,'" a colleague recalls. "He was looking for a girlfriend, but he didn't know the signals. It might have been a stewardess he had struck up a conversation with and now he didn't know what to make of it. He was very insecure as a man. He was generally perplexed by overtures, but there was a definite sweetness about him."

In one-on-one situations, even with those who liked him a lot, he had little to talk about unless the conversation centered on his radio show or himself. He was obsessed with the program. It *was* his life—so much so that the relative uncertainty for a while in 1990 over the show's long-term prospects prompted some to worry privately that Limbaugh would drop into a dangerous funk if it failed. Other self-absorbed talk hosts had varied lives and maintained relationships apart from their broadcasts; Limbaugh, on the other hand, seemed to live the show and to socialize only with those connected to his work and his politics.

He was amazed to be making so much money and doubly astonished to realize that even greater riches lay ahead. This prompted him to be generous, buying a new van for the Guardian Angels, the controversial New York street patrol, and treating the WABC staff and friends to a party aboard a pleasure boat that cruised New York Harbor. Asked by an old friend what it was like to be so wealthy, he cited only a modest reward, saying that he didn't have to worry about paying his phone bill each month. Nevertheless, the newfound affluence allowed him to keep a private car and driver on call throughout those evenings that he went to dinner with friends. The money also enabled him to indulge in often shameless purchases of movie videos, several hundred dollars' worth at a time, instead of putting up with the annoying ritual of renting and returning videocassettes for a fraction of the cost. Such extravagance on the outside suggested a deep-seated loneliness on the inside. The man who pounded out his views in front of a huge audience of people went home with enough cassettes to fill hour upon hour in the absence of real companionship.

To fill many of his weekends, he took to the road, playing to the crowds who listened to him Monday through Friday and earning still more money from their adulation. Like a presidential candidate who visits selected areas to solidify voter support, he made dozens of stops on his "Rush to Excellence Tour" to regions that were picking up his radio show.

Originally, the appearances were arranged by Paul Aaron, who had hired Limbaugh at KFBK and had since gone into the direct-mail business. Aaron contacted the affiliates and proposed that they pay Limbaugh's travel expenses and accommodations for a local stage show so that the stations could then profit from ticket sales and engender good public relations. Aaron acted as tour manager and travel agent. He helped promote the dates and he received Limbaugh's first-class airline tickets in advance of his departures from New York. Their paperless agreement then called for a split of the appearance fee, which started at $4,000 but rose in spurts to $25,000 as the radio show caught on.

Although the two men worked together for about eight months, Limbaugh set up dates on his own during that time before pulling away entirely and keeping all the spoils to himself. "It was commerce and public relations to go into the local markets to do a show," Aaron says. "But it became big commerce after a while with the sale of the T-shirts, coffee mugs, and videotapes. Rush never really made any big money before. Here he was in the Big Apple, early in his career, and he wasn't sure it was going to last. He wanted to make the money while he could. From the day I stopped arranging the appearances, I never heard from the guy again."

Between 1988 and 1991, he flew back and forth almost every weekend and at times for months at a stretch. Clad in tuxedo, with a towel nearby to wipe away perspiration, he would strut across a stage in a cartoonish, stand-up version of his lively radio broadcast—and sometimes twice as irreverent. After Washington homeless advocate Mitch Snyder committed suicide, Limbaugh's announcement to a Sacramento audience that he would now offer a memoriam was greeted with laughter. "Mitch assumed room temperature recently," he said in Limbaughspeak. "Mitch has finally earned a home." And he kept the ghastly bit going, as a lead-in to a backup appearance by Clarence (Frogman) Henry and band, whose old growler of a tune, "Ain't Got No Home," got a frequent airing on the radio show. Limbaugh then asked for respect as he intoned "a requiem mass for Mitch Snyder," solemnly singing, "AIN'T . . . GOT . . . NO . . . HOME."

In 1989, the booking fees and sale of souvenirs at such rallies combined to add around $250,000 to his income. In 1990, his week-ends and sales on the run increased his earnings by as much as $750,000. The shows in Sacramento were twice blessed, bringing out boisterous fans who remembered him when—and yielding two live-in-performance videos for sale to thousands more. Another 550 people paid $1,500 each to accompany Limbaugh on a week-long cruise through the Caribbean. He and EFM Media got a cut of ticket sales. As a high point, the vacationers got to join Limbaugh at the railing to scream insults at Fidel Castro as the ship passed near Cuba.

"Rush had nothing in his life but his career," says Lynn Samuels, a liberal with a withering Noo Yawk accent who became a friend upon joining WABC at the same time Rush did. "Being away on weekends was all part of it."

Beginning June 25, 1990, WABC doubled its daily dose of Lim-baugh by following his local show—finally—with the two-hour syndicated program that was making him famous around the coun-try. The latter broadcast previously had been blacked out in New York except for playbacks during off-peak periods. At WABC, adding the two coast-to-coast hours was viewed as another step in a transition to an all-network show. Limbaugh would no longer have to question whether he should repeat WABC bits during the two syndicated hours.

Four days later, a choice opportunity for growth of the syndicated show presented itself when ABC Radio announced that it was abandoning Talkradio, which eight years earlier had revived the concept of network programming during the daytime. After putting up with an unimpressive affiliate lineup and meager financial re-turns, ABC planned to scuttle a schedule of two-hour shows that now consisted of counselor Joy Browne; Gordon Elliott, a mischie-vous Australian familiar to the local viewers of "Good Day New York," and Barry Farber, a veteran New York radio broadcaster known from decades of nighttime work on WOR and WMCA. ABC also prepared to junk an overnight show hosted by Bob Aaronson. (Browne and Farber, joined by liberal broadcaster Alan Colmes, managed to hold on to many of the ABC affiliates carrying their shows when they staffed Daynet, an independent daytime network based in New York.)

Left unsaid by ABC amid its embarrassment over Talkradio's failure was that a two-hour independent show, fed over the same network satellite from noon to 2:00 P.M. Eastern Time, between Browne and Elliott, somehow claimed 235 affiliates. That dwarfed the 50 to 100 stations reportedly claimed by ABC's own people. The success story, of course, was Limbaugh.

"Did Rush kill ABC Talkradio?" asks Maurice Tunick, the network's vice president for talk programming at the time. "I think it was that Rush's impact was not fully understood at ABC when he was catching on."

"Would ABC have folded Talkradio if not for Limbaugh?" asks Mark Mason, the former WABC program director who later moved to WFAN. "I don't know, but he sure did hasten its demise."

"There was a lot of jealousy," says David J. Rimmer, the Talkradio program director at the time of the announcement. "Here we had fought so long and so hard to keep Talkradio in business, and Ed McLaughlin was able to get a guy who would have saved our asses and made us all heroes in the process."

The same network that had passed up the chance to claim Limbaugh as one of its own was now irritated by his success. The talk internally was about finding "the next Rush Limbaugh," even though ABC was loath to authorize the kind of cross-country expedition on which McLaughlin had signed the real thing two years earlier.

Limbaugh's show was already being carried by many of the one hundred or so stations affiliated with Talkradio. But with the actual shutdown of ABC's daytime schedule only three months away, McLaughlin now stood to pick up still more airtime on those stations scrambling to fill gaps in their lineup. "I probably had ten times the audience with Rush as ABC did with its top show," McLaughlin said. "It comes down to talent. For some reason, ABC couldn't find the talent. They should have been able to build around us, around Rush and Dean Edell."

McLaughlin took advantage of the situation by expanding Limbaugh's national show to a third hour, which was made available beginning July 30. He would become the undisputed king of the daytime hill. And the summer only got sweeter.

In August, KMBZ-AM in Kansas City, which had made Limbaugh a talk personality six years earlier and then fired him with little appreciation for his combative bombast, not only carved out a two-hour space for his syndicated show but added the third hour as well. In San Francisco, McLaughlin's hometown, a big hole in Limbaugh's blanketing of the nation's airwaves was filled when KNBR agreed to carry him live, nine to noon local time. The station eased out KGO, which had been presenting pretaped—and pre-edited—shows only on weekends in the belief that Limbaugh's act wasn't broad enough to sustain an audience on the opposite coast.

In San Francisco and New York, members of GLAAD, the Gay and Lesbian Alliance Against Defamation, a group that pays close attention to the broadcast media, raised objections to what they considered a high volume of antigay remarks by Limbaugh. The broadcaster, it should be noted, had been championed for the pivotal job he held at KFBK by a gay man, news director Norm Woodruff, who later died of AIDS.

Nevertheless, on the national show, Limbaugh used the word "faggot," and claimed at one point that homosexuals wanted a cure for AIDS so they could continue to pursue a deadly life-style. He even introduced an "AIDS update" with such songs as Dionne Warwick's "I'll Never Love This Way Again." A staple of his stage show was "safe talk," in which he stretched a condom over the stage microphone, and made with the bawdy asides, in an attempt to show that the audience was no more protected from his comments into the sheathed mike than gays were safe by using condoms instead of abstaining from anal sex.

After a week or so, Limbaugh apologetically dropped his AIDS updates and admitted that they were cruel. "That was mistargeted," he confessed. "It was too broad. And it was making fun of or impugning people who are dying. . . . It's the thing that I do regret most and it's gonna stick with me a long time . . . that episode alone has resulted in the reputation I have now as a gay basher. Which I don't do."

But a GLAAD task force won promises of improvement in his posture from WABC executives and McLaughlin. "Our concern is that he's mainly dehumanizing people," a GLAAD member said, whereas the station countered that Limbaugh's comments were mainly directed at gay activists, such as those who disrupted his March appearance on the Sajak show. WABC also agreed to help GLAAD produce public-service announcements for the station to air. (Limbaugh was not the only target of GLAAD's ire. GLAAD also met with the general manager of Howard Stern's station to urge a toning down of the morning man's gay material. In 1993, the group helped to extract a public apology and a conciliatory statement from Marky Mark after accusing the rap singer of condoning antigay remarks made by another performer during a British music program.)

Flareups such as the one with GLAAD did not bar Limbaugh from being taken seriously by one of the mainstream media heavyweights he usually had fun jabbing. On November 9, 1990, amid the largest military buildup since the Vietnam War, Ted Koppel, a listener to the radio show via WMAL in Washington, brought Limbaugh to "Nightline" to argue in support of the Persian Gulf deployment opposite columnist Mark Shields. No shtick, no rock-and-roll riffs, no heh-heh-hehs. Just a talking-head Limbaugh standing his ground on the subjects of Saddam Hussein and the use of American might.

"I disagree with Mark as to say our objectives are not defined," he told Koppel. "They're twofold. We're going to turn back aggression and we are going to maintain the free flow of oil at market prices. And I think those two objectives are noble and valid and I think the American people support them."

Shields noted that, in the absence of a draft, "no son of an American senator, no son of a CEO, no son of an anchorman and very few syndicated columnists' sons are at risk there." He also prompted Limbaugh to revisit the matter of the Vietnam-era draft, which the broadcaster himself had managed to avoid two decades earlier and now conceded was porous with exemptions and exceptions. Shields said: "I don't know how long Mr. Limbaugh's basic training was in the Marine Corps. Mine at Parris Island was thirteen weeks."

The value Limbaugh derived from his appearance on "Nightline" had to do with his acceptance by so esteemed a news broadcast. He also took pride in the way he fended off Koppel's apparent and repeated suggestion that the radio listeners who voiced support for American involvement were less informed about the stakes involved in a possible war and were instead giving a visceral response to the crisis. "But I enjoyed it, nevertheless," Limbaugh said. "I had a good time doing the program and I was proud that I was not taken out of my game and proud that I was not because of pressure, doing a national television show, that I didn't compromise my belief just to make Koppel happy."

Watching the joust in Cape Girardeau was Rush H. Limbaugh, Jr. He was now seventy-two years old and severely weakened by the complications of diabetes, which had thinned his once-considerable size through the years and now required vigilant attention. Impressed by his son's toughness and conservative resolve, he turned to his wife and said, "Millie, where did he get that?"

"I told him, 'Where do you think he got it? He got it from *you*,' " Millie remembers. "He was so proud."

Finally, finally, the father realized that his namesake had not wasted his own intelligence after all. There he was on "Nightline," for God's sake, doing himself proud.

"Rush's dad was always going to be right," Roxy recalls, "but he loved his son very much."

The love Limbaugh had not doubted. But his father's respect he had always craved. When his mother told him on the phone about the reaction to "Nightline," he saw almost at once that his father finally had given that respect, and it thrilled him.

Sadly, less than a month later, his father died. Rush eulogized him at length on the radio.

Chapter 12

BREAKTHROUGH

As a sales representative for the publisher Simon & Schuster in Minnesota and Wisconsin, Raymond Jay spent a lot of time in his car traveling between dozens of bookstores and wholesale distributors. He passed his midday hours on the road by listening to Limbaugh's show over KSTP in St. Paul.

In the fall of 1990, he read that the station's ratings were moving up. What's more, in visits to the supply rooms and business offices at the stores he serviced, it seemed that more and more employees were listening to Limbaugh, as more and more stations added his show. "I'd go into these stores and there would be people throwing things at the radio because of something Limbaugh said," Jay recalls. "A lot of bookstore people in Minnesota are liberal. I'd say, 'Hey, the radio has an off button, why don't you just turn the guy off if you don't like him?' But they'd say, 'No, we love to listen to him, but we hate him.' "

Sensing that there was something to this Limbaugh character, Jay phoned Irwyn Applebaum, then the president and publisher of Pocket Books, a division of Simon & Schuster, and suggested that the company look into doing a book with the talk host. In Applebaum's New York office, only a few blocks from where Rush originated his broadcast, the publisher had to confess that he had no idea who Limbaugh was. After the call, Applebaum asked members of his publicity department if they knew much about Limbaugh. They, too, were unfamiliar with his show, perhaps because the talk host did not interview authors, like many other radio personalities, but more likely because Limbaugh had received little attention in the New York media. He cut only the faintest profile in the city where he worked.

It was a classic illustration of Limbaugh's early success; he was shaking up the heartland while toiling in relative obscurity in the Big Apple, the epitome of "making it" in network radio. His was a Broadway show that did better business on the road.

But then, to the surprise of those New Yorkers who had never heard of Limbaugh, but prided themselves on being one step ahead of the curve, *The New York Times Magazine*, which usually offered serious pieces on issues and men of letters, anointed him with the full treatment in December. "A large new noise echoes across the invisible cacophony that is talk radio," the piece said, ". . . and after only two years on the national dial, he has more listeners . . . than any other talk-show host and a list of stations . . . that grows every day."

A friend of Jack Romanos, then the president of Simon & Schuster's mass market operations, likewise urged him to sign Limbaugh to do a book. Convinced, Romanos put senior editor Judith Regan on the case. Before joining Pocket Books, she had worked for Geraldo Rivera and as a writer at the *National Enquirer*, which went after stories with singular determination. So she was well cast to pursue Limbaugh. For weeks, she dined with him and drank with him and relentlessly tried to persuade him to sign with the company.

Rush, however, was reluctant. Although he once wrote a column for the *Senior Spectrum Weekly* in Sacramento, he was not an enthusiastic scribe. And this had caused embarrassment around the time that Pocket Books was wooing him.

Late in 1990, it was revealed that Limbaugh did not write the front-page column that appeared under his byline in the *Sacramento*

Union. A newspaper staffer routinely taped the day's broadcast and then cobbled together a column from his remarks and one-liners. Limbaugh received a faxed copy and reviewed it before publication.

"What difference does it make?" he said when a reporter from the competing *Sacramento Bee* called him in New York for comment. "It's hot, it's honest, and it doesn't threaten America."

The paper's editor also deflected questions about the practice, arguing that the column contained Limbaugh's own words and often the broadcaster rewrote the copy faxed to him.

The ghostwriting was disclosed by radio host Christine Craft, a self-described "middle-aged, feminist liberal" who several years earlier had filed a famous lawsuit against a Kansas City TV station that fired her as a news anchor for looking too old. She told Sacramento about the Limbaugh column during her afternoon radio show on KFBK, his former employer and current affiliate. "The latest Milli Vanilli is right here in Sacramento," she said, referring to the pop duo who did not record the hit vocals sold under their name.

Still, Regan pressed her case.

A few TV talk shows followed the *Times* and began to feature conservatism's self-described "harmless little fuzzball," thus jogging the memories of those who had long since forgotten disc jockey "Jeff Christie" and that funny guy with the unusual first name who used to be in public relations with the Kansas City Royals.

"When I found out that the chubby, happy-go-lucky guy who worked for the Royals now had a national show, I was floored," said Ken Rhodes, a newscaster on Long Island's WBLI-FM who had known Limbaugh in 1984. "In fact, the first time I heard him on the radio in New York, it didn't dawn on me for weeks that it was the same guy. I remembered his persona, but not the voice. Then, when he mentioned the Royals one day, I thought, oh my God, that's the guy."

Royals star George Brett said he heard from a mutual friend that Limbaugh was doing a national show, "and would be on radio in New York and Kansas City every day. I started listening. I didn't know he was so bright. He never dropped the big words on us, he didn't have the answers to solve problems."

No less an authority than Walt Bodine, one of Kansas City's veteran radio broadcasters, was unaware that Jeff Christie, the mellow rock jock who had worked on KUDL in the 1970s, was the one and the same Rush Limbaugh. "So Christie was Limbaugh?" he said. "I'll be damned."

Same thing with Joe Abernathy, who had employed Jeff Christie briefly on KFIX-FM in Kansas City. He did not understand why I wished to speak with him about Rush Limbaugh, whom he listened to from time to time—then was shocked to learn the all-but-forgotten Christie's real name.

Ditto with Jim Gallant, who was the program director at KFIX. When I tracked down Gallant in 1993, the broadcaster learned for the first time that the Jeff Christie he had remembered employing in 1978 was Rush Limbaugh. True, Limbaugh's voice on the radio in recent years always seemed familiar to Gallant for reasons he could never explain, but he did not draw a connection to Christie.

Paul Leonard, the station manager at KMBZ when Limbaugh was fired in 1984, was still working with Bill Steding, who had authorized the dismissal. Now they were with Star Media, a Dallas-based broker of radio stations. Noting Limbaugh's success, Leonard told Steding: "You fired him." And Steding replied: "Rush Limbaugh? I didn't even know I knew him."

Bob Harper, who had brought Jeff Christie to Pittsburgh's KQV in 1973, heard from KFI program director George Oliva that Limbaugh's show was coming to the Los Angeles station. "Wait a minute," Harper said to him. "Is this Rush Limbaugh from Cape Girardeau in Missouri?"

When Harper finally caught the show, he recognized that Limbaugh was goofing his way through the broadcast as if to spoof the idea that he was on the air in the first place—just like Jeff Christie used to do on KQV. Nevertheless, Harper was surprised to hear what a political animal Limbaugh was. Back in the days of Three Dog Night, who knew?

Jim Quinn knew Jeff Christie in Pittsburgh before leaving him the job at KQV, but the two had been out of touch a long time. Years later now, Quinn's mother told him about a guy on the radio who always asked of his Pittsburgh callers, "How's Jim Quinn doing?" The guy's name was Rush Limbaugh. One day, Quinn's mother called him and said, "He's on 'Geraldo' right now!" Quinn turned on the set and there he was, Jeff Christie. Same guy. "I'll be damned."

Mary Jane Wolf had worked with Jeff Christie at WIXZ in McKeesport. When Rush Hudson Limbaugh reached her radio via KDKA in Pittsburgh, she marveled at how he didn't have one of those made-up radio names—like Jeff Christie. Then again, there was something about Limbaugh's laugh that sounded so familiar. She called another WIXZ graduate, Rick Toretti. "Could this Rush Limbaugh be . . ." Before she could finish, Toretti said: "Yes."

"I was surprised and pleased," Wolf recalls, "but I think back then that Jeff thought he was better. I think he believed that he would go on to better things. Those seeds were already planted. He was so interested in what was going on in the world."

In Cape Girardeau, Limbaugh's former college instructor in American government, Peter Bergerson, found himself vacillating while listening to the show on KZIM. "I would go from being entertained to being frustrated to cringing to yelling back at him," he says. "The intolerance he displays and the way he sometimes picks on people bother me. But I guess you have to keep in mind that he's trying to be entertaining with politics."

Bill W. Stacy, who had watched a cocky, nineteen-year-old Limbaugh try to breeze his way through Speech 101 at Southeast Missouri State, later became president of the university and was now being recruited to head a new campus of California State University at San Marcos. For a nonacademic reference, he listed his old friend Rush Limbaugh, Sr., SEMO's former attorney and a revered figure in Missouri. "After I got the job, one of the California trustees said to me, 'So you know Rush Limbaugh?' And I said, 'Oh yes, he's simply the greatest guy, he was president of the Missouri Bar Association,' and so on. And the woman just looked at me. She had no idea who my Rush Limbaugh was. It turned out that she was from Sacramento and remembered the grandson from when he was on the radio there.

"So I had failed to turn Rush on to college, and here it was years later and he helped me get a job as a college president."

Louise Adams, the secretary who had worked alongside Limbaugh during his years with the Royals and came to feel like his surrogate mother in Kansas City, could not recall hearing him in any political discussions during their years together. But she grew proud of him as his politically minded show picked up listeners over KMBZ. In the summer of 1991, she flew out to Long Beach, California, to attend the National Conservative Forum, a day-long gathering organized by Limbaugh and featuring former Secretary of Education William J. Bennett, Gary Bauer of the Family Research Center, ultraconservative Rep. Bob Dornan of California, columnist Mona Charen, and other lights of the right wing. "I couldn't believe the following he had," she recalls. "People just went nuts when he walked into the room. And during the luncheon, when I told the people at our table that I knew Rush, well, I became an instant celebrity. They couldn't get over it."

"I thought it was marvelous that he became as famous as he was because he finally accomplished his dream—and was getting paid well to do it," his first wife, now Roxy Baker, says. "I heard him on the radio and I could see that he was more comfortable with himself. He had grown up.

"Friends knew I was married to him. Others who found out would say, 'You were married *to him*? Wasn't he miserable to live with?' "

Hearing the big mouth of conservatism was one thing. But for some of these same people, seeing was not believing, at least not right away. They were unprepared for the first sight of their old friend on television after all those years. My, but he had gotten big. "I remember he went up and down with his weight, but he was never *that* heavy," one recalls. "But the first time I saw him on the TV, I almost fainted."

He had carried about 240 pounds or so on his five-foot-ten frame while employed by the Royals and KMBZ in the early 1980s. He then seesawed through several diet plans, at one time dropping about sixty pounds in two months while acting as a commercial spokesman in Sacramento for the Nutri/System weight-loss program. But he regained the size and reached 270, with a forty-four-inch waist, by 1988. He told *Sacramento* magazine that "when I am heavier and not looking at myself in the mirror all the time, I truly believe I've done my most creative work. But I also know that heavier people risk losing some degree of credibility because of their size." In addition, there was always the risk of diabetes, as his father had learned.

Going to New York in 1988, Limbaugh expanded at an alarming rate—to 320 pounds by 1991. He would add one hundred pounds in all during the first four years in Manhattan before heading downward again. The commercial diet plans didn't seem to help much and he wasn't one to exercise. And it showed, in the rivers of sweat that flowed down his face during live appearances, in the abandonment of golf because he concealed the tee with his girth, in the need to hail a taxi for short distances rather than cover them on foot. A reporter who accompanied him on one of his weekend speaking trips described a gluttonous span of several hours in which Limbaugh ate a hot dog, a box of popcorn, and a diet soda at the airport; a corned-beef sandwich, potato salad, pie, crackers, cookies, chocolate mints, a double Crown Royal, and then a second drink during the flight; followed by a pass at a salad bar after reaching his destination.

The reaction got cruel at times, particularly on New York radio. Howard Stern said that Limbaugh was "a big, fat dope. He's not even entertaining. Rush's mom named him that because he was always rushing to the fridge." Another time Stern remarked: "Rush Limbaugh, here's a guy who can't even reach around to wipe himself when he's on the bowl."

On WFAN's "Imus in the Morning," host Don Imus presented one of his spoofs of raspy-voiced local disc jockey Scott Muni, who was made to say of Limbaugh: "I knew he was a big guy, but, gee, he's a (bleep) theme park. . . . It's bad enough that he sounds like Mussolini, but does he have to look like him, too?"

Still, Limbaugh was happening. When disc jockey Scott Shannon, an originator of the wild "Morning Zoo" format on WHTZ-FM in the 1980s, made a heavily hyped return to New York radio in the spring of 1991 over WPLJ-FM, his rocking and rolling premiere also featured the rocking and rolling Limbaugh from across the hall at WABC. Limbaugh was known primarily for his politically incorrect harangues, but as a former rock jock he projected a continuing devotion to the music in his choice of the Pretenders' bass-thumping "My City Was Gone" as a theme song, his use of rock riffs such as the Eric Clapton classic "Layla" to punctuate each radio show, his quirky friendship with heavy-metal star (and avowed hunter) Ted Nugent, and his stated appreciation of diverse sounds, including the dreamy New Age music of Mannheim Steamroller. This rock-and-roll sensibility went a long way to explain Limbaugh's solid appeal to men over twenty-five, desirable listeners who, like himself, grew up with the music. He sat down opposite Shannon and a street-corner blues band and traded lines in front of the rock audience.

WPLJ, whose ratings had plummeted in recent years, would have been lucky to have a fraction of Limbaugh's numbers. In May, EFM Media announced that the talk host now had 350 stations carrying his show, with nearly 1.8 million listeners each quarter-hour, or 80 percent more than in 1989. His increasing popularity was a cause for special joy at affiliates such as KFBK, KMJ in Fresno, WHAM in Rochester, and WWL in New Orleans, all of which were posting big gains in his time slot that in turn trickled down to the bottom line in the form of premium ad rates. The broadcast also claimed a total of 7.1 million listeners a week while reaching ninety-two of the top one hundred radio markets in the country, compared with seventy-nine of the top one hundred the year before.

Rush often expressed the view that the political content of his show was less of an audience draw than the fun he offered. As he put it, listeners turn on the radio for three reasons—"entertainment, entertainment, entertainment." He told *Radio & Records:* "A turning point in my career came when I realized that the sole purpose for all of us in radio is to sell advertising. I used to think radio was for me to become a star and get my ego thrills. I wasn't listener-oriented, I was me-oriented. As I got a little older, I realized the key to my success was making the audience *want* to listen to me." By offering them fun, that is.

He even tried to have fun with Anita Hill, the law-school professor who came forward in 1991 to challenge Judge Clarence Thomas's nomination to the Supreme Court by alleging that he had repeatedly engaged in sexual harassment of her when they worked together in the federal government. Limbaugh had expressed his support of Thomas well before Hill emerged. The National Conservative Forum that he convened on July 27 in Long Beach, California— because, he said, "conservatives need to be rejuvenated"—focused on the Thomas nomination (and yielded another videotape for sale). Robert H. Bork, the conservative who had been rejected for a seat on the top court in 1987, predicted to the two thousand attendees that Thomas would face similar hostile questioning from liberals in the Senate but would end up being confirmed. Moreover, Bork argued before the crowd that Thomas "has to be confirmed" so that he could provide a crucial fifth vote needed to overturn the *Roe* v. *Wade* decision that upheld abortion rights. Bork said he was also pleased that Thomas opposed affirmative-action programs. He received two standing ovations. Limbaugh, of course, concurred.

Hill's riveting, televised testimony before the Senate Judiciary Committee two and a half months later enraged Limbaugh, who called her "a psychotic liar"—and then some. He added five thousand dollars to a pool of reward money that was being offered by two groups seeking to identify who had leaked Hill's original accusation to reporters Timothy Phelps of *Newsday* and Nina Totenberg of National Public Radio. (The leak was not traced conclusively.)

He later threw the bright spotlight of his radio show on a lengthy article in *The American Spectator*, a conservative magazine, that portrayed Hill as a flake who had made other charges of sexual harassment and shown bias against her male students. In Limbaugh's view, the *Spectator*'s searing report illustrated that the major media had been blind to Hill's credibility problem when her charges held the nation rapt; the piece neatly supported his recurring us-against-them theme, which held that most journalists were liberals pursuing their own agenda. His heralding of the story by reporter David Brock, who later wrote *The Real Anita Hill*, prompted a blitz of listener calls to the magazine. Editor in chief R. Emmett Tyrrell, Jr., cheered that Limbaugh "had given voice to the unspoken concerns of millions."

"My guess is she's had plenty of spankings, if you catch my meaning," Limbaugh snickered on the air. Of course, Hill is "purer than wind-driven snow," he said with sarcasm at a speaking engagement. Then, in a mimicking of Hill's friend Susan Hoerchner, who had testified on her behalf, he continued: "Senator, Anita told me that she has never even in twenty years had a bowel movement. Senator, Anita said to me that it is never necessary for her to even bathe. So I ask you, how can you not believe Anita?"

As heavy-handed as Limbaugh acted in the matter of Anita Hill, his impassioned anger obscured the fact that polls showed most people did not, in fact, buy her story. Initially, respondents said that Thomas was the one they believed. Only later did opinion shift in favor of Hill. By that time, Limbaugh was fuming over Hill's newfound role as a symbol of feminism, one who would dare make a New York appearance alongside Gloria Steinem. He could not let go.

In the wake of allegations from a navy woman that a gauntlet of drunken flyers had abused her and others at the infamous Tailhook convention in Las Vegas, a caller from Philadelphia told Limbaugh: "Sexual harassment is getting to be a crime only less heinous than mass murder."

"Well, I agree with you there," Limbaugh replied. "I think that sexual harassment has assumed a level of chicness now that is perhaps more than it should be. But I think this case, with what I've heard happened to her . . . hey, look, people are resigning here left and right. Nobody is trying to say this woman is wrong or not telling the truth about it. I think this is a clear case. Let's be consistent here: I much more believed her than I believed Anita

Hill, for example. . . . And let it be known that Clarence Thomas was not present at this convention."

While Judith Regan continued to bait Limbaugh for Pocket Books, Irwyn Applebaum encountered further grassroots evidence that the broadcaster would be a great catch. In December, Pocket Books had a meeting with its sales force in Fort Myers, Florida. While Applebaum and his team were preparing their presentation for the next day, the publisher excused himself and headed for the men's room.

"I must have taken a wrong turn or something, but I came upon this table loaded with Dittohead paraphernalia, and inside the ballroom was Rush in front of about eight hundred people," Applebaum recalls. "The local radio station had brought him in, in the middle of the day on this weekend. I was amazed that he could fill the ballroom. It convinced me more than ever that he was our man. And when I got to talking to our sales reps, people who spent a lot of time driving around in their cars, it turned out that they were big Rush fans, too."

Limbaugh finally agreed to do the book. He went in to meet Applebaum and Jack Romanos, filling the latter's office couch only slightly less impressively than had the rotund actor Dom DeLuise, another of their authors. During the get-together, Limbaugh made it clear that he did not want to write an autobiography because he was too young for that just now, but would try to re-create in book form the kind of fun and arguments that he traded in on the air. Pocket Books paid him an advance of around $150,000. And the company also gave Raymond Jay a finder's fee.

Publication was set for the fall of 1992.

Indeed, 1992 was shaping up to be a more than promising year.

Just as Pocket Books had been steering Limbaugh into print, media consultant Roger Ailes, a battering ram for presidential candidates Richard Nixon, Ronald Reagan, and George Bush, was working to put the broadcaster on television.

Limbaugh's interest in the small screen had wavered. A year

into his national radio show, when Lorimar TV taped the "Talk Wrestling" pilot with him and feminist Gloria Allred that went no further, he said that he wanted to do a television show that would mix issues with humor. "I'd like to be a comedian and I don't mind being a serious talk-show host," he told a reporter. "I want to do both."

But his disastrous appearance as host of "The Pat Sajak Show" in March of 1990, when the CBS producers seemed to welcome his on-air confrontation with gay activists, soured him on TV. It angered him that his radio show could become successful as a solo vehicle, and yet people in TV preferred to put him in a debate. One morning he appeared on Regis Philbin and Kathie Lee Gifford's TV show in the innocent belief that they wanted him to discuss President Bush's newly declared war on drugs, but fellow guest Jimmy Breslin, the tough New York newspaper columnist, fumed at being paired with a mere radio host and instead attacked him as fat and worthless. Though stunned, Limbaugh remained calm.

"I never debate," Limbaugh maintained to *Talkers*, the radio publication. "That's not what I do. . . . I think that my strength on TV would be the same as it is on radio. I happen to be an entertaining personality. Put me on and let me do what I do. TV hasn't found a way to do that."

In short, he didn't have much fun when he went on TV. He added: "I don't know that what I do on radio is compatible with TV—no guests, a spontaneous program. TV just can't function with spontaneity."

However, in September of 1990, Ailes started to cultivate Limbaugh with an eye toward devising a TV format on which he would be comfortable. They talked several times, and by the following March, in a development that received little media attention at the time, they signed a letter of agreement. Ailes would develop and produce the show, and had ninety days to find a studio, a network, or a syndicator to distribute the venture.

Although Ailes did not score right away, Limbaugh liked him, and he agreed to extend their agreement beyond the three months as the search continued. By the fall of 1991, Ailes felt a tug on his line from Multimedia Entertainment, a division of Multimedia Inc., which published fifty-two newspapers, owned radio and TV stations, and operated cable systems in four states. As TV syndicators went, Multimedia Entertainment was little more than a boutique, but one with two fashionable properties, "Donahue" and "Sally Jessy Raphael," which generated estimated revenues of $90 million and $60 million a year, respectively.

Limbaugh called his brother, David, and asked the lawyer to work out the details on his behalf. After weeks of back-and-forth between David and Multimedia's general counsel, Steven S. Fadem, the self-described "country lawyer" from Cape Girardeau flew into New York to close the deal. The week chosen also happened to be when David was scheduled to attend a seminar sponsored by the *National Law Journal* on how to negotiate a contract in the entertainment industry. More specifically, the session presented a mock negotiation on structuring a TV talk show.

Among the faculty panelists: Fadem, who had contributed a sample Multimedia contract for inclusion in the seminar textbook— a textbook now being read by David Limbaugh, whom he would face across a negotiating table later in the week.

"I had not met David, but I knew he was going to be in the seminar," Fadem recalls. "I tried not to reveal any more trade secrets than I had to."

Neither lawyer believed that his hand had been strengthened or weakened by the classroom encounter, but they agreed that the talks afterward constituted one of the more arduous days of law practice in their experience. Gathered in Fadem's Rockefeller Center office on that Halloween of 1991, besides the Multimedia lawyer and David, were Graham Coleman, the attorney for Ailes, and Richard Mincer, a senior vice president with Ailes Communications whose quarter-century in TV included seventeen years as executive producer of "Donahue." Robert L. Turner, the president of Multimedia Entertainment, also stopped in.

They started to finalize the three-way agreement among Ailes, Rush Limbaugh, and Multimedia after lunch. On the one hand, Mincer and Ailes already had talked with Multimedia to enlist the company as a syndicator for the show. This, therefore, put Ailes and Limbaugh in adversarial positions when it came to working out the remaining fine points, but not so that it impeded progress. "I was ninety-nine-percent sure we would resolve all the stumbling points," David recalls.

By dinnertime, they were still talking, and they kept talking, in Fadem's office and in huddles around a table in a nearby conference room, until about 10:00 P.M. In the end, David had one agreement between his brother and Ailes that made them coequal partners, as well as a three-year deal covering their relationship with Multimedia. The language guaranteed a salary for Rush Limbaugh out of the show's budget as an advance against his share of the anticipated profits. The terms were then faxed to Ailes and to Limbaugh, who approved the fruits of the day-long negotiations.

The deal was announced the next day by Turner, who hailed Limbaugh as "a modern-day Will Rogers." The new show would be an Ailes Communications/Rush Limbaugh/Multimedia Entertainment coproduction, he said, with Ailes as executive producer and Mincer as senior producer. Although the program was scheduled to go on the air the following September, it remained unclear just what in the world viewers would see. The format would come to be written on cocktail napkins. Limbaugh hinted that there might be guests, but they would be on hand to ask him questions.

"The show will not be about what anyone thinks, but about me, and what *I* think," he told me at the time. "I don't think there's a TV show on the air that combines irreverent humor and a serious discussion of the issues. That is what I do and that's what we'll try to do with the show. . . . I will not be deferential. There will be no pretense toward journalism. It will be an entertainment show."

Limbaugh said he believed that much of the friction he felt during his previous appearances on television stemmed from the liberal orientation of those who worked in the business. For this reason, he characterized his professional marriage with Ailes, a fellow conservative, as "profound." He also sought to downplay the suggestion that Ailes might be distracted by Bush's upcoming reelection drive. "Roger will always be a name that they call, but I doubt that that will happen because now Bush has a whole White House bureaucracy in place, and Roger is branching out on the entertainment side."

Rush, meanwhile, prepared for the launch of his TV show by

touching up his smile. He visited an Upper East Side dentist special-
izing in cosmetic work and had some crowns done to beautify his
teeth for the close-ups to come.

He had earned up to $3 million in 1991. "The Rush Limbaugh
Show" had 440 affiliates and about four million listeners a week.
Even without the book and the TV show, the radio program headed
into the election year as a formidable media player unto itself.

The ABC Radio Networks and EFM Media ended their sales
and marketing relationship, which dated to the beginning of the
syndicated show. As of January 1, 1992, no longer would the commercial time on Limbaugh's show be sold by ABC personnel.
McLaughlin explained that ABC wanted to focus more closely on
its own remaining radio networks, now that Talkradio was dead.
This view, reported by industry publications, echoed a belief inside
ABC that its 15 percent cut of Limbaugh's commercial revenues,
though standard in the business, seemed like small change when
set against the networks' larger revenues and was insufficient to
justify a continued sales effort. McLaughlin likened ABC to Macy's
and EFM Media to a boutique.

At the same time, the breakup with ABC and the shift of the
sales operation to MediaAmerica Inc., a four-year-old New York
firm with salespeople representing far fewer radio shows, hinted at
more hardball from McLaughlin. He was dissatisfied with ABC's
sales performance on behalf of Limbaugh's show, as well as EFM
Media's weekday health program hosted by Dr. Dean Edell. Believing, too, that Limbaugh was too powerful a sales tool to be
packaged for sale with so many other ABC programs, McLaughlin
was finally persuaded by MediaAmerica that it could better serve
the show.

Gross ad billings for the Limbaugh and Edell radio shows totaled
about $6 million in 1991. In the year to come, the gross would soar
to $12 million.

Chapter 13

TALK RADIO

A s a distinct type of programming, talk radio took a form that would be recognizable today during the 1940s, when late-night interviewers such as Jack Eigen and Barry Gray hobnobbed with show-biz celebrities in front of starstruck audiences. Sometimes in those early years, they would even pass along questions phoned in by listeners, whose remarks were not put on the air, but instead paraphrased by the hosts to the featured guest.

Jack Eigen started broadcasting from New York's Mardi Gras restaurant in 1945 and had a long string of stops as a so-called talk jockey. He packed the Copacabana for years, later had a Manhattan venue of his own, and also worked in St. Louis and Chicago.

In New York, he was kept apprised of possible guests by a network of maître d's he had befriended who would tell him who was in town. In addition, listeners were just as likely to hear the host speaking with Martha Raye, calling Eigen's table from London, or be told what Bob Hope was saying as he waited for a train connection in Chicago.

Barry Gray came to prominence as a wee-hours host on New York's WOR in the mid-1940s. He chatted up celeb royalty, played records (smashing to bits on the air those he didn't like), and griped about whatever was on his mind. Gray "has the biggest sucker racket on the radio" a writer observed in 1946. "People love to hear others insulted. Particularly the kind of people who listen to Gray." He shifted to a newsier orientation in the 1950s and kept at it into the 1990s.

Arthur Godfrey also emerged as a compelling personality in the 1940s. The red-headed broadcaster was brought from CBS's Washington affiliate, WJSV (now WTOP), to New York, where he ended up doing three daily shows on the network—one in the morning and two at night. He had a natural, easygoing, and believable manner, particularly while delivering commercials ("Aw, who wrote this stuff? Everybody knows Lipton's is the best tea you can buy. So why get fancy about it? Getcha some Lipton's, hot the pot with plain hot water for a few minutes, then put fresh hot water on the tea and let it just sit there"). The humorist Fred Allen called Godfrey "the man with the barefoot voice" and "the Huck Finn of radio."

Godfrey's wake-up shows aired opposite Don McNeill's "Breakfast Club," which ABC distributed from Chicago to stations around the country and an audience of millions. "Good morning, Breakfast Clubbers, good morning to ya," McNeill would say to kick off his program of corny jokes, birth announcements sent in by listeners, sentimental poems, singers backed by Eddy Ballantine's house orchestra, and even a moment of silent prayer. When the King of Corn signed off at the end of 1968, he had been at it for thirty-five years.

Informational radio talk as Gray and a few others practiced it was seen by the 1960s as a viable programming option, particularly as stations sought specialized formats to replace their department stores of music, talk, sports, concerts, and more. In 1960, for example, Robert Hyland, Jr., general manager of KMOX in St. Louis, dropped all of the station's music shows between 3:00 and 7:00 P.M. in favor of so-called information programs—a move that later prompted *Broadcasting* magazine to state that Hyland invented the talk-radio format. One of KMOX's first talk shows was "At Your Service," begun in 1960 by Jack Buck, later a popular CBS network sportscaster.

The format took a major step forward in the early 1960s, when technology and looser regulations combined to put listeners' calls on the air. Their phoned-in remarks were broadcast following several seconds of taped delay, to prevent any obscenities from slipping through, and were punctuated intermittently by a high-pitched beep tone that the FCC ordered inserted during all taped dialogue. In opening up the format, talk stars, now dubbed "phone jockeys" by some writers, arose in markets around the country.

At KABC, an also-ran in the Los Angeles market, an all-talk format was implemented in 1960 to reach those thousands who spent hours and hours driving to and from their corner of the sprawling metropolis. "It was new and totally off the wall," Ben Hoberman, KABC's general manager at the time, reminisced in *Beating the Odds*, the autobiography of ABC founder Leonard H. Goldenson. "I thought it would be distinctive and appeal to a small, quality audience, which would give us enough to sell. We could then make some money."

Hoberman hired Joe Pyne, one of the first shock jocks, later described by an essayist as "a Cro-Magnon Rush Limbaugh." Pyne hammered home his ultraconservative views and attacked callers mercilessly. So incendiary were his statements that Hoberman ordered him to take a week off following President John F. Kennedy's assassination, lest he say something in the midst of national mourning that the station would regret.

Commentary on KABC through the years was provided by Edward P. Morgan, Paul Harvey, John Cameron Swayze, and others. Ray Briem, Ira Fistell, David Viscott, and Michael Jackson hosted shows. The British-born Jackson, who had started out on American radio as a rock jock in 1958, was working five hours a night on Los Angeles's KHJ when talk was catching on in 1964. He advised callers on personal problems and once alerted police in time to save a woman who announced that she had cut a wrist. Joining KABC in 1966, he established himself as a Los Angeles insider; his access through the years included interviews with Hollywood lights and world figures such as Archbishop Desmond Tutu and Prince Philip. In the 1990s, still going strong, Jackson maintained the top-rated talk show in southern California until Limbaugh passed him via KFI.

In Miami, where Brooklyn-born Larry King had gone to break into radio, the disc jockey was brought in to interview Bobby Darin, Jimmy Hoffa, and other names from a table at Pumpernik's restaurant over WKAT in 1959 as a way to generate more breakfast business. A year later, King was talking nights from a houseboat berthed on the Intracoastal Waterway for WIOD (which would be his Miami outlet and his link to Jackie Gleason and a world of other guests all but continuously until the Mutual Broadcasting System launched his national show, beginning with a couple of dozen stations, in 1978).

In March 1964, NBC's flagship radio station, WNBC in New York, took the bold step of firing all but one of its disc jockeys and instituting a call-in format. The station's first talk hosts included Pyne (in an hour-long taped rebroadcast of his Los Angeles show), actor Robert Alda, Lee Leonard, the authoritarian Brad Crandall, student of the occult Long John Nebel, and sports maven Bill Mazer, who was brought down from Buffalo's WGR.

The concept was novel. "The first day I'm there at WNBC, I start answering calls on the air," recalls Mazer, who discussed sports for three hours, 4:00 to 7:00 P.M., and in the 1990s was doing a morning show on New York's WEVD-AM. "I had no idea about talk radio. I did it without any sense that we were inventing a form. When I went on, I had no guide, no anything."

Jerry Williams, an influential voice in New England via Boston's WRKO-AM, places the beginning of "real, two-way talk" at around 1957, when he started broadcasting in the city on WMEX. He counted John F. Kennedy and Malcolm X among his most frequent guests and even lured Richard Cardinal Cushing to his studio. "I had Malcolm on about twenty times," he recalled. "One of those nights, our tower was bombed. But that was our entertainment, to have these people on. It was exciting radio."

Unlike Limbaugh, who confined his activist role to strident radio preachings after going national in 1988, the dean of Boston talk has occasionally stepped out of his glass booth to press for change. In 1986, Williams helped lead the successful fight to repeal Massachusetts's seat-belt law, and he is widely credited with directing the tea-bag revolution of 1989. Talk hosts around the country followed his lead in encouraging listeners to send the packets to Washington in symbolic protest of a 50 percent raise in congressional pay. In the end, thousands of tea bags were mailed to lawmakers, and a pay raise was thwarted in February 1989. At least for a few months, that is.

Of course, after moving from KABC to New York radio in 1970, Bob Grant became famous himself for pit-bull assaults on those he found stupid or just plain ill informed. "You creep," he said to one caller. "Get off the phone or I'll punch your nose down your throat!" In the 1992 presidential campaign, he (like Limbaugh) introduced George Bush at a local rally held late in his reelection drive.

By the end of 1992, talk radio had become the second most popular format on the AM dial in America, with around six hundred stations offering some form of news/talk programming, according to *The M Street Journal*, a weekly newsletter that monitors the Federal Communications Commission and industry trends. This was twice the number of three years earlier.

An analysis of the fall 1992 ratings of The Arbitron Company, as done by the firm and *Billboard* magazine, also showed that the news/talk format gained in national listening so that it was now in second place, with a 15.2 share of the total audience, behind adult-contemporary music. Among listeners twenty-five to fifty-four years old, news/talk ranked third in popularity.

Besides the homegrown talk lineups offered by many stations, and the widely traveled broadcasts of King and financial adviser Bruce Williams made available by Westwood One, numerous lesser-known talk shows were being beamed at low cost to affiliates by satellite-equipped syndicators. These included Daynet, Sun Radio Network, Independent Broadcasters Network, and burgeoning networks established by individual stations such as WOR in New York and KVI in Seattle. And, of course, there was EFM Media Management, the much-envied syndicator of Limbaugh.

As Rush's show took off in 1988, replacing psychologist Joy Browne on WABC, it quickened the movement of the pendulum away from the hand-holding, problem-solving, personal-advice programs that proliferated through much of the 1980s. Toni Grant, Susan Forward, Judith Kuriansky, and Dr. Ruth Westheimer, doyenne of the frank "Sexually Speaking," were among the other radio practitioners of this form.

"Hot talk," with all its screaming and controversy, was now in. Yet Rush Limbaugh's brand of hot talk stood apart from most others because it eschewed the use (and abuse) of guests, so-called experts, and the day's newsmakers to maintain the pace and let the host shine. Limbaugh wanted to be the sole reason that people tuned in. Even his callers, plentiful though they were, played a secondary role. As a result, he seemed to violate the rules of the format; he ignored the vague premise in the industry that a talk show should somehow make a stab at offering equal time to opposing arguments.

So what, he told an interviewer: "Everybody can get any guest and I'm not going to do any better with them than the best inter-viewers. . . . So why slice that pie any further? I wanted to carve out a niche that focused on me. And I've been real fortunate, it worked."

His show was a one-man performance. Boasting about this, he also recognized that some of his colleagues "think I'm violating the sacred format of what talk radio ought to be. . . . And I've really set it up that I want to do two things on this show . . . I want to combine the serious discussion of issues and analysis provided by me, with irreverent humor."

The criticism that Limbaugh referred to, or perhaps it was simply a case of professional jealousy, was evident when he attended the 1991 convention in Seattle of the National Association of Radio Talk Show Hosts, a group that mainly consisted of broadcasters from small and medium-sized markets. Although he had rearranged his schedule to be there and was now the top gun in the field, the other hosts were standoffish during the opening-night reception. He also was subjected to a harangue from a man in the audience at one point during his keynote speech at the next day's luncheon.

He urged his colleagues to believe in themselves and to broadcast with commitment. Overall, however, the atmosphere was one of: *Why him and not me?*

Chapter 14

"UNCLE LAR"

After Limbaugh's syndicated show hit the air in 1988, older listeners heard splashes of Arthur Godfrey in the newcomer's freewheeling style. It was Godfrey, a superstar on CBS Radio in the 1940s before he started doing TV as well, who wanted to take the preachiness out of the announcer's trade. He playfully mocked the stuffiness of his scripts and gave a "hu'um," a whistle, or a laugh before moving on to his next feature. It was Godfrey of whom *Newsweek* wrote: "Even the metallic microphone can't hide the man's naturalness or the genuineness of his laugh. And to most, his pleasure in beating sacred cows is refreshing and clever. Of course, he has enemies, too. In some homes he is snapped off as being crass, rude, silly and dull. But this, to Godfrey, is the controversy that helps build a showman's success."

This was in 1947—forty-one years before writers would be saying the same thing about Rush.

Limbaugh insisted that his brash style was all his own and patterned after no one else's. "I don't listen to other hosts or shows," he told a reporter in 1988. "There's no originality left. Why copy people?"

As the show caught on, however, he said that he didn't listen to other talk programs for a different reason. "And it's not because

I'm effete or elite about it, but rather, when I started out in this business as a disc jockey . . . I ended up copying Larry Lujack at WLS, trying to be the next Larry Lujack, and stunted my own growth," he explained to *Talkers*. He said that Lujack was the only person he ever copied.

Candid as this confession was, it suggested that the copying had ended in Limbaugh's disc-jockeying days of the late sixties and early seventies. Lujack, a legendary broadcaster once described as "the Great Cynic of Chicago radio," quit the business in 1987 and so was no longer on the air to invite comparisons. But in fact, one of the loosely kept secrets about Limbaugh's rambunctious style on the air concerned the level of debt he *continued* to owe Lujack.

Here's Lujack on WLS counting down the top hits of 1968: "WLS Hit Parade award winner Aretha Franklin, by your votes the top female vocalist of the year 1968—'LS jock serving humanity tonight Larry Lujack . . ."

And then there's Limbaugh, who often says that he, too, is "serving humanity."

Lujack: ". . . by the way, reprints of this address will not be available so perhaps you will like to take notes."

Limbaugh (by way of his show's staff announcer): "Tapes of 'The Rush Limbaugh Show' are provided to heads of state internationally for use in their daily briefings."

Lujack: "Five-thirty in Chicago. Time for the clunk letter of the day . . . *Da-da-do, da-da-do, da-da-da!* . . ."

Limbaugh intoned *"dadalup, dadalup, dadalup!"* to introduce his trademark "updates" on the homeless, the joys of cut timber, and other topics designed to grate on the liberal opposition. He all but claims a copyright on *dadalup* in his book: "This is my attempt to approximate the stirring sound of a trumpet fanfare and alert listeners that something important is coming."

Besides phrases and bits such as these, Rush Limbaugh's debt to Larry Lujack extends to the talk host's calculated use of the dramatic pause, the stretch of so-called "dead air" that has long been considered taboo in the medium of sound. Lujack's pauses were particularly striking because he toiled in Top 40, a format that typically called for a high-energy, rat-a-tat delivery without breaks of any kind. Lujack may have been the first disc jockey to understand the power of silence and its way of luring people in. During his pauses, the listeners could hear the laconic broadcaster rustling and paging through papers in front of him, thereby giving his show an air of informality and reality, much as Limbaugh later did when he began to audibly finger and snap the faxes and news clippings brought into his studio.

Lujack also spoke of himself in the third person ("The opinions expressed by Mr. Lujack . . ."). So did Limbaugh—and sometimes in similar fashion ("The views expressed on this show by the host will soon become federal law").

And Lujack laid down the hits with a self-parodying pomposity: "After all, he is Superjock and he always will be. Other disc jockeys come and go, but Superjock just keeps coming!"

As did Limbaugh: "I am Rush Limbaugh, your guiding light in times of trouble, confusion, murkiness, despair, and presidential tumult."

Lujack, doing his last broadcast on WCFL in 1976 before a format change: "Mr. Lujack's last major address to the nation from this radio station follows this selection. . . ."

David Limbaugh recalls that his brother used to listen to Lujack on WLS, whose 50,000-watt, clear-channel signal reached as far away as Florida and Texas. A veritable temple of rock music for much of the Midwest.

Sometimes, Rush also went around imitating the disc jockey's on-air style. "To work at WLS was one of Rush's lifetime goals," David says. (It became the Chicago affiliate for his talk show.)

Similarities run throughout the two men's lives. Lujack, like Limbaugh, grew up in the Midwest and went into radio full-time after only a year of college. In Lujack's case, he was enthralled by the idea that a station would actually pay him to sit back and play Buddy Holly records. An early stop was KRPL in Moscow, Idaho, in 1958. The studios stood alongside Paradise Creek, so the announcers said they were "broadcasting from the banks of Paradise." He was fired a lot in the beginning for not sounding friendly enough on the air. "Some of those stations had a sign up near the microphone that said 'Smile,' but I was never into that because it just seemed so phony," he recalls. "Disc jockeys from that day were all very up, bubbly and bright, which I could just never do. Whatever I am that day, that's what goes on the air, take it or leave it. That was very different back then."

After kicking around on a string of other stations, Lujack reached Chicago's WCFL in 1967 as host of an all-night show. During the next twenty years, he did a morning program on WLS while Limbaugh was in high school and college, then bounced back to WCFL in afternoon-drive (while his young fan was by now working professionally himself) before returning to WLS. Lujack was only forty-seven years old in 1987 when he let the Cap Cities station buy him out of an eight-year, $6-million radio contract for a reported $1.5 million.

"Uncle Lar," as he sometimes called himself, had been disc jockeying for nearly thirty years and said during his final broadcast: "I don't wanna do this anymore."

In the years that followed Lujack's retirement, which was page-one news in Chicago, various celebrities told of their appreciation for his laconic and often inventive radio style. While David Letterman was attending Ball State University in Muncie, Indiana, he would get out of bed early enough to tune in Lujack and partner Tommy Edwards's popular "animal stories," which described the lightning bug's sex habits, ways to protect a lawn from dog waste, and other matters of importance. No doubt an influence on the "Stupid Pet Tricks" segments that air on Letterman's late-night TV show.

Before "Saturday Night Live" made Bill Murray a star, the Chicago native used to punch up jukebox selections in a Chicago barroom and then offer his own imitation of how Lujack would introduce the tune.

And then there was Limbaugh, whose remarks to NBC interviewer Bob Costas in 1991 about Lujack were reported by broadcast columnist Robert Feder in the Chicago *Sun-Times*. Reading the piece at home in the suburbs, Lujack was pleased but not surprised. Others who remembered the disc jockey's air work also had been telling him that this fellow Limbaugh was copying his licks.

"I rarely listen to radio anymore, because it's not enjoyable, so I've never heard Limbaugh," Lujack told me in early 1993. "However, I have seen his TV show once or twice. Frankly, what he copied, I can't pick out what it is on television. I am by nature sarcastic, at times caustic, if that's what it is."

Moreover, Lujack said he was mystified as to why Limbaugh had become so successful. "His appeal escapes me," he said. "What he does, he does well, but I don't see anything there or hear anything to justify the humongous success he has. I have less desire to listen to Howard Stern than to Limbaugh, but I can understand Stern's success. But the country must be more conservative than I thought for him to be so big, the silent majority and all that."

Weeks after speaking with me, Lujack called back to decry Limbaugh's snide treatment of Chelsea Clinton, the new president's twelve-year-old daughter. Limbaugh himself had cut no godlike picture as a youngster, and he was previously reprimanded by his mother for mocking the appearance of former President Jimmy Carter's daughter, Amy. Now, Lujack had come upon Limbaugh again on television and this time watched him make fun of Chelsea's frizzy-haired looks.

"My God, that is so pathetic—how cruel," Lujack said. "This kid has been through enough with all the sex allegations about her father during the campaign. She did not ask to be a public figure." Lujack went further: "Why doesn't he pick on someone his own size?"

Chapter 15

A VERY GOOD YEAR

Rush Limbaugh's national radio career had begun in the summer of 1988 on McLaughlin's educated, entrepreneurial hunch and with the syndicator's own funds. There were no ratings to measure performance against and only a few dozen affiliates to muster an audience.

Limbaugh's starting salary of $150,000 was guaranteed by McLaughlin against the distinct possibility that the whole enterprise might wither away for lack of interest from stations and listeners. Rush's jolly high jinks and "homeless updates" would count for nothing if big-city affiliates shut him out, or if the listeners ignored his bold attempt to supplant local daytime programming with something else entirely. For without desirable affiliates, as well as meaningful ratings, advertisers would withhold their commercials and thereby deny the program vital means of support.

All of these ifs had receded in memory by 1992.

The new year brought great news from the West Coast. Limbaugh's three-hour show, as carried 9:00 A.M. to noon by Los Angeles station KFI, had just toppled KABC's Michael Jackson, an institution on the dial for twenty-five years, to become the new leader of late-morning radio in the country's second-largest radio market. In the newly released fall ratings, Limbaugh's average audience of 100,000 listeners per quarter-hour surpassed Jackson's 90,000 during the hours they competed. The evidence suggested that people had not tired of Jackson's even-handed interviews but that the noisy conservative was luring defectors from other shows.

Nevertheless, the victory prompted Limbaugh to cluck. He told the *Los Angeles Times* that Jackson's show was boring by comparison. "Michael Jackson is a premiere broadcaster and always has been . . . a standard-setter and so forth. But it's formula."

Jackson conceded that he sometimes was too polite to guests. Not that Limbaugh was a Visigoth; in fact, around this same time, etiquette expert Marjabelle Young Stuart placed him on her list of America's best-mannered citizens, right up there with George and Barbara Bush, Oprah Winfrey, weatherman Willard Scott, Paul Harvey, and a few others. Based on a total of 827 nominations from journalists to chauffeurs, the author and lecturer said that people found Limbaugh to possess "dignity and grace."

KABC executives said they wanted to aim for more entertainment during Jackson's dignified show, so as to counter the three reasons that Limbaugh claimed people listened to him—"to be entertained, to be entertained, to be entertained." But Limbaugh's Los Angeles audience continued to grow. (By the winter of 1993, he was attracting 237,400 people per quarter-hour, to make his the most-listened-to program in the market.).

In San Diego, the Limbaugh ascendancy was also bad news for Michael Reagan, the son of the former president. Two years into his stint as afternoon host on KSDO, he was dropped by the station to make way for a taped playback of Limbaugh's program. KSDO had been lobbying hard for the show and won out when XTRA-AM decided to switch to a sports format. In all of Limbaugh's praise for Ronald Reagan, on a show that *Broadcasting* magazine called "Reaganism with a rock 'n' roll beat," he never imagined that an echo of his hero's views would overpower a member of the former president's family.

In March, "The Rush Limbaugh Morning Update," a ninety-second weekday commentary, was made available for airing between 6:00 and 8:00 A.M. An adjoining minute was reserved for a commercial sold by EFM Media, though affiliates were allowed to air the feature two other times before 10:00 A.M. with their own local sponsorship. Translation: Limbaugh was able to reach morning listeners who until then may have been unfamiliar with his act, and a new revenue stream started flowing to EFM Media from the sale of commercials during the more desirable wake-up hours.

Later in the month, *Inside Radio*, an industry tip sheet, reported that EFM had begun to charge a radio station in a small, unrated Northeast market $250 a month to carry Limbaugh's show seeing that the affiliate would not show a quantifiable audience response that the syndicator could then build into its own ad rates. The charges came to affect about 130 stations by 1993. The other affiliates, at least for now, received the program free of charge and had only to carry four minutes an hour of EFM's commercials. As *Inside Radio* noted, "The take from the commercials, the videos, the cruises . . . and the personal appearances adds up to a capitalist's dream."

And why not? More than 3 million people were listening at a given moment and a total in excess of 12.8 million tuned in each week. "The Rush Limbaugh Show" had increased its number of affiliates tenfold. Those five-hundred-plus stations, including recent additions WBAP-AM in Dallas and WTIC-AM in Hartford, Connecticut, now resonated Limbaugh's trumpet blast of conservatism across the entire country—"100 percent coverage," as they said in the business.

Outside of the big cities, listeners would be amazed to pick up his show simultaneously at several different points on the dial. A drive well north of Dallas, for example, would allow Limbaugh's saturation presence to boom on through to a car radio from stations in Texas, Oklahoma, and New Mexico, as if from a thick cloud that remained ever overhead.

The omnipresence of the conservative registered with Dale and Susan Paget, writers who had been traveling around the United States for three months, confronting the congested suburbs of southern California and marveling at the farms and buffalo herds found in the wide open spaces. In concluding their series of travelogues for the *Los Angeles Times*, they observed: "Like it or not, we couldn't escape country music or Rush Limbaugh on our AM radio, fast-food places and mosquitoes."

Even *Vanity Fair*, the oh-so-hot monthly magazine that profiled the new, the decadent, and the powerful, noticed Limbaugh's presence on its own highly selective radar screen. In the same May issue that splashed a bosomy Ivana Trump, America's best-known divorcée, across the cover ("Ivana Be a Star!") and profiled novelist-to-the-hip Jay McInerney and Hillary Clinton, Limbaugh also received lengthy and serious attention, complete with photographs taken by celebrity shooter James Hamilton.

"Bull Rush" was written by the magazine's Peter J. Boyer, a former television writer for *The New York Times* and the author of *Who Killed CBS?* The piece asked: Is Limbaugh "just the court jester of the disaffected politically incorrect, or the secret weapon of the Republican rebellion?" Yet with striking testimonials, Boyer left little doubt that Limbaugh's rumblings across the fruited plain were being felt in the halls of influence, Washington, Hollywood, and New York. "Ted Koppel is a Washington fan, if not a philosophical sympathizer, often laughing out loud as he rides to work; ditto Hollywood producer Don Simpson." The latter told Boyer: "I'm not exaggerating, I listen to him every morning."

On June 29, 1992, the Supreme Court, by a 5–4 vote, reaffirmed a woman's constitutional right to an abortion while also allowing some state-mandated restrictions on the procedure. Limbaugh, who had always condemned "the prochoice crowd," went on the air two hours after the ruling was issued in Washington and reviewed its language while also holding his ground. He noted that the high court found parts of Pennsylvania's law to be constitutional, including a twenty-four-hour delay on an abortion after a woman hears a presentation regarding alternatives, plus a need for unmarried women under eighteen years old who do not support themselves to receive an approval from a parent or from a state judge. The court struck down the need for a married woman to notify her husband of her intent to undergo an abortion.

The states "can enact restrictions, but they cannot proscribe it," Limbaugh said, cutting to the essence of the ruling. "In other words, they can't outlaw it. And this is not bad. I think this, in essence, is good because we all know, ladies and gentlemen, that the vast majority of abortions occur primarily for the purposes of birth control. They don't happen because of rape or incest or the victimization, the unwanted victimization of a woman. And there is a responsibility that is inherent here and I think this decision will allow states to get to that."

At the same time, vocal groups on both sides of the fractious issue were dissatisfied with the decision—from Operation Rescue, the militant antiabortion group, to the National Abortion Rights Action League, whose president, Kate Michelman, found the ruling to be more antiabortion than it appeared—"devastating for women," in fact. She had an ally in Patricia Ireland, president of the National Organization for Women, who maintained that the constitutional right to an abortion had received a "flimsy stay of execution."

Such impassioned reactions on the prochoice side once again inflamed Limbaugh and prompted him to hurl the most daggerlike of his epithets—*feminazi*. Disputing Ireland's contention that the latest court decision placed obstacles in the way of abortions, he said that Ireland was the model of a feminazi.

"A feminazi is a woman—a feminist—to whom the most important thing in the world is that as many abortions as possible take place," he argued. "How else to explain feminists who get angry when a woman who's decided to have an abortion is talked out of it and instead has the baby? Why do they get so mad? Here is another example of that. Here is Patricia Ireland, upset at anything which stands in the way of a woman on the way to having an abortion. You have to ask yourself why, why this rage, why this anger . . . *Roe* versus *Wade* is still the law of the land."

What in the world is wrong, he asked, with a woman's being

told about fetal development? "How does it violate her right to an abortion?"

Feminazi. By now the term had come to reflect the pugnacity of Limbaugh's views as clearly as his belief that global warming was a bogus scientific concept. But he was challenged on his coining of *feminazi* by a broadcaster who was more than up to the task.

"It is the suffix that drives people crazy," ABC newsman Jeff Greenfield said during his 1992 appearance with Limbaugh at the 92nd Street YM-YWHA in Manhattan. "*Feminazi.* I mean, that is a movement that did not simply want to silence people, it killed people, by the millions. It is a very powerful, memorable phrase. I think it did you much good in terms of defining you as a person with a colorful and bold turn of phrase. Any regrets about that particular term?"

No, Limbaugh replied, making it clear that *feminazi* did not apply to all feminists, but maybe to twenty or so. "I happen to be prolife. I happen to think life is the most sacrosanct thing on the planet, human life. I think that if we cheapen it, or devalue it in any way, then other societal ills result. I do not think it is wise for a society to kill for convenience sake, and I think that is what abortion has become. . . . A feminazi is a woman, a feminist, to whom the most important thing in her life is seeing to it that all abortions possible take place. That's why there aren't very many. I don't know more than twenty in the whole country. A feminazi is a woman who gets mad when a woman decides to have a baby, is talked out of having an abortion. I don't understand that, if choice is what this is really all about." He added that the millions of abortions performed in the United States were comparable to a holocaust.

If there were twenty feminazis in the whole country, Greenfield asked him, then why go after them? "It does strike me that that's a howitzer for a flea."

"Because they drive the movement," Limbaugh said. He wondered why there was "such anger" that a pregnant woman might decide to deliver her child.

"Rush, I gotta tell you," Greenfield pressed on, "I really don't know who in the feminist movement, other than people who last disappeared in 1969 when we were all a little wacky, who are angry when a pregnant woman chooses to have a baby. Is it Gloria Steinem? Is it Kate Michelman? Who are you talking about?"

"Yeah, well, I think those are a couple of names that you see," Limbaugh said.

Many in the audience groaned.

"Who are angry?" Greenfield said. "I mean, I really want to get this clear because it's important."

"Sure," Limbaugh said.

"When a pregnant woman chooses to have a baby, is it your view that somewhere in the recesses of their souls, Gloria Steinem or Kate Michelman are angry? Would they really secretly want these children aborted?"

Limbaugh countered by singling out the opposition of "militant, prochoice people" to the twenty-four-hour waiting period on an abortion. The excuse they give is that the delay may cause undue economic hardship, he said, but the same people want twelve weeks' unpaid leave to have a child. "And if you can afford twelve weeks, how come you can't afford twenty-four hours?"

"I have to tell you, there may be three members of some witches' collective somewhere up in New England that think this, I don't know where they are," Greenfield said. "I don't think it's Gloria Steinem, I don't think it's Kate Michelman, I don't think it's any leader of the movement." Greenfield told him that *feminazi* was "the one phrase that you use that puzzles me."

Limbaugh backed off a little—a rare moment witnessed by the few hundred people in the auditorium: "My attitudes on this are not such that I want to force my view on anybody. Never have, never would. If I were married and my wife got pregnant and wanted to terminate her pregnancy, I'd try to persuade her heart and mind, and if I failed, I wouldn't stop her. . . . Now perhaps *feminazi* is too much like Operation Rescue's finger-in-the-face 'you murderer,' and I don't intend it. I mean it to describe the attitudes of some of the leaders of the political movement that guides abortion. I hope you won't deny that that does exist."

Not at all, Greenfield said. Nevertheless he sought to get off

the subject by summing up his view that the use of feminazi
"evokes . . ."

Limbaugh cut in: "Provokes."

"No, no," Greenfield insisted, "*evokes* a memory that is the most
extreme example . . ."

Limbaugh looked relieved when Greenfield then changed the
subject.

Chapter 16

ENTER THE KINGMAKER

Limbaugh's political influence was enriched handsomely by his partnership with Roger Ailes, who was paving the broadcaster's way to national television just as Ed McLaughlin had placed him on radio stations across America.

Roger Ailes. One of the tough guys in American politics. A five-foot-nine, 240-pound sultan of a man with a wicked sense of humor. A press-bashing manipulator of the media who helped elect three Republicans to the White House.

The self-described "middle-class midwesterner," a factory fore-man's son from Warren, Ohio, got started in politics with Richard M. Nixon. It was a fluke. At the time—1967—Ailes was executive producer of "The Mike Douglas Show," having risen to the Phila-delphia-based TV talk program after working at stations in Parkers-burg, West Virginia, Middleport, Ohio, and Cleveland, where his responsibilities at KYW-TV included the station's children's pro-grams.

The affable Douglas would have Edward Teller and dancing bears on the same show, the common denominator being that both the renowned physicist and the circus act happened to be in Phila-delphia at the same time. As Ailes himself told the story in a 1992 interview: "One day, my associate ran in and said, 'We have Richard

Nixon, the former vice president, coming in the front door and we have Little Egypt the belly dancer with a snake in the greenroom. What do we do?' And I said, 'Put one of them in my office.' And I forgot about it, and went to rehearsal, and when I came back upstairs, there was Richard Nixon sitting in my office.

"I always said, had they put Little Egypt in there, I'd have had an entirely different career, and perhaps a lot more fun."

Nixon, who was angling for the Republican nomination for president the following year (1968), got into a long discussion with the twenty-seven-year-old Ailes about television and politics during the hour before airtime. Actually, the former vice president irked Ailes by saying it was too bad that a candidate had to rely on what he called "gimmicks"—that is, television—to get elected. Ailes assured Nixon that he would lose again if he held to that view.

Nixon then warmed to Ailes's comments about the various interview shows, the importance of lighting and makeup, and other fundamentals. The producer clearly made an impression, for two days later Nixon's people called to ask Ailes if he would produce television shows for the '68 campaign. Ailes agreed. He became a part-time consultant at first, but he left the Douglas show to become a full-time member of the Nixon team on the eve of the GOP convention in August.

Among Ailes's contributions in Nixon's defeat of Hubert H. Humphrey was to keep his candidate from projecting what the producer called an "overimpression," an image that might be interpreted as phony by sophisticated TV viewers and therefore alienate them. Ailes regarded TV as an artificial medium that made one's natural actions and speech seem artificial as well; the challenge, he thought, was to find a way to sidestep this problem.

To this end, Ailes sought to counteract the widely held perception, fueled by the televised debates with a more vigorous-looking John F. Kennedy in 1960, that Nixon appeared awkward on TV. In the shows that Ailes produced in 1968, he put Nixon in an arenalike setting, with studio guests seated on both sides of him and a panel of other ordinary citizens in front to pose unrehearsed questions. The setup was designed to show Nixon, who knew both victory and defeat, back in the combat of the arena, but at ease, and in command of the issues raised by his questioners. Perception was everything.

After Nixon's victory in November, Ailes said: "Never again will a man be elected to office without TV. . . . Now, one of the questions a candidate's backers will ask is if the man can make it on Johnny Carson."

Ailes's shrewdness was not forgotten by Nixon. The following year, as an unpaid presidential adviser (but a paid TV consultant to the Republican National Committee), Ailes answered Nixon's call and flew to New York from Cincinnati, where he was producing a talk show starring Dennis Wholey, to give the president speaking tips right before his address to the United Nations General Assembly in quest of diplomatic assistance to end the Vietnam War. "He told Mr. Nixon to be wary of the hall's lighting," *The New York Times* reported. "It was not diffuse television lighting, designed to flatter the face, but directly overhead, he said, so the President would be advised to stand a foot away from the lectern so the lights would not deepen the shadows of his eye sockets. Moreover, standing back from the lectern would enable the President to avoid casting shadows across the notes for his prepared speech."

Ailes considered lighting "one of the most important things of all." And his advice to Nixon on how to work with it, indeed his role as a kingmaker, was spelled out in writer Joe McGinniss's subsequent best-seller, *The Selling of the President*, which maintained that candidate Nixon had been marketed no differently from a car or a brand of toothpaste.

Ailes charged that the book was mostly fiction. He said it was nonsense to suggest that Nixon the candidate was "sold" to the American people. "If such a thing could really be done, it would be a dangerous thing for our country and I'd have no part of it." He took particular issue with McGinniss's contention that the real Nixon differed markedly from the product pitched to the voters.

Manipulation? Phooey, Ailes said. "If you're a lawyer, you must learn courtroom techniques; a doctor must know how to deal with a patient; a man on TV must learn how to be effective in that medium. What's wrong about that?"

Still, the Nixon connection weighed on Ailes after the disgrace of Watergate. "Everybody wants to talk to me about him," Ailes said in 1977. "It's an albatross." At the time, Ailes was pursuing opportunities in show business, as a producer of a live satirical revue in New York and as a coproducer of an Off-Broadway hit, *The Hot l Baltimore*. In remarks that seemed prescient when Limbaugh reached TV two decades later, Ailes said that someday he wanted to do a completely improvisational show.

In the meantime, now weighing much more and sporting a rakish mustache and goatee that never would have passed muster in the Nixon White House, Ailes continued to advise candidates on how to navigate the media, as he himself remained very much a part of it. He counseled Republican Senate and congressional hopefuls while also serving as executive producer of NBC's late-night interview show, "Tomorrow," with Tom Snyder—a situation that the network did not see as a church-state conflict.

In 1984, after President Reagan appeared to stumble in his first televised debate with Walter Mondale, Ailes was brought in by the president's camp to prepare their man better for future TV appearances. In 1988, the Bush campaign turned to Ailes to help counter the candidate's wimp image. The assignment found Ailes spending hours with the vice president in an effort to take the whine out of his voice and to help him exhibit greater forcefulness with his hand gestures, which up until then looked awkward and clumsy. The makeover was illustrated tenfold during Bush's bristling and combative on-air interview with CBS anchorman Dan Rather, who sought in vain to get answers about the Iran-contra scandal. In the moments before the live exchange, Ailes pumped up Bush for battle. "He's gonna sandbag you," Ailes warned.

As vividly chronicled by CBS newsman Bob Schieffer and Gary Paul Gates in *The Acting Presidency*, what viewers soon saw as a seemingly spontaneous bout on the evening news was largely scripted. Ailes stood next to the TV camera and scrawled large clue words for Bush to mouth back at Rather. "Not fair to judge . . . Yours" came out as ". . . it's not fair to judge my whole career by a rehash on Iran. How would you like it if I judged your career by those seven minutes when you walked off the set in New York?" It was mud in Rather's eye over the anchorman's having caused

CBS to go dark after a televised tennis match when, reportedly in a fit of anger, he was not in place to begin his newscast. In short, Bush dug in and threw punches. The look of a fighter played well. Wimpishness be damned.

Ailes ran Bush's media campaign against Massachusetts governor Michael Dukakis, going at it seven days a week. He said he "micromanaged" the campaign, having a hand in every decision. But he emphasized forever afterward that he had no role in the decision to produce and air a controversial commercial that tied Dukakis to Willie Horton, who had terrorized a couple, raping the woman, while on furlough from a Massachusetts prison. Although dragging Horton, a black man, into the race was seen by many as a racist stretch, the crimes he committed on Dukakis's watch were cited by the Republicans to considerable advantage during the campaign.

"Willie Horton," asked WCBS-AM newsman Art Athens in 1992. "Did you do it?"

"No I didn't," Ailes said. "Well, the media has a tendency to invent things and then fall in love with their own inventions. I've offered money to anybody who can prove that I had anything to do with the Willie Horton commercial. It was produced by an independent expenditure in 1988."

The Horton spot was created outside the Bush campaign by a right-wing maverick named Floyd G. Brown. The commercial effectively blamed Dukakis for Horton's crimes as it also sought to stoke white voters' fears. However, Ailes's denial was a matter of semantics, for he did deliver another TV commercial that showed prisoners passing through a revolving door, just as Horton did. Although the by-now-infamous Horton was not mentioned by name in Ailes's spot, the Horton connection was more than clear.

"By the way, I have nothing against attacking Willie Horton," Ailes said. "I think he was a bad guy. He murdered people, he raped people. I just didn't happen to do that commercial, and the media hates it when I want to say those things and they want to defend Willie Horton. . . . The press always defends criminals against the victims." (Ailes had an ally in Limbaugh, who dismissed the idea that the controversial ads pandered to racism. Limbaugh wrote in his book: "It's almost as if Willie Horton were a victim—

of the media, of the Republicans, and so on. We don't hear about what Willie Horton actually did.")

After working for two losing Republicans in 1989, New York City mayoral candidate Rudolph Giuliani and New Jersey gubernatorial contender Jim Courter, Ailes continued to voice anger at the media. He accused reporters of "brutality" for focusing on his negative campaign tactics while also reporting every charge leveled by his clients.

By 1992, Ailes said that he was through with politics and told everyone that he had broken the news to Bush the previous November. The presidential campaign four years earlier had taxed his wife to the point where she nearly suffered a nervous breakdown, he disclosed, and his daughter was physically attacked at college "simply because she was my daughter." He was quitting at his family's insistence rather than dig in for another long, hard haul.

On the surface, Ailes's whirl of other activities lent credence to his claim that he had put the political life behind him. He was launching the Limbaugh TV show, marketing a political board game developed by an associate, and promoting singer Kelly Garrett at New York nightclubs. It was also announced in 1992 that Ailes would expand his marketing role on behalf of Paramount Pictures' TV shows, including "Entertainment Tonight" and "Hard Copy."

But all of Ailes's show business merely masked the counsel he continued to provide Bush and his reelection cause. He was among those at the turn of the year who urged the president to shake off indecision and mount an offensive to win the White House once more. *New York Newsday* gossip columnist Liz Smith, an old friend of Ailes, reported in June that the White House was "chasing . . . begging [Ailes] . . . to come back and pull its chestnuts out of the fire." Ailes's labeling H. Ross Perot "looney tunes" also fueled speculation that the media man wanted more of the fray.

"You talk to George Bush?" Athens asked him soon afterward.

"Yeah, in fact, I saw him last week," Ailes replied. "He and I went to the theater, went to Kennedy Center together. We're friends, and I'm friends with many of the people around him. I saw Barbara a few days ago, but I just don't want to be a political guy anymore."

But, again, Ailes's denial was a matter of semantics. For the night at the Kennedy Center—June 3, 1992, to be precise—involved more than Bush and Ailes. Limbaugh was also the president's guest at a performance of the musical *Buddy*, and afterward the broadcaster spent the night in the White House, bedding down in the Lincoln Bedroom. The chummy encounter helped clinch Limbaugh's coveted support for the president's sagging reelection bid.

Bush extended the invitation to Limbaugh through Ailes, who persuaded the president to link arms with a potentially invaluable supporter in the tough campaign ahead. But others also recognized the radio broadcaster's value. In their May 20 column in *The Washington Post*, Rowland Evans and Robert Novak began: "The air of grim foreboding hovering over Republicans today explains surprising advice from one of the party's most prestigious figures: President Bush, in order to save himself, would do well to imitate the style of Rush Limbaugh. This Republican leader, a longtime Bush backer, was not entirely sure that the president would know the name of the popular right-wing radio talk show host. So, instead of approaching Bush himself, he went to Press Secretary Marlin Fitzwater and urged him to compile a tape of Limbaughisms that the boss might study."

The column went on: "The notion of the patrician head of state emulating a talk-show shtick to regain his popularity conveys two grim facts of life increasingly accepted in the upper strata of the GOP. First, the inevitability of the president's reelection is gone. Second, Bush simply may not be up to getting himself another term."

As a result of this uncertainty, Limbaugh enjoyed an unforgettable evening. Despite Limbaugh's embarrassed protest, the president of the United States insisted on carrying his guest's overnight bag to the Lincoln Bedroom. There was dinner, then they were off to the Kennedy Center. Although the president and his wife, along with Limbaugh and Ailes, left the musical story of rock-and-roller Buddy Holly during intermission, their night was far from over. Back in the president's quarters, Bush slipped in a videocassette of Dana Carvey's merciless portrait of H. Ross Perot on "Saturday

Night Live" and laughed as if he was seeing it for the first time. Then Ailes urged Limbaugh to do his own takeoff on Perot, getting Bush to laugh some more.

When everyone retired for the night, the Bushes to their room and Ailes to the Queen's Room across the hall from Limbaugh, the wide-eyed guest reached for the phone. "You'll never guess where I am," he said to his brother back in Cape Girardeau. He dialed again. "You'll never guess where I am," he said to his mother.

Limbaugh remained awake into the wee hours so that he could study and savor every detail of the Lincoln Bedroom—a Republican, no less, Lincoln. There was the sixteenth president's desk and there, too, his only signed and dated copy of the Gettysburg Address. He was awed.

For all of the respect and influence that Limbaugh's grandfather commanded as a longtime lawyer and leader in the state of Missouri, for all of his father's muscle as a Republican power, the man who led Richard and Pat Nixon down Main Street, it was Rusty, the once-wayward son, who got to advise the president while relaxing with him at 1600 Pennsylvania Avenue. His father would have been so proud.

Certainly, it would now be harder to be hard on George Bush.

But was Limbaugh being co-opted? Nonsense, he said, there was no attempt to win his support.

Nevertheless, Limbaugh responded in writing to *The Washington Post*'s queries about the visit in language that was uncharacteristically wooden and defensive: "The president never once asked me about the views of my listeners. . . . He did, however, ask me for my views on a few things." Bush "did not ask me to discuss anything at all on my radio program. He inquired very little about the program, other than how I got started. I discussed my program only when answering his questions about its history." In a remark that eventually would seem hollow, Limbaugh added: "I did not ask him to guest on my program."

Beyond that, Limbaugh said it would be inappropriate to discuss any more specifics—he ended up doing so within days, of course— "but our conversation ran the gamut from baseball, to politics, to the campaign, to his press conference the next evening, to my life history."

During the presidential primaries earlier in the year, Limbaugh had voiced his support for Bush's more conservative challenger, Pat Buchanan, the former speechwriter for Nixon and Reagan who recently made his living as a syndicated columnist and provocateur on CNN's "Crossfire." Before the February balloting in New Hampshire, Limbaugh urged Republicans to vote for Buchanan as a protest against Bush's about-face on new taxes and his acceptance of civil-rights legislation that conservatives considered flawed. It was an endorsement that thrilled the upstart Buchanan, who said he would name Limbaugh director of communications. As Limbaugh put it, Bush had "let down people who elected him."

Buchanan ended up humiliating the president by scoring a healthy 37 percent of the Republican vote to Bush's 53 percent. But Buchanan's crusade faded after subsequent primaries. Nevertheless, Limbaugh did not automatically extend his support to Bush in the looming bout with "Slick Willie." And while he also did not join the populist parade forming behind Perot, a somewhat obscure interview published by the Heritage Foundation showed that he admired the third-party Texan as recently as two days before walking into the White House.

"I think Perot convinces people that they matter again, that they're relevant, that what they want is what should happen," he told his good friend William J. Bennett, the former education secretary and drug czar in the interview conducted June 1 for the foundation's *Policy Review*. "Say what you want about his lack of specificity, he's also the one candidate who doesn't run from a problem. . . . I talk to Perot people on my show, and meet them when traveling around the country. They are upwardly mobile, middle- and upper-middle-class people, who are just fed up with what they see as the decline of the country. They may not be able to voice it, it may be in their subconscious, and Perot is bringing it out."

Republican insiders were fretting. They wanted Rush Limbaugh in their corner.

Limbaugh acknowledged that his Bush bashing, specifically his urging the president to voice a more conservative message if he wanted to win, probably had shaken up the Republican camp— and probably enough to expedite his invitation to the White House. Yet after the sleepover, it was striking to see how effective the president's courtship had been. Everything suddenly turned warm and rosy between the president and the commentator. A mutual admiration society took shape and its two members went out of their way to praise each other.

Two days later, Limbaugh was back in Cape Girardeau to address the 1992 commencement of Central High School, his alma mater. He told the graduates that "I have just spent the night discussing politics and the future of this country with the president of the United States." Not bad for a kid who had split town twenty-one years earlier without so much as a college degree.

And then, five days after enjoying Bush's hospitality, Limbaugh turned up on the "Today" show, where Ailes periodically appeared as a political pundit. Like a schoolboy back from a trip to the capital, the broadcaster was urged on by cohost Katie Couric to give a kind of verbal home movie of his visit. Following Couric's cues ("How did this happen? Dinner at the White House? . . . That must have been very cool"), he offered a glowing testimonial for that "genuinely nice guy," George Bush, and an earnest defense of the president that could hardly have sounded more positive had the president scripted it himself.

In the matter of the Earth Summit in Rio de Janeiro, Bush, he said, "expressed frustration that as much cooperation as he seems to have given his enemies, the Democrats in Congress, the environmentalists, he says it's never enough, and I think that's the lesson to be learned. He, I think, should understand that they are not out to get along with him, they're not out to strike consensus deals. Rather, they're out to defeat him politically. And so trying to get along with them, and trying to mollify them, is—is only exacerbating his problem. And I pointed this out, again with—I thought, I'm going to get kicked out of here after saying this, 'cause I wasn't asked. But that's the kind of night it was, and I—I'll treasure it always and I'll never forget it."

Recalling that his own Perot impersonation got a chuckle out of Bush, Limbaugh became even more flattering: "I think this president is—he's a nice guy. This is the thing about him that . . . somehow gets lost. . . . He's a genuinely nice guy and a family-oriented man who really is trying, I think, to please people at the expense of following his own inclinations . . . and I think he really just needs to go and as I told him, I said, 'You realize the media is not going to be your ally here.' I pointed out how he made his offering of 150 million to the forests. Network news gave him nine seconds, and then five people following him got nine seconds each to trash him, why it was too little, too late, and that kind of thing. 'This is going to happen to you throughout the campaign, and it has been. Your passion's going to have to override all that.' And I think in time that that's what will happen. I hope. I think that's the only thing that will work for him."

And then, seven days after the White House visit, Limbaugh snickered at Perot's cause when he told his listeners: "And don't expect me to get on somebody's bandwagon just because the bandwagon seems to be moving fast."

Weeks later, when the president phoned a Limbaugh affiliate, WOOD-AM in Grand Rapids, Michigan, while flying in to a local campaign appearance, he told morning man Gary Allen: "Well, Rush is a very sound man and he's got good, strong, conservative principles and, of course, I have a lot of respect for him, and we all learn from him, even those that disagree with him out there listen to him because they like his wisdom. Even though they don't disagree [sic], they know that he's a man of integrity and honor."

The minuet rankled some of Limbaugh's colleagues. To watch fellow radio broadcaster Larry King receive all but incessant media attention because of his news-making interviews—on CNN—with Perot was one thing. After all, King still remained within the bounds of the emcee. But they were unaccustomed to the idea that one of their own had become the president's soulmate—and in an election year.

At the annual conference of the National Association of Radio Talk Show Hosts, a group that was itself compromised by its acceptance of sponsorship from the American Petroleum Institute and other corporate interests, Jerry Williams of Boston's WRKO presented the group's Big Mouth Award to Bush's former chief of staff, John Sununu, who had since replaced Buchanan on CNN. "Anyway, this working relationship between Rush Limbaugh and Roger Ailes indicates why Ross Perot is not getting quite a break on the 846 stations that Rush seems to be on," Williams scoffed during his talk. "But there wouldn't be anything corrupt about that, would there? Anyway, they're very small stations except for the one in Boston, which we ignore."

Williams continued to rail against Limbaugh in the lobby of Washington's Mayflower Hotel after the presentation: "The most insidious thing is that his new TV show is going to be produced and run by a private company led by Roger Ailes. Now, Roger Ailes is a consultant to the president of the United States and there is a cabal there and a plan for Rush to batter Ross Perot on behalf of George Bush. I mean, that's what's really going on. I mean, that's a wild conflict of interest."

Consumer advocate Ralph Nader, whom Limbaugh derided as "a human handkerchief," also addressed the conference: "Any talk-show host that has a pronounced agenda that's consistent, thematic and focused—for example, Rush Limbaugh is clearly pushing George Bush. He's pushing George Bush by going after Perot, et cetera. Now he's close to George Bush. Anyone who has a pronounced agenda like that seems to me has an obligation to expose that view to callers or to guests on the show.

"You can't simply say, as Rush says, he's only an entertainer. That's a copout. That's a way where he, in effect, reduces our expectation of his impact and he says, 'Well, I'm just an entertainer, I'm not a commentator,' et cetera, where images of the fairness doctrine's right of reply would come in. The same is true for Paul Harvey. It isn't exactly a talk show unless you would consider talking to oneself a talk show. But where you start naming names, attacking people or representing a partisan political agenda in a systemic manner, I think there's an obligation to let some people in to challenge you and to have the two-way communication that is often associated with talk radio most prominently."

To enthusiastic applause from the broadcasters, Nader said: "He ought to be man enough to stand up to challengers and let them on [his show]."

In recapping the night at the White House, Rush reiterated on the air that his visit would not lead to a guest appearance by the president on the radio show. "I don't have guests anyway," he said.

True, but not for much longer.

On July 8, bomb-sniffing dogs and solemn Secret Service agents combed the New York studios of WABC, seventeen floors above Madison Square Garden. Vice President Dan Quayle was coming to Limbaugh's "patriotic center of the universe" for a precedent-breaking guest shot.

Quayle recognized the impact that the unfiltered talk media were having in the 1992 campaign. Talk radio offered particular value to politicians in need. Former California governor Jerry Brown spent hours on local radio stations in Connecticut explaining his views and went on to win the state's Democratic primary. Arkansas governor Bill Clinton's laughing exchange with WFAN's Don Imus helped humanize the candidate just in time to win the crucial New York primary. Before going on Limbaugh's show, Quayle also had phoned Imus's program and the liberal Lynn Samuels on WABC. Quayle even went so far as to address the Washington gathering of talk-show hosts in a blunt bid to sell a proposed aid package to Russia. "I need your help on this and so does the president," he told them. "So I hope that you will at least maybe quote me and give me one minute of time and help convince your listeners who in turn will hopefully convince the legislators in our Congress . . . to support the president on this important issue."

But doing the Limbaugh show, with its millions of listeners across the country, was doing prime time. For a conservative pol on the stump in 1992, it didn't get any better than this.

Seated at a microphone across from the headset-wearing Limbaugh, Quayle spoke about the task facing the Republicans: "Our trick, Rush—not a trick, our challenge—our challenge is to make the American people comfortable with the leadership George Bush will offer in the next four years."

Limbaugh pressed Quayle on whether Bush could pull off a victory after reneging on his read-my-lips, no-new-taxes pledge—an unhealed sore spot with the host. To which the vice president said Bush would be able to follow through on his proposals if the voters ousted the Democratic majority from Congress. And Quayle did not leave the studios without receiving an endorsement of his highly publicized campaign for "family values," a mission fired up by the birth of a child to TV's unmarried Murphy Brown. Limbaugh assured him that any negative reporting of Quayle's views represented a "malicious attempt" to ruin the vice president's image.

It would not be the last time that Limbaugh and Quayle conversed on the air before Election Day. But for now, a radio powwow with the accommodating broadcaster had generated good spin before the conservative faithful.

"You knew you were hitting our kind of people," David Beckwith, Quayle's press secretary, told a reporter. Indeed, an audience profile prepared for Limbaugh's syndicator the previous fall by Yankelovich Clancy Shulman, a leading research firm, found that 77 percent identified themselves as Republicans, 13 percent as independents, and only 6 percent as Democrats.

Perhaps of greater value to the Bush-Quayle cause, 79 percent identified themselves as conservatives, 17 percent as moderates, and only 1 percent as liberals.

"If your goal is to reach the unconverted or the undecided, you might be better off somewhere else," Beckwith added. "That was especially good for the vice president because one of our jobs was to rally the base, and people who listen to Rush tend to be our base."

To the Republicans' relief, Limbaugh was on board.

Chapter 17

UNCONVENTIONAL SPECTATOR

F or a week in July, The Enemy encamped in Limbaugh's base-
ment. The Democratic National Convention took over Madison
Square Garden and the adjoining Paramount theater, both located downstairs from the WABC studios where he preached to
America daily.

The gathering and its proximity gave Limbaugh great fodder for
his show. He visited the convention on its second night to do a
program with his friend Bill Bennett and drew stunned greetings
from reporters, who never expected to see the two conservative
Republicans venture into the lion's den. The next day, Limbaugh
labeled it "one of the longest weeks of my life" and called the
assembly "the most disorganized mess." His visit also prompted
him to recall a recent story about a zoo veterinarian who won a
prize because he was able to identify more types of animal feces
than anyone else. He suggested, "The networks ought to hire this
guy as an analyst for the Democratic National Convention because
what was going on in there was nothing but a whole bunch of . . ."
He let his listeners complete the thought.

Limbaugh was especially incensed by Jesse Jackson, who roused
the Garden with a fiery endorsement of the Clinton-Gore ticket
in which he also mocked Quayle's family-values crusade. Jackson

compared the vice president to Herod, the biblical king who ordered the slaying of infants in hopes of killing the newborn Jesus Christ in the process. Jackson described Mary and Joseph as a homeless couple and said, "If Mary had aborted the baby, she would have been called immoral. If she had the baby, she would have been called unfit, without family values. But Mary had family values."

Limbaugh summoned his own knowledge of the Bible to dispute the idea that Mary and Joseph were a homeless couple when Jesus was born. Rather, they fit squarely into Limbaugh's civic-minded scenario—a couple who were going to register themselves so that they might pay taxes. Furthermore, Jackson's reference to abortion put new spring in Limbaugh's unyielding contention that the Democrats were downright craven:

"I would suggest to you that the party that can't wait to fund every abortion in the world, that cannot wait to see to it that every woman who gets pregnant, and even thinks about having an abortion does so, with your tax dollars, I say they have more to answer to on this charge than Dan Quayle does. . . .

"If the Democrats and their ideology reigned supreme in biblical days, since Mary's was an unwanted pregnancy, they would probably be demanding that she have an abortion."

When it appeared to Limbaugh that his eight morning newspapers had nothing but praise for Jackson's speech, the talk host fumed over the idea that the polemic went unchallenged: "This is exactly what I mean when I tell you that the dominant media culture is a willing participant . . . to impugn and make fun of the things that most people in this country hold dear."

It was vintage Limbaugh: on the one hand, making an outrageous assertion, such as that the Democrats "can't wait to fund every abortion in the world," yet also giving bellowing voice to a belief among many listeners and nonlisteners that the news media tilt so far to the left that they ignore a multitude of sins. It was no secret, as *New York Newsday* columnist Sydney H. Schanberg would later concede, that "the public already holds us in fairly low repute, having defined all too many of us as whiny, arrogant and elitist." Yet as big as Limbaugh's show had become, with a total number of listeners greatly exceeding, say, the million-plus circulation of the influential *New York Times*, he still carefully positioned himself apart from the "dominant media" that he professed to scorn.

And standing apart, while in one-on-one touch with the like-minded callers to his program, he had come to fill a role as their ambassador in a culture of resentment that held opinions well to the right of the liberal media.

The material provided by the Democrats' activities in New York seemed to pale when Perot upstaged the convention by announcing July 16 in Dallas that he was dropping out of the race. The billion-aire concluded that he could not win the election and would only "disrupt the political process" if he kept going.

Limbaugh went on the air an hour later and could barely contain his I-told-you-so. He gloated that he was the one who had predicted that, if Perot quit, "it cannot be his fault." He said it was "bogus" for Perot to claim that he feared throwing the election into the House of Representatives. "It's the most convenient reason he can find to avoid blaming it on himself."

To the chagrin of those Perot supporters in his radio audience, Limbaugh accused the ex-candidate of having "a performer's ego . . . The one thing this proves is that politics is a business . . . and Ross Perot is not a politician."

He even fired at colleague Larry King, on whose CNN show Perot had offered himself as a candidate months earlier. To those listeners who accused Limbaugh of helping to undermine Perot's cause, he said: "You people think that Larry King has given birth to a candidacy and I have killed one? I wonder how Larry King does feel. . . . You were bamboozled along with everybody else, Lar. He was, he was." (Weeks before, King had said of Limbaugh in *Vanity Fair*, "Gay-bashing, bashing women, 'feminazis,' bashing blacks. I don't think that's funny.")

The Perot withdrawal also spurred Limbaugh to share a footnote to history, what he called "off-the-record remarks" made by Bush during their night together the month before. "In a conversation about the Perot candidacy, the president didn't really seem inter-ested in what those of us at the table were saying. . . . The president said—and I don't remember the exact words—but after a period of time, he finally threw up his hands and said, 'Look, would you cut with the Perot stuff, he's not gonna last. Perot's not going to be there. . . .' He said, 'I'm gonna tell you guys, it's never been otherwise, and the reason I'm not getting going right now is because it's going to be Clinton. You guys had better keep your eyes on Clinton. That's who we're all going to have to keep our eyes on.' "

Limbaugh was chewing red meat, saying that Perot's exit was the Democrats' worst nightmare and signaled the return to a traditional campaign—"socialism versus America. The Democrats versus the Republicans." He sneered at the Democrats' attempt to make the party appear more centrist: "The liberals are not going to take this attempt to make them look like archaic dinosaurs lying down."

He said that the strategy recalled the Democrats' 1988 convention, "but eventually George Bush and the Republican party did the media's job for them in correctly identifying Michael Dukakis and the Democrats as liberals. Remember: When races come down to liberal versus conservative, conservatism always wins. And with Perot now gone, ideology makes its reappearance."

In retrospect, Limbaugh accurately heralded the plan to raise taxes in a Clinton administration. He said that the Democrats declined to assault Bush for breaking his own no-tax pledge "because they're going to do it again and again and again. You people don't know what being shafted is, until this bunch gets the White House. . . . In a political situation I find this incredible. What are the Democrats focusing on? Quayle. Family values. S-and-Ls. Unequitable treatment of blacks and stuff that does not ever win elections and hasn't.

"All they gotta do is say George Bush lied. They don't even have to say about what. They're not even attacking that and the reason they're not, and this is why you ought to be—if you're mad at Bush, you ought to be scared because the Democrats aren't talking about what he did 'cause they plan to do it even more."

For one who claimed to be an entertainer first and foremost, the wild turns in the campaign now found Limbaugh pounding home dry political dogma. Over and over. And the election was still four months away.

The passion undercut his contention that he did not try to use his three hours on the air as a platform for change. "I have a political slant which I have an opportunity to share," he told an interviewer. "I happen to be a political junkie and a conservative and I have the freedom and good fortune to be myself [on the air]. I do not look at this radio show as a means of instituting change. I resist that. I don't look at it as I'm right and they're wrong and they ought to agree with me. That may happen, and that's icing on the cake."

The Republicans came together in August and Limbaugh, the most prominent Republican in the media, would not miss it for the world. He planned to do his show from Houston affiliate KSEV and to partake of the hoopla. But even before he touched down in Texas, signs were pointing to the kind of adulation he would receive from the GOP faithful throughout the week. Seated in first class en route from New York, he was spotted and then swarmed by admiring local fans from the Westchester County delegation.

On the ground, he was hailed and sought after and honored day upon day. He was cult leader within the larger Republican sect, an undeclared convention mascot who held a warm spot in delegates' affections while bashing the dominant-media types who recorded most of his moves with something approaching astonishment. Limbaugh's fans were stuck with the mainstream press to feed them their headlines, but they had Rush to tell them what the headlines really meant and what was missing from the front page. And now he was among them, Rush Limbaugh himself, going from place to place in a stretch limousine longer than most had ever seen.

A Tuesday party and rally at the Wortham Center sponsored by the Republican National Coalition for Life drew the GOP's elected and unelected conservative heavyweights, including Quayle, Sununu, the Reverend Jerry Falwell, ex-candidate and televangelist Pat Robertson, and the group's chairman, Phyllis Schlafly. But it was Limbaugh who upstaged all the others and was kept at the microphone for about twenty minutes by the $75-a-head hundreds crying for more. Even the outspoken Schlafly had to confess that Limbaugh was the one they came to see. To skeptical reporters covering the event, it was a revelation to observe Limbaugh outshining the other conservative stars.

"BLAME IT ON THE MEDIA" read a popular T-shirt on sale in Houston. Indeed, Limbaugh picked up on what he called "the theme of the convention" and told his fans to ignore the savaging of their gathering by the liberal press. "I look at this crowd and see happy, upbeat faces," he said. "But according to the media, you are forlorn, you are depressed, you are divided. . . . The news is that it's you who are responsible for the doom of the Republican party. They say you are a nerd, a kook, that you're sick, you're an oddball. . . . That is the exact opposite of the truth, and I admire you for sticking to your guns! I don't want to be labeled a media basher. I am simply responding. We wake up every day, we see the institutions and the traditions that we think made this country great under assault. We respond. We are defending what we believe in! . . . You represent a majority!"

It was a familiar refrain, and carefully constructed, this angry notion that "they" were slandering and maligning the GOP, political haven for straight arrows such as himself and the assembled. How dare they do so under the guise of being objective journalists! At least Limbaugh was honest enough to decry and rail against the Democrats without any pretense of objectivity. To this audience, Limbaugh's was a complaint of exhortation and it worked in the best tradition of political rhetoric. "Ditto!" they shouted in accord.

He urged them to "stay confident and not give up the fight." Only Ronald Reagan would have whipped up lustier cheers.

"I listen to Rush off and on, I'm not a real good radio listener," Schlafly said later. "But it was almost like a rock concert. I've never been to a rock concert, but they tell me it was like one, the way they responded to him."

That evening, it got even better. "Rush, Rush, Rush!" went the chant inside the Astrodome when he took his place in Quayle's private box of blue chairs reserved for family and friends. There was Falwell seated behind Marilyn Quayle, Robertson on her left side, and Limbaugh on the right, at one point arm-in-arm with her as she glowed.

"Rush, Rush, Rush!"

These were his people and he was their hero. He was having a blast while blasting away at the opposition party and the woman who would be its first lady. In the mischievous spirit of "Saturday Night Live'"s earnestly fake commercials, the Limbaugh show's staff announcer, John Donovan, provided an especially sinister narration pitching a new "movie" based loosely on one that the host had just seen:

"Hillary Clinton seemed simple and unassuming, until she moved into the White House. *Then*, she became a maniacal, power-hungry psycho, in *Single White Female*. 'You said the F word, Family Values. Go to your room, Willie.' . . . She's married to Bill Clinton, but she has the ability to cause more damage than any single woman in history. . . ."

Meanwhile, away from Limbaugh's antics, Roger Ailes worked hard to dismiss reports that he was ending his retirement from politics to assist Bush once more. Getting people to believe him was almost as hard as getting Bush reelected.

As far back as the spring, Ailes had become so irritated by the sluggishness of the Bush campaign that he urged the president's advertising advisers into quicker and more combative action. He did this privately; publicly, he said only that he spoke with Bush regularly, but had little influence on his campaign.

Then, whispers to the effect that Ailes was back for keeps made their way into print days before the convention, when it became known that he would coach the president on his acceptance speech. In Houston, the story intensified on Wednesday when *The New York Times* and other newspapers reported that Ailes had, in fact, assumed an expanded role in the Bush campaign.

"Not true," Ailes told James Brady, the columnist for *Advertising Age*, at breakfast.

Well then, what about the president's speech? That same morning, on the "Today" show, Bryant Gumbel asked Ailes if he had seen it.

"No," he said.

"Are you helping him with it?"

"No. Not—I haven't."

Gumbel: "Not yet. Not even as a friend?"

"Oh, as a friend, I'll do whatever they ask me to do."

Technically speaking, Ailes may not have seen the speech that Bush would deliver the next night. But as *Newsweek* would report months later, Ailes was more than privy to the writing. According to the magazine, Ailes saw one version and "said it read like a mattress tag." So with the convention proceeding at full tilt, and Bush still in need of a finished product, campaign superchief Jim Baker reportedly drafted Ailes and the president's newly hired chief speechwriter, Steve Provost, to pull the contributions together— and fast.

Mission accomplished by Thursday evening, Bush passed the moments before he ascended the podium by relaxing in a holding room with GOP chairman Richard N. Bond and the fighter's faithful trainer—Ailes. There he was.

And why did Ailes protest so much about being identified as a campaign operative? For one thing, there was the ticklish business of being executive producer on Limbaugh's upcoming TV show, which needed at least the appearance of being steps removed not so much from Bush's principles, but from his presidential campaign. Ailes had taken some heat a decade earlier for producing NBC's "Tomorrow" show while also representing candidates seeking office. More specific, however, were the terms of the deal launching the new show. "I would break the contract if I went back [to the Bush campaign]," Ailes told Brady. "I also have a contract with Paramount Television. . . . That would also preclude me from going back."

Appearances, it seemed, were everything.

"I'm not an adviser in any capacity," he told Brady again.

And appearances would have to be maintained.

Pat Buchanan, the vanquished candidate, was unbowed in his speech to the convention Monday night. He dished out crisp zingers as he espoused conservatism with a scowl:

"Like many of you last month, I watched that giant masquerade ball at Madison Square Garden—where twenty thousand radicals and liberals came dressed up as moderates and centrists—in the greatest single exhibition of cross-dressing in American political history. . . . Bill Clinton's foreign policy experience is pretty much confined to having had breakfast once at the International House of Pancakes. . . . Friends, this is radical feminism. The agenda Clinton and Clinton would impose on America—abortion on demand, a litmus test for the Supreme Court, homosexual rights, discrimination against religious schools, women in combat—that's change all right. But it is not the kind of change America wants. It is not the kind of change America needs. And it is not the kind of change we can tolerate in a nation that we still call God's country."

Buchanan visited Limbaugh's radio show on Wednesday amid considerable negative reaction to his speech beyond the Astrodome. In that morning's *New York Times*, for example, appeared a hostile op-ed piece from Michael Lind, executive editor of *The National Interest:* "The William F. Buckleys and Irving Kristols who detoxified the right are being succeeded by a generation of Buchanans and Rush Limbaughs setting up a retox ward." That Buchanan, like Quayle, was even welcomed into the radio studio reflected the ex-candidate's bond with the host, though Limbaugh felt compelled to explain the exception to his no-guest format: "That's the beauty of this show. We can do what we want to do here. We don't have to plug ourselves into a formula and rigidly stick to it. We can be flexible and we have."

Limbaugh also heaped on the flattery: "I mean, you are on a high and you should be. That speech was tremendous." He said that the addresses by Buchanan and Reagan on Monday night, the latter being far more conciliatory, were a reminder of "exactly what won three landslide elections for the Republican Party in eighty, eighty-four, and eighty-eight."

However, after passing that night as a guest in the Bush family's convention box, seated next to former first lady Betty Ford, Limbaugh toned down his appreciation of Buchanan. This came on Thursday following Bush's acceptance speech. Going on PBS's "Charlie Rose," which was then being carried only by New York's

WNET-TV, Limbaugh agreed with the host's assertion that Buchanan and Reagan showed the "two faces of conservatism."

Well then, Rose asked, "which one are you with?"

"I'm with Reagan," Limbaugh said, choosing his words carefully. "There are certain matters that Buchanan chooses to express in ways in which I wouldn't, and there are attitudes he holds that I don't necessarily agree with him, but I like him and we get along."

Curiously, he withheld this more qualified assessment from his national radio show, which Buchanan and everyone else in Houston could hear via local station KSEV.

To cap off the festive week, Friday was Rush H. Limbaugh Day in Houston. Mayor Bob Lanier issued a proclamation to that effect, noting, "Mr. Limbaugh is the epitome of morality and virtue while saying more in one second than most people say in a lifetime."

Gratified by all the attention but weary from late nights and little sleep, Limbaugh left the city pleased that Bush now seemed "engaged" for combat. He also believed that the president ultimately would win reelection by four to six points, saying, "The polls are coming down in spite of this media imbalance." He figured that sooner or later the voters would share his conviction that Clinton's projected image of moderation was a charade.

"Here you have fifteen thousand media people here, and one of us happens to tell the truth about what's coming out of this convention—me."

Chapter 18

ROMANCE AND A NEW DEAL

Back in New York, the radio business continued to go Limbaugh's way. At this point, that was no surprise. But the period was noteworthy because, after griping a few months earlier that "just having a relationship is a fantasy," he met a woman whom he dated with interest.

It was one of the more unlikely pairings. Donna Dees was a CBS News publicist whose responsibilities included "48 Hours" and "The CBS Evening News." Not only did the pretty blonde work for the dominant media culture that Limbaugh so often castigated on the air, but she represented Dan Rather, one of the anchor gods of broadcast news.

Dees originally had recoiled at the idea of a blind date with Limbaugh when it was suggested by a mutual friend, his Pocket Books editor, Judith Regan. His right-wing politics appalled her. But one summer night, Dees and Limbaugh both happened to be dining at Patsy's, an Italian restaurant that counted Frank Sinatra among its customers. Regan was with Dees at the time, so Limbaugh came over to their table for coffee and dessert. He further enlivened the evening by doing imitations of Ross Perot and William F. Buckley, Jr. As a result, Dees was charmed by the bubbly, yet self-effacing man after all. When he phoned days later to ask her to dinner, she accepted.

In a city where couples more often rendezvous at restaurants or under theater marquees, Limbaugh began their evening the old-fashioned way by picking up Dees at her apartment. When she came down on the elevator, his car and driver were waiting outside the building, but he was pacing nervously in the lobby, like a schoolboy romantic. It struck her as a sign of his sincerity and absence of airs. And so they were off, but not, it would turn out, by themselves.

A celebrity of Limbaugh's size and rectitude could not expect to take Dan Rather's publicist to dinner at the celebrity-studded "21" and escape the attention of New York's twenty-four-hour gossip mill, especially considering that he also spoke of Dees afterward, albeit anonymously, on the radio. *Daily News* gossip columnist Richard Johnson, who numbered Regan among his friends, became intrigued by word of a blossoming romance. He learned who Limbaugh's date had been, called Dees for comment, and then led his column with six paragraphs under the headline, "LIMBAUGH'S RUSH HOUR WITH DEEDEE." Johnson wrote that Dees "spent a good part of the meal explaining to Limbaugh what really happened—from a woman's point of view—between Anita Hill and Clarence Thomas. Limbaugh, gentleman to a fault, listened politely without interrupting. But there were mitigating circumstances that might have made Limbaugh more quiet, and more charming, than usual. He'd had root-canal work earlier in the day."

Dees had expected one or two throwaway lines to be buried in Johnson's column. Instead, when her evening led the page, it turned up heat from politically correct friends and associates who were stunned to read that she was seeing the Genghis Khan of the right. And the spotlight did not lift, for five weeks later she was taken aback to find herself *again* under Johnson's byline, this time in an item saying that she and Limbaugh had necked in public. The columnist said that their "romance" was "ripening," and he went on to describe a Sunday walk in Central Park with Regan during which the couple managed "some unguarded moments together.

How else would Regan know that Limbaugh 'is supposed to be a great kisser'?"

Limbaugh, now cast as a bona fide stud by one of New York's leading gossip columnists, laughed off the bawdy remarks that greeted him later that day in the press box at Giants Stadium when he showed up to watch the football team play. Roger Ailes caught the item and called to tease as well.

Meanwhile, Dees felt mortified. Her walk with Limbaugh and Regan in Central Park bore little resemblance to the one in Johnson's account. Moreover, she wondered angrily who had supplied the details. Even Rather picked up on the Sunday in the park with Rush and said to her, "It's nice to see that romance isn't dead."

Clearly, however, Limbaugh ate up the attention, which he may have had a hand in generating, perhaps inadvertently, through his friendship with Regan. For instead of simply ignoring Johnson's latest blurb, which appeared in the New York paper on a Sunday, he opened his Monday show by talking and laughing about it to an audience spread over fifty states. In what seemed an obvious case of one who doth protest too much, he explained that "it isn't true. There's no romance to ripen."

But he continued: "I am a great kisser. The secret is out, that's the point of this. It's absolutely true. I don't need much practice to be a good kisser . . . these things are instinctive."

He still did not let go: "It's an official denial of the rumor. I did go walking in Central Park, but it was for exercise, not romance." As he told it, Regan and her baby daughter had pulled away to view the *Alice in Wonderland* statue at the boat pond while he and his lady friend remained seated on a bench.

"There was nothing but conversation. I am not into PDAs, public displays of affection. Judith has to be the source of this."

In the *Vanity Fair* profile that appeared four months earlier, he had complained: "I still get up and read the New York papers and see my name not mentioned and think I'm a failure, that I'm not mattering, that nobody knows who I am in the city I live in, and it bugs me greatly. I just sit here and get depressed."

Now, portrayed as a Lothario for all of New York to see, he told friends that he felt as if he had finally "made it" in the hard-bitten town after all. In many ways, it was an all-too-obvious male response. But in Limbaugh's case, there was something else. Though he apologized to Dees for the embarrassment the item had caused her, he who had been publicly rejected in a high-school game of spin-the-bottle, and divorced twice by women who found him wanting, must have drawn from the item a balm for those psychic wounds. Doubtless it felt as good, if not better, than his career success.

Weeks later, when *USA Today* gossip columnist Jeannie Williams described another Patsy's get-together between Limbaugh and a "stunning blonde" (Dees), he used his TV show to refute the writer's claim that he had referred to the woman as "my sweetheart." He continued to give broadcast attention to the gossip references, as if trying to convince the public that he was involved in an enviable relationship.

In fact, however, he and Dees had since become no more involved than good friends.

ABC Radio, McLaughlin's old network and the one that had let Limbaugh slip through its fingers, was seeing dreary returns in the talk business. In 1987, when ABC Talkradio was languishing in terms of profit and clearances, the network had gone into evening talk to fill a perceived need among stations and to reestablish its own image as a credible provider of such programming. ABC launched nighttime shows hosted by Sally Jessy Raphael, who came over from the rival NBC Talknet, and former TV interviewer Tom Snyder in a one-two punch of a strategy. But by the summer of 1992, ABC was getting out of evening talk for much the same reason that it had scuttled the daytime lineup two years earlier.

Limbaugh, however, kept marching merrily along.

Philadelphia, the nation's fourth-largest radio market, finally fell neatly into place in September when an FM station, WWDB, started airing his three-hour program live. The decision effectively ended a local blackout of Limbaugh's show, which had been heard only in weekend rebroadcasts on WCAU-AM. WWDB's owner, an adamant holdout until then, told *The Philadelphia Inquirer* that he was eating his previous words of resistance. As he explained, "We had to ask ourselves, 'Can 500 cities be wrong and we're right?' " (Three affiliates within hearing distance outside the city would lose Limbaugh as a result of an exclusivity agreement with WWDB.)

In addition, WWDB picked up Limbaugh's show out of a prudent concern that another station eventually would add him and thereby pose competition that could have been avoided. No one was more aware of the risks than WWDB's program director, David J. Rimmer, who had been programming ABC Talkradio when Limbaugh got away from the network.

And within three months, WWDB saw its decision pay off. The Arbitron ratings for the fall of 1992, the first report card after Limbaugh's arrival, showed that the station was attracting the kind of desirable listeners who had been toughest to reach—specifically, adults twenty-five to fifty-four years old and men. The gains in Limbaugh's noon-to-three time period were more than 50 percent higher than in the months before WWDB added his program. "I expected it to work, but not as fast as it did," Rimmer says. Nationwide, the fall ratings showed that Limbaugh's audience in an average quarter-hour totaled 3.8 million people—up 58 percent from February and double the size of two years before.

With the tremendous growth and strength of the franchise came inevitable signs of strain between McLaughlin, who had been a player in network radio for twenty years now, and Limbaugh, who relished being able to stand his own ground outside his mentor's once-protective shadow. Privately, especially after those times when McLaughlin had urged him to ease off subjects such as feminism, Limbaugh sniped that his own work was making the syndicator rich. Speaking with a friend, the talk host downplayed McLaughlin's contribution by saying, "I make him look good. He brings nothing to the table." It was Limbaugh's view that his own celebrity, built on his growing political value and show-biz stature, had opened a few doors that McLaughlin now followed him through. Previously, it had been the other way around. There was also a suggestion in Limbaugh's corner that McLaughlin at one time may have regarded the radio show as little more than a preretirement venture, instead of a bonanza whose potential had yet to be fully tapped.

So it surprised those who were aware of this friction when McLaughlin announced on August 31 that EFM Media had signed Limbaugh to a new, multiyear radio contract. In a prepared statement, McLaughlin gushed that Limbaugh was "the radio phenomenon of the nineties. He is an enormous talent whose achievements are unprecedented and historic. Rush's new contract reflects this. And he is only four years into his national radio career. We look forward to working with Rush for many more years and in making 'The Rush Limbaugh Show' even more successful."

Limbaugh returned the compliments: "EFM Media has always permitted me the freedom to do all I need to make 'The Rush Limbaugh Show' the greatest radio talk show in America. I'm convinced that I'm associated with the absolute best."

Limbaugh's brother, David, once again served as his lawyer in the negotiations. He dismissed evidence of a split between the broadcaster and the syndicator, saying they had cordially disagreed at one time on their respective visions for the radio show but remained close. He said their business relationship was harmonious. "There were growing pains in the relationship, but they were not related to any questions about Ed's integrity," David said. In fact, the very timing of the new contract, which paid Limbaugh a signing bonus and increased his percentage of the profits, reflected how close McLaughlin wanted them to remain: It went into effect eighteen months before their initial agreement was to expire.

The contract they had signed in 1988 extended until December 1994. Now, the new one instead became retroactive to July 1, 1992, superseding the earlier pact with one major exception: Bruce Marr, the consultant who had introduced Limbaugh and McLaughlin four years earlier, would continue as a third party in the partnership under terms of the 1988 accord but would exit the picture in December 1994, when that original deal was to expire. From that point on, the riches of "The Rush Limbaugh Show" would be split between the host and McLaughlin.

McLaughlin said the new agreement was designed to reward

Limbaugh for the program's success and would lock up his radio services for most of the 1990s. Limbaugh said that his compensation would now consist solely of a share in the profits—in other words, no more minimum salary, as was guaranteed in the 1988 deal.

The new contract would not jump Rush ahead of Paul Harvey, the $10-Million Man, but McLaughlin said he believed that eventually his partner would exceed the riches of shock jock Howard Stern, who was then earning in the mid-seven figures as his outrageous New York morning show was being picked up by more and more out-of-town stations. Limbaugh appeared to concur when he said that he was earning about $3 million a year and could go as high as $5 million in 1993 if the advertising held up.

Publication of Limbaugh's first book, the launch of a monthly newsletter, and the debut of his TV show were scheduled to follow.

But first, there was a moment in the spotlight to savor.

In the previous two years, Rush had been nominated for one of the National Association of Broadcasters' prestigious Marconi Awards in the category of network/syndicated personality of the year. Both times, he went to the NAB's annual radio convention in hopes of taking home the honor. Both times, he lost. In 1992, Limbaugh was nominated again, along with Larry King, Casey Kasem, CBS commentator Charles Osgood, and disc jockey Dick Bartley, who had started up two oldies shows with ABC the year before. But this time, at the New Orleans Convention Center, Limbaugh was represented by McLaughlin, attired movie-star elegantly in a tuxedo with a white silk scarf. And this time, Limbaugh won.

McLaughlin rose to accept on Limbaugh's behalf and the audience rose with him in a standing ovation. Among those who knew McLaughlin, and those who marveled at his incredible success since losing out on the presidency of ABC Radio six years earlier, the standing ovation was intended as much for him as for the talk host whose antics he had championed.

Chapter 19

PRINTING MONEY

John Fund, an editorial writer with *The Wall Street Journal*, collaborated with Limbaugh on his book. He interviewed the broadcaster and prepared a draft manuscript that was also reviewed by David Limbaugh.

"At a certain point, as word got around that we had signed Rush Limbaugh, some of the liberals in the company were not so keen on the idea," recalls Irwyn Applebaum, who left Pocket Books for the top job at Bantam Books as the volume was being written. "They were upset not because they heard that Rush was antifeminist or antigay, but they felt that we should not supply a forum for such a voice.

"I spoke to Rush. I wanted him to understand that we were not a conservative book club and some people in the company were not thrilled with the idea of publishing him. He said he didn't need any hassle like that. He made it clear that he was an entertainer, not a philosopher, that he had no political agenda or master plan. But I assured him that once the book came out, we as a company would get behind it and market the hell out of it."

To Limbaugh's great fortune, publication of *The Way Things Ought to Be* coincided with a tidal wave of interest in the author and impassioned support for his politics in the 1992 campaign. In Dallas;

Topeka; Florence, Kentucky, and other communities across the map, restaurants and other lunch spots were setting aside Rush Rooms, and piping in the radio show, so that fans could keep up with Limbaugh while putting down a sandwich. Others were arranging to have his program taped during the day for playback when they got home from work.

With a following like this, sales of the book were so strong so swiftly that those outside the Limbaugh loop were mystified.

Beyond the question that still lingered in some quarters—Rush Who?—was the book itself. It offered little more than a printed keepsake of the same polemics on feminism, Anita Hill, the failure of liberalism, and other favorite topics that he addressed time and again on the radio. Autobiographical reflections were surprisingly few, he contradicted himself in places, and non sequiturs abounded. A five-page recollection of his controversial "caller abortions" read like a partial transcript of his 1989 appearance in Sacramento—an appearance that had already been captured and sold on videotape.

But these were meaningless quibbles to a following whose response certainly would not be governed by book reviews or Limbaugh's adherence to the kind of outline he was expected to prepare back in Speech 101. As reported by *Publishers Weekly*, Limbaugh announced on the air September 9 that his "upcoming bestseller" finally had reached stores, and listeners phoned him within hours to say that it had already sold out at their local store. Outlets that had ordered cautiously were quickly depleted of their supply and had to scramble for more books from wholesalers and resuppliers. By the end of that first day, reorders prompted the publisher to print another 175,000 copies in excess of the initial print run. The next day, the publisher called for 50,000 more, raising the total to about 465,000 and putting the printer in Scranton, Pennsylvania, on overtime production. Jack Romanos, by now the president of Simon & Schuster's consumer group, described Limbaugh as "just a bit right of Attila the Hun" while noting that the barbarian's book was the fastest seller in Pocket Books' four years of publishing hardcovers.

By way of comparison, the sales rate equaled the early performance of Andrew Morton's *Diana*, which became number one on

Publishers Weekly's best-seller list after only ten days, mainly because of insatiable media interest in the princess's marital woes with Prince Charles.

With a new book and a new TV show to celebrate, Limbaugh was now a member of the dominant media that he professed to despise. Fittingly, it seemed, Multimedia and Pocket Books threw a party for him at "21," the famous and famously expensive Manhattan restaurant that exuded establishment power. Arthur Godfrey, the broadcasting heavyweight of an earlier generation, used to dine there. As president in exile, Richard M. Nixon often presided over a table of guests. Now, too, the influence symbolized by a fete at "21" extended to Limbaugh, a sometime patron until that evening. Dozens of guests and roving camera crews packed several of the restaurant's private rooms, noshing on canapés and sipping cocktails. He welcomed the mantle bestowed by the A-listers even though their congratulations and the elegant setting seemed vaguely at odds with the ham-handed, up-with-taxpayers polemics he bellowed to the heartland on the air.

But there they were: Ailes; Phil Donahue; Georgette Mosbacher, the Washington socialite and wife of the Bush campaign's general chairman; James Brady, the observer-about-town whose columns were among Madison Avenue's favorite features in *Advertising Age*; *Newsday* TV critic Marvin Kitman; PBS interviewer Charlie Rose; and Richard B. Stolley, the editorial director of Time Inc.'s magazines.

Limbaugh liked this party business. Later, at a private affair held at the elegant Le Cirque to celebrate publication of TV host Kathie Lee Gifford's autobiography (*I Can't Believe I Said That!*), he was out in circulation again, along with Barbara Walters, Diane Sawyer, Donald Trump, John McLaughlin, Sen. John Warner, and Neil Sedaka, who sang "Love Will Keep Us Together." Limbaugh huddled in conversation with Alan Alda and he fenced with Shirley MacLaine.

The actress, whose liberal and feminist politics were well known, came up to him, studied his chest for a moment and said, "I'm looking for your soul." When asked by Limbaugh what she meant, she answered, "I've heard horrible things about you."

Limbaugh countered by asking what it would be like if he sized up her talents without ever seeing one of her movies. To which MacLaine said, "I see your point."

Meanwhile, like the Energizer bunny, his book kept going and going . . . number one on *Publishers Weekly*'s September 21 list of hardcover bestsellers . . . number one on *The New York Times*' September 27 list of nonfiction bestsellers . . . 725,000 copies in print by September 28 . . . 1,080,000 copies by October 2 . . . number one on the *Times*' list of October 11 for the third week in a row. Even Limbaugh's audio version of his book was setting company records, with 85,000 cassettes in circulation within a month of release.

He especially savored his book's position atop the *Times*' list, a summit reached without a review appearing in the paper of record (and one did not run until February 21, 1993, when the book already had spent months as number one). "The liberals are furious," he proclaimed.

What was happening here? More than just Rush whipping up enthusiasm for the book on the air.

As reporters covering the GOP convention in Houston had seen, his unsubtle put-downs and conservative war cries on the radio had uncorked a wellspring of support and enthusiasm among millions of listeners. Now, with his book in stores, they got the chance to vote for Limbaugh at the cash register, and many voted more than once as they went down their holiday gift lists. "It was one of those books that brings many nonregular book readers out of the hills and the farms and the countryside and into the bookstores because they hear that there's a book out that they might want to see," Applebaum says.

The Wall Street Journal's reviewer alluded to the phenomenon as he sized up the volume, writing that "it is clear that Mr. Limbaugh's critics are wrong to tie him to the teeming anthill of scorn. Instead, the author comes across as a sensitive fellow, an old-style reformer, in fact, a man who is amazingly civil considering the burden he is forced to bear. . . . Nevertheless, there are those who are sure that

Mr. Limbaugh hobbles about on cleft hooves, and the only use they will get from this book is as kindling. But there are many others— a growing and faithful horde—who consider Mr. Limbaugh to be a true national treasure: The human bug-bomb who has detonated himself in Hysteriaville's town square."

Other critiques were far less kind; some of the writers used the occasion to dissect not only the book, but also the Limbaugh phenomenon.

The *Seattle Times:* "It is not that this collection of redundant conservative wit is simply a bad book (although it is), it is not really a book at all."

The Los Angeles *Daily News:* "It is an exercise in self-importance."

Don Imus, the WFAN morning man, mentioned on the air that Limbaugh's book was a runaway hit and said: "It's a crime they cut down a tree to print this thing."

The *Los Angeles Times* called Limbaugh "a corn-fed P. J. O'Rourke, sharing the Ivy League–bred humorist's contempt for compassion and do-gooderism. Rush, however, lacks O'Rourke's rapier wit. He doesn't thread the needle—he hits his targets with a thick plank." Reviewer Patrick Goldstein was exactly right about that plank; but in Limbaughland, each thwack generated a round of applause.

As media critic Jon Katz expressed it in his *Washington Post* review, "Limbaugh has no desire to be taken seriously by journalists or reviewers. But as more Americans are learning every week, Limbaugh ought to be taken seriously."

Katz, a former CBS News producer and ex-newspaperman who was writing provocative analyses in *Rolling Stone* about the rise of the "new media," such as talk radio, and the death of network newscasts and newspapers, complained that Limbaugh "mostly rehashes his radio commentaries." But he also dared to say what may have been unacceptable to many of his colleagues; he called the book "important reading for citizens, journalists and politicians struggling to grasp the cultural civil war that seems to be raging during this presidential campaign."

And then came Madonna.

Her sexually graphic *Sex*, priced at an audacious $49.95, was published in October after a drumroll that seemed to last for months. The New York tabloids in particular had fought for hard-to-get leaks about the book's contents and then outdid themselves when a half-million copies of the closely guarded volume finally flooded into stores.

It had the makings of a publishing sideshow, the explicit sexual romps of the Material Girl now vying for sales dominance with Limbaugh's sermons on family values and morality. "Given the controversy raging in the New York public school system regarding sex instruction, I think they have found their first-grade textbook," Limbaugh said.

But Madonna was up to the challenge—at first. *Publishers Weekly* reported in November that *The Way Things Ought to Be* had sold more than 68,000 copies in two weeks at those outlets monitored by the magazine, compared with 75,000 copies of *Sex* during the same period. Madonna leapfrogged to number one on the *Times'* list . . . but on November 29, Limbaugh was back on top after a three-week absence. And stayed there. By December, *Sex* was fading.

Entertainment Weekly was amused by the development: "It's a vindication for anyone coveting a bumper sticker that reads *Buchanan in '96*. A switch that will delight the ever growing crowds who consider Madonna more annoying than a grass stain on a new Gaultier shirt . . . What Rush's return seems to indicate is that America prefers its bombast packaged in the form of a paunchy suit-clad politico rather than a raunchy unclothed chanteuse." The *Times* put it this way in an end-of-year wrapup: "*Sex*, with Steven Meisel's photographs of Madonna in harness and barebacked was tops for three weeks till Rush Limbaugh (yes, Rush Limbaugh) pushed it aside."

The momentum of *The Way Things Ought to Be* made the book the fastest-selling hardcover in history and put it within sight of *Iacocca*, the autobiographical phenomenon by auto executive Lee Iacocca. Published in the fall of 1984, the latter book sold 2.6 million copies and became the most successful nonfiction hardcover, but it set that record over a period of two and a half years. *Publishers Weekly* reported that Limbaugh was up to 1.9 million copies in print in only three months, far beyond the nearly 1.2 million copies of Desert Storm commander H. Norman Schwarzkopf's highly touted autobiography, *It Doesn't Take a Hero*, for which Bantam Books had reportedly paid the general $5 million. Limbaugh also led Magic Johnson's *My Life*, part of a three-book deal with Random House that was earning the basketball star $5 million as well. The audio version of Limbaugh's book turned into a 140,000-copy best-seller by year's end.

Pocket Books had hit a gusher. Naturally, the publisher wanted to drill again. Calls were made to the author and to the First National Bank building in Cape Girardeau, where his brother, David, had his law office. In late December, they struck a deal for a sequel to be called *See, I Told You So*. This would be the book Limbaugh had vowed to write if Bill Clinton was elected president. Scheduled for publication in the fall of 1993, it was expected to be a cannon blast at the first months of the new administration. This time, instead of an advance in the low six figures, Pocket Books agreed to pay Limbaugh $2.5 million against anticipated earnings.

A fat fee, surely. But if the momentum of the first book carried over, $2.5 million would seem like a meager investment to Pocket Books. For at $22 a copy, *The Way Things Ought to Be* was grossing for the publisher around $12 million per one million copies sold.

For Limbaugh, the book-biz mathematics meant that if all 1.9 million copies in print at the end of 1992 did indeed sell, he would net about $8 million for himself. Paperback and audio sales were expected to add six-figure sums on top of that.

Conservative beliefs had been good business for Rush Limbaugh. He said he made no apologies "for having money and earning it."

When the publisher prepared to pay him his first royalties in December, he insisted that there be no bank-to-bank transfer, no wired exchange conducted by mainframes in the cold halls of finance. No, he wanted a check. Something he could look at and smile at and show off and photocopy and frame.

The check was for $3 million. He was amazed to be making so much money. He was amazed there was so much money to be made. And for one who still presided in his crowded lecture hall of conservative studies, there was a lot more where that came from, and it was close at hand.

Limbaugh had said a few times that he wanted to have his own syndicated column. He read a bunch of newspapers daily and liked to read the arguments pro and con that stretched across the opinion pages. He was impressed that writers such as William Safire and William F. Buckley, Jr., had carved out whole realms for their passions, politics, and punditry via the printed page.

But Limbaugh had no real passion for writing, as he first discovered when the *Sacramento Union* put together the column that appeared under his name and as he rediscovered in stitching together his book. He was a man of the spoken word and the reflexive response. He had a microphone three hours a day with which to convey instantly much more than he could ever hope to condense within the confines of a column. And besides, there was little financial incentive to knuckle down at his word processor. Syndicators wooed him with offers to go as high as a fifty-fifty split of the fees that they would charge subscribing newspapers, but such a generous cut would still net him only a five-figure sum at most. Hardly worth the grief.

As an alternative—Limbaugh sometimes pegged it as his warmup to a column—he and EFM Media came up with the idea of producing their own newsletter. After all, the fans had shown that they wanted product. Their eager purchase of mugs, bumper stickers, videotapes, and other goodies authorized by Limbaugh, who held sole rights to their sale, went a long way to ensure his seven-figure income. Why not offer them some printed material as well?

In the summer of 1992, EFM Media shopped around for someone to help launch the publication to coincide with the release of Limbaugh's book in September. One more-than-qualified suitor proposed that his firm take Limbaugh's input and then go off and publish the newsletter as a soup-to-nuts contractor, thus sparing EFM the nuisance. Similar suggestions had come in as far back as

1989. But nothing doing. The suitor had completely misread the intentions. EFM wanted firm control of its latest enterprise.

In August, it hired Diana Schneider, a senior staff editor at *Reader's Digest*, to edit *The Limbaugh Letter*. She called EFM "just about the most adventurous place to be in the communications industry. Rush Limbaugh brings to print his unique talent to inform and entertain. There's simply no one else like him on the scene." John Axten, the president of EFM, said that *The Limbaugh Letter* would "make it easier for listeners to quote Rush and to share his opinions."

As for Limbaugh himself, he proposed another benefit of his latest effort. "Because I do not have guests on my radio program, I can also share now with my listeners my conversations with important people in public life," he said. "And as usual, all with half my brain tied behind my back, just to make it fair."

But this would be no glossy monthly charging subscribers $15 or $20 a year. This would be an eight-page monthly newsletter charging glossy-monthly prices and then some—$29.95. Another revenue stream. Subscriptions were advertised on the radio show, Limbaugh's daily gathering of the converted.

Volume 1, Number 1, dated October 1992, opened with a message from editor in chief Limbaugh saying it was "arguably the most successful startup publication in history. I want to proudly announce from the outset: *this newsletter is printed on non-recycled paper*. A grateful nation acknowledges the countless trees eager to sacrifice their sweet virgin pulp to support my words." To the "environmental wackos" and contemptible "tree huggers" on his list, this was a splinter in the eye.

The newsletter then opened to a two-page interview with Charlton Heston, who was becoming one of Limbaugh's favorite celebrity soulmates, "a man of deeply held values and moral purpose." The actor echoed his questioner's often-stated opinion that the power brokers in Washington and New York, as well as those in the Hollywood film community, "just do not understand that people don't think the way they do . . . most actors are not fully informed about the issues on which they become spokespeople." The hodgepodge of other published items included some of Limbaugh's one-liners ("Anita Hill: Has the hottest legal briefs in the business") and a page that noted where to phone for merchandise and videotapes.

Within two months, EFM Media reported that *The Limbaugh Letter* had wooed 85,000 subscribers—a remarkable showing for a steeply priced eight-pager. Two months later, the number of paying customers had grown to 113,000, thus representing a staggering gross of around $3,390,000. Roughly a quarter of the subscriptions were paid up for two years, or $49.95, which added another $565,000 to the till. By February 1993, with Rush continuing to flog subscriptions on the radio, saying "you need *The Limbaugh Letter* to stay in touch with the truth," another 77,000 came in.

Gross revenues? More than $6 million. And counting.

Minus salary and negligible printing costs, the publication was no longer a revenue stream, but a raging river. A no-brainer representing millions of dollars in profit, with the expectation at EFM Media that renewals would be automatic and thereby become a handsome annuity.

A typical caller to the radio show was Jeff, from Clinton Township, Michigan. He phoned in February 1993, to dispute Limbaugh's adamant stand against Dr. Jack Kevorkian, the controversial suicide facilitator dubbed "Dr. Death" by the host. But first Jeff made it clear that he had become "Rushed" months earlier, then bought Limbaugh's book and subscribed to the newsletter. Which represented a total outlay of nearly $52.

Limbaugh's fans were making him richer by the day.

Chapter 20

TIME FOR TV

In the weeks after the Republican convention, a juggling act became Limbaugh's new routine. Besides his three-hour radio show, he began rehearsals for the TV program in advance of its September 14 premiere. Radio from WABC in early afternoon, then TV from the Unitel studios into the evening.

The TV venture came together with far greater ease than the radio show launched on only a few dozen stations four years earlier. But the risk was high; the new program stood to open a new phase of his career, or to relegate him to the heap of other radio personalities, such as Rick Dees and Jonathon Brandmeier, who crossed over to the small screen only to fail in the ratings.

In TV syndication, talk shows were as vulnerable as they were potentially lucrative. Distributors hungered for the tens of millions of dollars in advertising available for a fraction in production costs.

Oprah Winfrey's weekday talk show was believed to earn her production company and syndicator King World $100 million a year in profits. The program hosted by Sally Jessy Raphael, a Multimedia colleague of Limbaugh, reportedly netted $40 million annually for the distributor. Phil Donahue, who marked twenty-five years on the air in 1992, clearly had generated hundreds of millions of dollars in revenues along the way. But for all the riches generated by these long-termers among the fifteen syndicated talk shows on the air in the fall of 1992, there were other broadcasts that did not make it that far.

"Kitty Kelley," featuring interviews with the gossipy biographer, had lined up only twenty-eight TV stations covering 30 percent of the country when syndicator MCA Inc. yanked it from the market in advance of its fall premiere. A show hosted by Ron Reagan, the former president's son, had been shut down by MCA a year earlier. "Jane," a youth-oriented talk show hosted by Jane Pratt, the sassy editor of *Sassy* magazine, was canceled by Twentieth Television after eleven weeks of syndication warmup on New York's WNYW-TV. "The Dennis Miller Show" was stricken from the night by Tribune Entertainment Co. after nine months of poor ratings.

At the same time, Viacom Enterprises was airing "Montel Williams" on fifty-one stations around the nation, while Multimedia also had former Cincinnati mayor Jerry Springer primed for the talk market. Even in public television, the late-night "Charlie Rose" was poised to go national from New York station WNET in January. Johnny Carson quipped during his farewell appearance on "The Tonight Show" that the earth's population had grown by more than two billion in his thirty years as host, and "half of those . . . people will soon have their own late-night TV show."

However, while the format's menu of prurience, pop therapy, and celebrity glitz seemed to shut out Limbaugh's brand of muscular politics and pranks, the early reception suggested otherwise. Two months before the premiere, Multimedia announced that it had placed Limbaugh on 170 TV stations blanketing 95 percent of the country, one of the highest clearance rates among 1992's new crop of gabfests. A total of 185 stations were on board by the time it aired. This was Multimedia's most successful launch—a rate slightly higher than that for Genesis Entertainment's upcoming "Whoopi Goldberg," which would also compete in late-night.

Limbaugh pointed not so much to Goldberg's Hollywood ties, but to her liberal orientation, in explaining where he himself was heading on TV. He said that his views would appeal to those who had tired of TV's liberal slant, as he saw it offered by Goldberg, Arsenio Hall, and David Letterman. Ailes, his executive producer, stressed that the Limbaugh show would aim for entertainment, not politics (as if anyone didn't know that in this case they were one and the same).

Limbaugh also conceded that he had had nightmares about his chances after the TV show was announced a year earlier. "People kept saying, 'It's not going to work, you haven't got a format. You're a perfect creature of radio, but [you can't translate] that to television.' Then I started doing the rehearsals, and I don't have those nightmares anymore."

Despite his self-confidence, the odds makers were far less certain of his prospects, especially considering the nightly show's uneven placement—in New York on WWOR in the bleary-eyed slot of 12:30 A.M., in Los Angeles on KCOP at 3:30 P.M. and again at 1:00 A.M., in Philadelphia on WTXF at 1:30 A.M. In Washington, it had no affiliate (until WDCA picked it up twice daily on March 1, 1993). "Could it be," he asked, "that they don't want Congress to see this show?"

"Radio fans don't connect to television," *The New York Times* observed after interviewing eighteen advertising executives, TV producers, other syndicators, and network officials. "His controversial cant may scare off advertisers and stations. Industry buzz: He won't go the distance. 'Who wants controversy? Look at Morton Downey. And if Rush softens his edge, he doesn't have a show.' "

However, unlike Downey (whose name seemed repeatedly linked to Limbaugh's ever since the latter succeeded him on KFBK in 1984), the TV newcomer did not trade in an outrage per day so as to numb and ultimately bore the audience. Limbaugh also had enough bits and musings to sustain three hours of radio a day—no small feat in itself and certainly a rigorous warmup for doing a mere half-hour of daily television. And perhaps most significant of all, Limbaugh had a vast audience, now tuned to 520 radio stations, just waiting for his TV offshoot to succeed. Cultivating a startup audience would be a cinch. All he had to do was talk about the TV show on radio. Which, of course, he did.

On the day of the launch, with listeners still calling to ask where and when they could find the show, he expressed disappointment over the dearth of TV commercials and other advertisements for the new program. He shared a curious suspicion that the affiliates "didn't want you to know about it." To help the show surmount what he said would be a liberal backlash, he urged his viewers-to-be to call and voice enthusiasm for the half-hour to their local station managers. "If you like this TV show, you're going to have to let them know," he said. "This is not promo hype. This is experience."

At the same time, the TV program had many advantages. Forty of the stations planned to air it twice a day. In Chicago, WGBO scheduled it for 10:00 P.M., an accessible slot. In New Orleans, WVUE had it ready to follow "Nightline," except during the "Monday Night Football" season, when it would have an even more attractive time period at 7:00 P.M.

The pilot of the show that Ailes had displayed in the supermarket of TV syndication, the annual gathering of the National Association of Television Programming Executives, presented Limbaugh without a studio audience. But the opener on September 14 included an off-camera collection of thirty or so guests who laughed and groaned through the half-hour.

Limbaugh opened the broadcast with a blue dot superimposed on his face—like the one that was used to conceal Patricia Bowman, William Kennedy Smith's accuser, in telecasts of his Palm Beach rape trial. The dot was there "because I demand anonymity for my own safety. Why? Because I stand accused of being one of the most heinous Americans alive today. Why? Because I believe in the power of the individual. I believe in limited government. I believe in you keeping more of your money. What does that make me? It makes me a conservative."

The spot lifted, and Limbaugh, looking trimmer at 270 pounds, presented a close, some might say claustrophobic, set that reminded more than one critic of a cable access show. It consisted of a den and an adjoining denlike workspace that included a round table at which the host sat and addressed the camera. Framed articles about Limbaugh adorned one wall; he had added to the egocentricity by putting copies of *The Way Things Ought to Be* on the dark bookshelves, which also contained scholarly-looking volumes.

Time for TV

In the twenty-two minutes not taken up by commercials, there were shots at Bill Clinton, shots at Al Gore, shots at Ross Perot ("I never believed this guy from the outset"), and a testimonial from Sen. Phil Gramm, who said he feared that Limbaugh would be lost to Hollywood once folks saw on TV how "pretty" he was.

Finally: "We're out of time. We've only just begun. If you love this show, let somebody know. We'll see you tomorrow."

On TV show number two, Rush paused to orient those viewers who were unfamiliar with him from the radio. "They call me the most dangerous man in America. Know why? Because I am . . . because I'm right and having a blast being right." And by the way, he said, holding up an already familiar prop, "this is a best-seller already." While the show played at times like a paid political advertisement for Bush-Quayle '92, it was well on its way to doubling as an infomercial to spur sales of Limbaugh's book.

The early returns were encouraging. The show opened to a 2.6 rating and an 11 share, then fluctuated over the next four days to average for the week a 2.5 Nielsen rating and a 10 share across the country. This meant that about two million households tuned in each weeknight, or 10 percent of those sets in use at the time the show aired. The report card reflected an improvement over the lead-in programs, but a drop of two points from the time-period numbers of the year before.

The more comfortable Limbaugh became in front of the camera, the more broadly targeted his show became. Beyond the swordlike conservatism that he espoused on the air, the program offered amusement and timeliness that transcended politics.

First, he came to borrow the more amiable techniques of his late-night colleague David Letterman by trading and jiving with the off-camera production staff, including the woman whose on-screen label read "Commie Makeup Babe," so as to poke fun at the very medium in which he was working. With his confused, now wide-eyed face cut into corners of the screen as taped clips aired, he also resembled Jonathan Winters, the original rubber puss. And by taping the show daily at 5:00 P.M. for airing that same evening in most cities, Limbaugh stayed on top of news developments and kept his agenda up-to-date, in the manner of a nightly wrapup, albeit one with a skewed point of view. Whoopi Goldberg, by comparison, reportedly was taping nine interview shows a week, in order to have a whole season's worth in the can by November.

And the response?

"There's none of the seeming spontaneity of his radio work," wrote Phil Rosenthal in the *Daily News* of Los Angeles. "The whole thing comes across about as real as the fat-free cheese and imitation butter whose commercials pay for the TV show."

John Koch in *The Boston Globe:* "Actually his compulsive self-promotion . . . is more endearing than egregious. . . . But are we having fun, too? And the answer, which has less to do with his political stripes than his one-note, essentially one-man format (very few guests, an occasional phone call-in) is no. . . . On television, by contrast, he seems less feisty than merely windy: a nakedly exposed blowhard casting about for a TV persona."

Rod Dreher in the *Washington Times:* ". . . to succeed, the shiny-faced Spanky McFarland look-alike will have to do something more than sit there and complain about multiculturalists and femi-Nazis."

Howard Rosenberg, the Pulitzer-winning TV critic of the *Los Angeles Times:* "After watching the first week of his new syndicated series on KCOP-TV . . . one must logically conclude that Limbaugh is the lead component of an insidious left-wing conspiracy to make conservatives look like clowns."

"*The Rush Limbaugh Show* may not change the face of TV or alter the course of human events," media watcher Edwin Diamond wrote in *New York* magazine. "But the man and the show deserve at least a historical footnote for being the latest and loudest fusion of politics and entertainment."

Joshua Hammer in *Newsweek:* "However long it lasts, Limbaugh's mad-as-hell message now has a seductively jovial face as well as a voice. And that's what makes it more unsettling than ever."

Robert Goldberg, in *The Wall Street Journal*, welcomed having a distinct point of view on TV, but complained, "It's static. It's uninteresting. Where are the visuals? Why is this man on TV?"

But did poundings such as these matter? No more than the dismissive reviews of his book hurt sales.

In its second week, Limbaugh's show grew to a 2.7 rating. In the third week, it was up to a 2.9, nearing the 3 that was reportedly guaranteed to advertisers. Goldberg, his lead-in in New York, was fading, down to a 2.0; it had been sold at a 4 rating.

Meanwhile, helping to fuel the ever-escalating interest in Limbaugh was George Bush.

Four days into the TV show, Mary Matalin, the president's deputy campaign director, phoned Rush to remind him that Bush would be in New York the following Monday. As Limbaugh told the story, Matalin then asked if Bush could stop by and visit his radio show. On being told that the program did not present guests, Matalin went silent on her end, until Limbaugh assured her he was joking when it came to U.S. presidents. "No, we'd be happy to have him by."

Secret Service agents immediately descended on the WABC studios to prepare for Bush's arrival days later. They installed two satellite dishes (in case one failed) for communications. They laid down oxygen canisters every few paces between the studio and the door. They brought in dogs to sniff around for bombs. On September 21, the day of the visit, they sealed off one of the building's elevators for the use of Bush alone. The measures appeared designed to ensure that the president would be constantly moving, not slowed or halted in any way.

Bush began his visit to Manhattan before a special session of the UN General Assembly, where he called for a widened peace-keeping mission for the world body and pledged greater United States involvement in the effort. Then, with busy 34th Street cleared of traffic to provide unimpeded access to the WABC studios across town, the president's motorcade swept him from the seat of world power to the podium of conservative power. After rising to the seventeenth floor of 2 Penn Plaza, Bush first sought out WABC's Bob Grant, in order to pay respects to another of his broadcast supporters, and then entered the studio where Limbaugh had been trumpeting the reelection cause for weeks.

"Rush, it's nice to see you again—just one more fan sitting at the table here," he began.

And then Limbaugh started lobbing the softballs. "The first thing I want to bring up is my conviction that people are not rabidly eager for Governor Clinton to be president. . . . What would you as president do, what can any president do to create jobs? . . . How would you define the differences between your health-care plans?" It was all too familiar territory for the president.

But the comments that perked up their exchange and prompted reporters to scribble notes more feverishly concerned the nagging matter of Clinton's Vietnam-era draft record. Limbaugh—who had only recently, and erroneously, attributed his own avoidance of the Vietnam draft to a 4-F classification, and had yet to be challenged on the subject—pointed to a published revelation that Clinton had contacted Arkansas Sen. William Fulbright's office "in an attempt to remove himself from potential military service." (In fact, however, Clinton had sought help from the lawmaker's office in 1969 when he was trying to win a slot in the University of Arkansas's Reserve Officers Training Corps.)

Bush, on the other hand, made repeated references to a Clinton letter from twenty-three years earlier in which the president claimed that the Democrat had referred to the military as "immoral." (Clinton never used that word, though he did state that the draft was "illegitimate.")

Nevertheless, the mention of Clinton's draft history set off Bush, a World War II fighter pilot who privately had been calling the governor a draft dodger. The president argued that "the fundamental difficulty is that he has not told the truth, the whole truth, and nothing but the truth. . . . I think the major point is the total failure to come clean with the American people on this very difficult question."

Playing devil's advocate, Limbaugh then asked for his guest's reaction to the idea that Vietnam was now old news. "What if people don't really care?"

"I'm not trying to make a big deal out of it," Bush replied. "But I have a different concept of public service and service to the country. Some say foreign policy, military policy doesn't matter. But there are still wolves in the woods. And someday, the commander in chief might have to make a very difficult decision."

In a score for Bush—and Limbaugh—the radio session made headlines. With photos.

"BUSH ACCUSES CLINTON OF 'FAILURE TO COME CLEAN' ON THE DRAFT" read the page-one head in *The Boston Globe*.

"BUSH TAKES UP DRAFT CRY" read the page-one head in *The Washington Post*, with the subhead, "Clinton Accused of Failing to Level With Public." (The UN speech was buried inside on page 15.)

The *Daily News* in New York played it: "BUSH: TELL TRUTH, BILL. PREZ POUNDS HIM ON DRAFT DANCING."

New York Post: "BUSH TO CLINTON: 'COME CLEAN' ON DRAFT."

USA Today: "BUSH STEPS INTO THE DRAFT FRAY."

Bush's attack came as the latest ABC News–*Washington Post* poll showed that Clinton was widening his lead, 58 percent to 37 percent among likely voters. The president's flareup was also noteworthy because seven months earlier Bush had suggested that Democratic candidates were being "quite unfair" in their assaults on Clinton's draft status. In addition, only 16 percent of those polled said that Clinton's seesawing explanations about the draft would influence their vote.

Yet despite the scant evidence that the draft mattered much, Bush's seizing on the issue during Limbaugh's show reflected a dogged belief in the GOP camp that Clinton remained vulnerable on the subject, if it could be linked to doubts about the Democrat's character. At the same time, in order to prevent a possible backlash over Bush's use of the word "trust" in knocking Clinton over the draft, the president's advisers had prevailed on him "to make the issue 'truth' instead of 'trust,'" *Newsweek* reported. Hence, there was Bush's refrain that Clinton "has not told the truth, the whole truth, and nothing but the truth."

Using Limbaugh's show as a launchpad for Bush's draft offensive may have been coincidental, but the echoes from the forty-five-minute appearance prompted the campaign to value the host and his broadcast even more highly. What other leading media outlet offered such a seal of approval?

"The show was an oasis in a pretty bleak media landscape," says David Beckwith, Quayle's press secretary. "It was also terrific for morale. Rush has a way of casting issues in terms that people can really understand. In many ways, he did a better job at that than we did ourselves."

So while the Republican campaign did not map out further appearances or phone-ins by Bush and Quayle, it looked to the radio show as a tool to help get the GOP base out to vote for the ticket. To that end, rather than wear out the show's effectiveness on Bush's behalf, the campaign also guarded against overexposing the candidates on Limbaugh's airwaves. Campaign strategists feared that the host's influence might wane if he was perceived as being courted too closely by the president and vice president.

As a result, even though footage of Bush's radio appearance was aired on the Limbaugh TV show later that evening, and the exchange was rebroadcast on radio October 5, the president returned live to the conservative's airwaves only once more. Quayle also was on a second time, calling the show from Cape Girardeau in the company of Limbaugh's mother and brother.

But Limbaugh had much more support to offer his candidate. He pounded Perot when the independent reentered the race on October 8. He contributed opinion pieces to *National Review* and *The New York Times* eviscerating Clinton and arguing the Republican cause.

Even so, Limbaugh toned down his enthusiasm for Bush when pressed in an unguarded moment. Although the broadcaster did not mirror the gloom of Ailes, who privately was knocking the reelection effort and saying the president's chances of victory were three in ten, he was laying a little distance. Appearing again on "Charlie Rose," which still aired only in New York, Limbaugh described Bush as a "fine guy" with "great intentions," but one who could not say what he wanted to say.

Then why, Rose pinned him, was he so enthusiastic?

"I'm not," Limbaugh said. "This is like the Super Bowl. Nobody's favorite team is playing, so you root for somebody to lose."

Hardly a ringing endorsement in front of the independent viewers of New York's public television station. But Rush was no fool. The election would be over on November 3, but he still had to live among these people.

Limbaugh's national audience, on the other hand, had no reason to doubt his support. Except during his October surprise.

In a masterfully acted hoax, Limbaugh sounded grieved and shaken as he stunned listeners with the about-face that he planned to vote for Clinton. "I can no longer ignore what is becoming obvious," he said. "It's necessary to have the courage to change."

And for nearly a half-hour afterward, the prank had people going, angrily so. How could he do such a thing? Even the Bush campaign called in search of an explanation.

At first, Limbaugh denied that he was fooling around. But eventually, he cracked a little and said: "How can you hold me to something I said seventeen minutes ago? That was in the past."

Limbaugh's echo of a certain Democratic presidential nominee was intended to cast an accusing light. In Limbaughspeak, the host was again illustrating absurdity by being absurd himself. Shortly before he concluded the broadcast, he confessed that it was all a sham meant to dig at Clinton. As Limbaugh's spokesman put it later in the day, "Rush made one statement, denied it, and caught all manner of grief from his listening audience. There is a governor running for president who has done that for twenty years and is leading in the polls."

Others, including his friend Bill Bennett, the former drug czar, later questioned the wisdom of perpetrating a hoax on such a serious-minded audience. Limbaugh, however, defended his stunt while apologizing to those whom it had upset. He seemed miffed that his "brilliantly conceived, flawlessly executed piece of broadcast excellence" was reported by only a few newspapers the next day. Nevertheless, he was pleased to have found vivid proof that he possessed the key to success—people believed him. In the hands of a demagogue, such credibility would be dangerous. In the hands of Limbaugh, it was an asset that the Republican organization cherished.

And so, Limbaugh battled down to the wire. On the eve of Election Day, he began his day at Bush's side before a rally in Madison, New Jersey. He was out of the glass booth and at the ramparts with his leader, along with four men in black shirts and pink ties who played Elvis Presley hits and other fifties tunes to warm up the crowd of commuters and other locals shivering in the morning cold.

"Governor Clinton would barely be above twenty percent if people listened to what he said," Limbaugh said in introducing the president.

Said Bush: "I've got a message for Saddam Hussein. 'You're [still] going to have to contend with me.' "

It was Bush's first stop on a sixteen-hour sprint through six states to cap the campaign. Win or lose, he said, "This is the last day I will campaign for myself for president of the United States or anything else."

His opponent had rallied in New Jersey the night before, flanked by an array of celebrities. "Last night, Governor Clinton was at the Meadowlands with Richard Gere and other Hollywood liberals," Bush said to a round of boos. "Well, here's a good deal for you: Let Governor Clinton have Richard Gere, and I'll take Rush Limbaugh any day!"

The crowd whooped with approval.

A few hours later, Limbaugh sat behind his radio microphone in New York and spoke on the air for six minutes with Bush, who by this time was aboard Air Force One in Akron, before moving on to Louisville. "Rush, I'm pleased to be here and, again, things are moving. We saw you this morning and now we're plowing away across this great country."

Limbaugh said that the undecided voters he knew were leaning toward Clinton simply because they felt a need for a change. "Mr. President, the Democratic team has succeeded profoundly in this campaign in making people afraid of their economic future. They have, in my mind, been misrepresenting the status of the U.S.

economy. . . . Should Bill Clinton win, let's turn it around, what are you most afraid of?"

"It's not so much fear as a conviction that we would go right back to what I call the misery-index days of the Jimmy Carter administration," Bush said, "because if the Democrats control not only the Congress but the White House, you are going to see the spend-and-tax philosophy result in interest rates of twenty-one percent—that's where they were under Carter—fifteen percent inflation, and a misery index . . . of unemployment and inflation up about twenty. It's half that now."

Bush described an upbeat mood aboard his plane, even among some of the reporters. "There's gonna be some red faces among the pundits come Wednesday morning. It's close, it's very hard to make predictions, but, Rush, I have never wavered in my conviction that we're gonna win because I think the people are gonna say truth, character, they count."

Limbaugh seized on what sounded like Bush's parting shot and would not let go. "This is your last day to drill that home to the undecided voters in America, that truth, trust, and character are relevant. Take your opportunity here and tell people why that's important in a president, do you think."

"First, as president, Truman was right: The buck stops there. You cannot be on all sides of every issue . . . I've tried very hard to uphold the honor and dignity of the White House. When we talk about family, Barbara and I have tried to exemplify the best in family values. . . . Then I hope that I've demonstrated the tough-ness that's required in the category character by making the right decisions on Desert Storm. . . . I think that I'll win this election."

On the day of reckoning, Limbaugh voted for the first time in two years. Though a devout Republican, he had made it a habit since moving to New York in 1988 to skip all of the party's primaries, and in 1991 he also sat out the November general election in which all fifty-one seats in New York City's newly enlarged city council were at stake.

At noon, he did his radio show before an additional audience that watched him on C-SPAN, one of his favorite media. The viewers were invited to get in on a presidential preference poll by dialing a 900 number for either Bush, Clinton, or Perot.

By 3:00 P.M., hundreds of thousands of calls were made, he said. At 85 cents a shot, the poll would have generated hundreds of thousands of dollars in revenues, although it was not made clear who exactly was to reap the harvest.

The vote: 4.5 percent for Clinton, 10 percent for Perot, and 85 percent for Bush.

Limbaugh signed off for the day:

"Courage."

Chapter 21

VICTORY IN DEFEAT

R oss Perot had the best showing by an independent candidate since Theodore Roosevelt topped the Bull Moose ticket in 1912. The Texan received more than nineteen million votes, or about 19 percent of those cast.

Bush, who took Texas and Florida by narrow margins, got 38 percent.

Clinton's 43 percent came in a broad-based showing that included sweeps of New England and the three Pacific Coast states, and wins in the large industrial states in the Midwest and mid-Atlantic region, as well as New York and New Jersey.

He would become the forty-second president of the United States.

Although Limbaugh had enthusiastically backed a losing candidate, he did not call Bush "The Loser," as he had Michael Dukakis after the Democrat's 1988 defeat.

Not at all. For Limbaugh snatched victory from the wreckage of defeat. About twelve hours after Bush offered a gracious concession to his successor, Limbaugh withheld his own hand and sharpened his bite.

"I want to begin this show today by telling you, that when it comes to analyzing why things happened yesterday the way they did, I was *not wrong about one thing*," he said at the outset of his show. "I was not wrong about anything. I was not wrong about why people voted the way they did. I was not wrong about what people are expecting. I was not wrong—I did blow the prediction [a Bush victory by four to six points]. I did blow the prediction, but let's be honest: I was simply remaining true to my cause."

Limbaugh said he was surprised only by the double-digit size of the Perot vote. It bolstered his refrain for the day:

"Six out of ten people in yesterday's election did not vote for Bill Clinton. Sixty percent of the electorate voted against Bill Clinton."

But it seemed foolish to think that the election's blow to Limbaugh's bluster would cause him to retreat or the foundation of his show to weaken. Rather, if Bush had won, and Limbaugh had gnawed at Clinton's political corpse a few dozen times, what meat would have been left to chew on?

No, as Limbaugh himself was quick to point out on that day after, his show had always been driven by the day's news and the issues behind the news. In breaking away from twelve years of Republican rule, the Clinton administration was sure to put issues in bold relief. And the 55 percent turnout at the polls showed that issues mattered.

Clinton's victory was a terrific development for Limbaugh. Four years of great material.

"We are only propelled by this," he pontificated. "This show becomes the focus now of the loyal, honest and good-intentioned, well-intentioned opposition to the monolithic power which will descend upon Washington, D.C. . . . Conservatism did not lose last night. . . . There is no mandate."

With thirteen million listeners a week, plus millions of book readers and TV viewers, Limbaugh—like Perot, with his nineteen million voters—was poised to become an even more potent voice on the outside. In the week before Election Day, his TV show scored its best ratings since the September launch—a 3.3, which was ahead of "The Arsenio Hall Show" and "Whoopi Goldberg."

Even Ronald Reagan passed Limbaugh the torch. "Thanks for all you're doing to promote Republican and conservative principles," the former president wrote to him after the election. "Now that I've retired from active politics, I don't mind that you've become the number one voice for conservatism in our country."

Limbaugh was already mining the election results for lines, saying that Clinton would make suicide doctor Jack Kevorkian the next surgeon general.

The only drag on Limbaugh's advance was the dearth of national advertising on his TV show.

While heading into the premiere, Multimedia was said to be having difficulty selling commercial time because of skittishness about what Limbaugh might do on the air—and the situation did not improve much with the growth in ratings and affiliates. With 194 stations in place after the election, it was not for want of coverage that few leading marketers besides Alka-Seltzer and Vaseline Intensive Care Lotion eventually were moved to place spots during the half-hour. The remaining commercial minutes were filled by the *Conservative Chronicle* and other dial-in sponsors familiar to his radio listeners.

And in the kind of publicity that a fledgling broadcast could definitely do without, Kevin Goldman, writing in *The Wall Street Journal*'s influential Advertising column, noted the shortage of top-brand commercials and suggested it was "a sign that advertisers don't want to offend anyone, pinko or redneck." He added: "In Mr. Limbaugh's case, no one is blaming the messenger, but rather the fact that he is delivering a message at all."

A Michigan-based publisher, The RadioGuide People Inc., found out just how much of a hot potato Limbaugh was when the company prepared to issue a free guide listing all of the broadcaster's affiliates around the country.

First, the Michigan Travel Bureau, a government agency, agreed to sponsor the *Rush Radioguide* and place a fall foliage map inside the giveaway at a cost of $55,000. After the deal was signed, state Democrats squawked to the governor. Gov. John Engler was a Republican, Limbaugh's Republican loyalties were just as well known, and 1992 was an election year. How dare the state use tax dollars to advertise in a publication pitching a partisan broadcaster, the Democrats wanted to know.

In response, the travel bureau's director apologized for the decision. In a see-through bit of window dressing, Limbaugh's name (but not his picture) was then stripped from all but the back panel of the guide; even above the list of his five-hundred plus radio affiliates, it said only, "Listen to Talk Radio . . . 'All Across the Fruited Plain.'" There was no sign of his name.

And yet Michigan's outlay of $55,000 placed its foliage map in 2.5 million copies of the *Rush Radioguide* and earned the state much more than that amount in commercial time on the two dozen stations that promoted the giveaway on the air and directed listeners where to get one.

However, lining up a retail chain to make the guides available in its stores presented the publisher with another headache. Without spending a dollar, the retailer would have its name printed in the *Rush Radioguide* and mentioned in the radio spots. The retailer also stood to gain new business from those customers who entered its stores to pick up a copy.

Nevertheless, one by one, Kmart and a few of the fast-food chains turned down the publisher's invitation to serve as a distributor because they wanted to avoid the appearance of endorsing Limbaugh's political views. True Value Hardware, which was already advertising on the radio show, declined to take the additional step of distributing the guide in its stores because, one of the retailer's media buyers explained, Limbaugh could be controversial and many of its outlets had yet to accept his program as an ad vehicle. On the one hand, True Value Hardware advertised on the show because it was pleased to reach his ever-growing audience; on the other hand, it appeared to have serious reservations about associating with Limbaugh himself.

With the Michigan Travel Bureau's embattled sponsorship of the guide in hand, but still no distributor willing to make the freebies available, Arthur R. Vuolo, Jr., president of The RadioGuide People Inc., called on yet another prospect—the Subway sandwich shops. When the chain heard that it would get free advertising and untold numbers of potential customers simply by stacking the guides in those Midwest outlets within driving distance of Michigan, it agreed.

Despite the difficulties Vuolo encountered the first time around, in the spring of 1993 he was planning to publish an updated edition of the *Rush Radioguide*. Seeking a new sponsor, he called on a hotel chain that advertised on the radio show. But the company nixed the idea because it claimed to have received letters from consumers who objected to the on-air sponsorship of Limbaugh.

"I knew Rush was controversial to some people," Vuolo said, "but I didn't realize the political ramifications."

Oh well, Limbaugh said in response to such obstacles, we'll just have to find those who *do* want to advertise on the TV show. After all, his people had done so on radio, in some cases bringing in sponsors suggested by Limbaugh himself, such as Snapple beverages and CompuServe, a computer-information service that had never advertised on network radio before. Although controversy was deemed by many leading marketers an inadvisable format in which to sell, the Limbaugh salespeople had posed the question: Controversial to whom?

They had their own research showing that only a minute fraction of the radio audience disagreed with Limbaugh—and that audience grew during the autumn months to a quarter-hour total of over 3.8 million listeners, more than half of whom were in the advertiser-friendly age group of twenty-five to fifty-four. In addition to the sales force's own data were the individual stations' ratings, and the packed houses for his speaking appearances, to demonstrate acceptance of his novel approach. As Limbaugh once put it, "the only way there would be controversy [cited by his listeners] is if all of a sudden I woke up and started spouting liberalism."

The idea, then, seemed to be that Multimedia would point beyond the supposed controversy surrounding Limbaugh and note the dramatic results that his radio show delivered to those who did advertise to such a harmonious audience. His listeners were so involved with the show and so supportive of his views that they responded to his sponsors and to his special testimonials on behalf of conservative publications, a manufacturer of portable spas, a maker of men's ties, and other advertisers.

Nevertheless, in an apparent bid to get around the difficulty of selling Limbaugh's TV time in a standoffish marketplace that was also inundated with barter deals for shows, Multimedia announced late in 1992 that it planned to seek payment for the program in the second season. Instead of Multimedia keeping three minutes per half-hour for its own ads and the affiliate stations keeping three and a half for local spots—the traditional barter arrangement— Multimedia wanted to retain only one minute and take cash from the outlets for the time it would now yield.

Because the show's ratings continued to rise, and were now up to an impressive 3.2, or nearly three million households, the switch to cash-plus-barter was thought to be an easy decision for the affiliates. After all, a survey by *Electronic Media*, an industry publication, found that TV stations considered the Limbaugh show and reruns of "Roseanne" their most rewarding acquisitions of 1992. Limbaugh outpolled "Designing Women," "Murphy Brown," "Whoopi Goldberg," and "You Bet Your Life." The latter, hosted by Bill Cosby, fell far below audience projections and was canceled, at a substantial loss to Carsey-Werner Distribution. "Limbaugh" was reported to be among only four syndicated shows, including "Inside Edition," "Baywatch," and "Star Trek: The Next Generation," that were meeting or exceeding the ratings guaranteed to advertisers.

But the cash-plus-barter idea did not fly. The word in the industry was that stations were unwilling to pay for Limbaugh's show because they were having a tough time selling the commercial minutes already available to them, perhaps because of the off-hours in which some of them were airing the broadcast. As a result, the stations wanted to continue sharing the advertising dilemma with Multimedia rather than pay up and be saddled with even more time to sell. They were unsure of making back in commercial revenue the sum they would have to pay in order to obtain the show in the first place.

In Philadelphia, for example, WTXF, which had launched Limbaugh at 1:30 A.M. before moving him to 11:00 P.M., bumped the TV show back again—to 1:00 A.M.—because the station had difficulty lining up commercials at the earlier hour. The station stuck to its decision despite an onslaught of nearly 1,800 viewer calls protesting the switch.

The ad problem raised the question of whether Limbaugh's TV future was indeed secure.

The Nielsen ratings amassed during the important November sweeps period showed that the program earned a 3 rating and a 16 share (percentage of TVs in use) nationwide. In New York, Limbaugh had a 1 rating in his original 1:00 A.M. time slot on WWOR and a 1 after moving to 11:00 A.M. on WNYW beginning November 16. In Los Angeles, the returns on KCOP were a 4 rating at 3:30 P.M. and a 2 at 1:00 A.M. In nineteenth-ranked Sacramento, the town where Rush had made his name, he posted a 6 at 11:30 A.M. and a 3 at 1:00 A.M. over KCRA (with a 10 and a 9 obtained by rebroadcasts on the weekend). Indeed, Limbaugh's ratings were far more modest in the largest urban centers than in the smaller metropolitan areas. As for the demographics of the audience, his TV following showed roughly similar numbers of men and women twenty-five to fifty-four years old.

And the viewers, like the radio listeners, were passionate about their man. In January 1993, when *USA Today* prepared to poll readers on their favorite late-night TV host, more than one thousand blitzed the paper's phone lines to protest the absence of Limbaugh's name from the printed list of choices. "It is the typical liberal bias of your newspaper and we're getting fed up with your continually biased news," one letter to the editor later fumed. The number of calls would have put Limbaugh in second place behind David Letterman, who received 1,381 votes. As Limbaugh noted on the air, "Do you people pack a powerful punch out there!"

The response was almost enough to help him weather Clinton's inauguration two days later. On radio and television, he was already poking fun at the Democrats' festivities in Washington, particularly their use of flattering staging areas such as the Lincoln Memorial ("looks like Lincoln is shining his approval and countenance down upon Clinton"), even though the choice of backdrops recalled the favorable showcasing of Ronald Reagan while he was president. Limbaugh also mocked the performances by seasoned singers such as Bob Dylan and Aretha Franklin. Dylan's rendering of his song "Chimes of Freedom" prompted the broadcaster to remark: "Who the hell's imprisoned here? Who the hell's living in oppression in this country?"

He found the days of celebration so image-filled "as to be surreal." Even a ceremonial ringing of the Liberty Bell in Philadelphia struck him as being not just ridiculous, but also devoid of symbolism.

But Limbaugh managed to have a last laugh on Inauguration Day. Working through White House channels in the final days of the Bush presidency, he had arranged for a greeting to be left in the Lincoln Bedroom for Harry Thomason and Linda Bloodworth-Thomason, the TV producers who organized the inaugural entertainment. When these old friends of the new president retired to the room on Clinton's first night in office, they found a note from Limbaugh that read:

"I was here first, and I will be back."

Chapter 22

THE BIG SHOT

In 1983, former disc jockey Rush Limbaugh was fired for the fifth time in twelve years when the Kansas City Royals removed him from a lowly marketing position that paid him around $18,000. So he turned again to radio, remembering after five years on the sidelines that life in the glass booth made him happy and offered the only real chance to display his oracular talents.

Ten months later, he was axed once more. Too outspoken for the Kansas City airwaves. But this time, he did not give up on radio. He believed in his gut that he had something to say and something worth hearing. And the determination paid off.

In 1992, Limbaugh earned around $12 million. Comprising this sum were $3 million in royalties from his enormously successful first book, $2.5 million as an advance payment toward his second book, about $4 million from his popular radio program, and $2.5 million from the TV program, stage shows, sale of merchandise, and subscriptions to his shockingly lucrative newsletter.

And there was more, much more, where that came from.

In 1993, when Limbaugh turned forty-two, sales of the first book would continue to yield millions as it hung on to the number-one position on the *Times'* best-seller list until March 14 and did well long afterward. The TV program, a ratings success despite advertiser reluctance, showed during the important February sweeps period that it was adding viewers. *The Limbaugh Letter* sought even more subscribers via an ad campaign planned for his TV show. And the radio program generated even greater profit as Limbaugh's syndicator, EFM Media, prepared to take the outrageous, but no less confident, step of charging larger stations a fee to air the broadcast.

For more than 400 radio affiliates—about 130 small stations had been paying for the show since 1992—carrying EFM Media's four commercial minutes an hour would no longer be sufficient. Not only would EFM continue to gross millions from the commercials placed on Limbaugh's show, but it now stood to receive a windfall in additional cash payments. Apparently, many of the affiliates indicated that it would be cheaper to handle a fee than to give EFM an extra minute or more of the commercial time that they were able to sell so profitably to local advertisers.

To handle his riches, Rush relied on Lazard Freres & Co., a leading investment-banking firm whose principals included, ironically enough, Felix Rohatyn, a financial adviser to Bill Clinton when he was running for president. Limbaugh told a friend that his money was being looked after by Rohatyn himself. Except for a Rolex watch, first-class airline tickets, and a driver whom Limbaugh retained to take him on his daily rounds, the broadcaster flaunted no outward signs of great wealth. He finally had all the money in the world to travel and to splurge, yet a measure of the man was that he could not think of any place he wanted to visit.

Nor did it appear that he had anything resembling a personal life. He had come to devote his days to work and his free time to work-related contacts, so that some of those who knew him well were left with the belief that having it all had not soured him, but it also had not made him happy.

"He's got no venom in him," says Lynn Samuels, the stridently liberal talk host who has worked with Limbaugh at WABC since he reached New York in 1988. "There's no meanness in that man at all."

Still, he gave the impression that he nursed an emptiness in his heart and sought to mask it by striving relentlessly after whatever level of success lay beyond his already-impressive hits in radio, TV, and publishing. Meanwhile, that success, though less than satisfying to Limbaugh, prompted others to follow the path he had cut so low and wide.

Infinity Broadcasting Corp., which had been placing the morning show of Howard Stern on major-market stations around the country, now saw an opportunity to spin off one of its Washington air personalities in midday syndication. G. Gordon Liddy, of Watergate break-in fame, was seen by the company as a good bet to steal away some of Limbaugh's younger male listeners.

Talk host Larry King gave up his late-night radio show after a run of fifteen years and began a daytime broadcast. The new three-hour venture began at 3:00 P.M. weekdays so as not to go head-to-head with Limbaugh's noon-to-three show, which had long since proven to King's handlers in parent company Westwood One Inc. that there was a market to be tapped by network programming aired during the daylight hours. To be sure, King's move to days generated an impressive starting lineup of 342 affiliates by the time the show began on February 1, 1993 (and Westwood then prepared to launch a lead-in hosted by Pat Buchanan).

Also in February, a voice from the left took to the radio—a counterweight to Limbaugh's views. Jim Hightower, a Texas populist who had served as the state's elected agriculture commissioner from 1983 to 1991, began a weekday commentary on a tiny base of eighteen stations. He picked up four more soon afterward.

It wasn't much of a start, but the colorful Hightower, called "a sound for sore ears" by Bill Moyers and "not a person who's at a loss for words, wit, humor, or the trenchant phrase" by the deadly serious Ralph Nader, believed in the "very democratic little box." Hightower saw radio as a tool that progressives had foolishly ignored as they tried to spread a message of empowerment, and he focused on kitchen-table issues overlooked by the major media. "These days, it's hard to be tuned into America if you don't know about Rush Limbaugh," he told me, "yet some movers and shakers still say 'Rush *who?*' "

Rush who?

Limbaugh's conservative theater of the airwaves had come to fill a compelling niche in American culture somewhere between the high-church musings of Washington think tanks and the cutting satire of "Saturday Night Live." Drawn to this niche was not so much a cult of followers (although his most devoted fans exhibited a cultish quality), but a hot and previously underserved market of consumers, voters, fellow conservatives, some liberal foes, and media junkies for whom his three and a half hours a day of "broadcast excellence" held the power to entertain and instruct, to confirm ideological passions, and to inflame a just-as-adamant opposition. If Limbaugh's unyielding attacks on the new president and his wife were a turnoff to some, the upward thrust of the broadcaster's ratings also appeared to suggest that Clinton's election was the best thing that could have happened to him.

Rush who? The smart ones knew who all too clearly.

Such as Kay Bailey Hutchison, the Republican state treasurer who in June 1993 won the U.S. Senate seat from Texas vacated by Lloyd Bentsen, Clinton's choice for treasury secretary. She had dined with Limbaugh at "21" in New York, and she played up a compliment from him in a campaign mailing. The "natural, red-blooded American guy" said he was "struck by her beauty." Unlike the "angry, bitter, scrunched-up-face . . . liberal women," Hutchison was among the Republican women he found "cool, calm and collected and competent."

Such as the Broadway producers of *The Will Rogers Follies*. They cast New York Mayor David N. Dinkins one night, and Limbaugh another night, in the role of Wiley Post, the pilot who died with Rogers in a crash at Point Barrow, Alaska, in 1935. Four times during the performance, Limbaugh's Post said from his seat in the audience, "Let's go flying, Will." For one night at least, Limbaugh and Marla Maples starred in the same show. Theatergoers waited for him afterward at the stage door, their *Playbills* and pens at the ready.

Such as comedian Mike Sullivan-Irwin: "One of the reasons Bill Clinton decided not to nominate Kimba Wood for attorney general is because he was afraid of the 'talk-radio backlash.' He stands up to Saddam Hussein, but he backs down for Rush Limbaugh."

Still others reacted to Limbaugh with alarm.

Humor columnist Erma Bombeck referred to him in print as "Rush Slimebaugh."

Washington Post columnist William Raspberry thought he was in an awkward position on learning that Limbaugh had agreed with something he had written—not once, but twice. Limbaugh, after all, was a gay basher and a demagogue, Raspberry said early in 1993. The columnist, who is black, also implied that Limbaugh was a bigot.

Then, letters and calls of protest poured in, as they usually did whenever Limbaugh was under attack. Raspberry said he stopped counting after 147. Three weeks later, he wrote a column of contrition: "I confess now that, apart from a couple of accidental listenings, I didn't know that much about Limbaugh. I still don't. My opinions about him had come largely from other people—mostly friends who think Rush is a four-letter word. They are certain he is a bigot. But is he?" Raspberry said he was embarrassed to realize that he could not cite a bigoted opinion held by Limbaugh.

On closer inspection, Raspberry went on, just because Limbaugh used his wit, his sense of exaggeration, and his knowledge to attack "those I consider 'good guys,'" did that necessarily make him any different from Art Buchwald or the editorial cartoonist Herblock.

"Limbaugh is often (for many of us) the hated opinion, but that doesn't, by itself, make him hateful. . . . Sorry, folks."

In a similar manner, on May 1, 1993, during the new president's first appearance at the annual White House Correspondents' Dinner, he appeared to identify Limbaugh with a racial agenda all too freely. Intending to get a few laughs from the black-tie audience, Clinton noted that Limbaugh had praised Attorney General Janet Reno for standing up to Rep. John Conyers during a recent congressional hearing over the Branch Davidian fiasco near Waco, Texas—but "he only did it because she was attacked by a black guy," the president said referring to the congressman. Limbaugh, who happened to be at the dinner as a guest of *USA Today*, cried foul, saying afterward, "It's not funny. . . . I'm the absolute furthest thing from a racist."

Oops, the White House responded after *USA Today* told of his anger on page one. Clinton's director of communications, George

Stephanopoulos, said: "As for the joke about Rush Limbaugh, the president meant to be funny, and it wasn't." This was an explanation, but certainly no apology to the president's most outspoken foe.

Limbaugh's showboat prominence on the political scene was by now viewed as a well-entrenched example of how talk media were displacing the sleepier craft of journalism in all its "Meet the Press" seriousness (even though "Meet the Press" welcomed Limbaugh as a guest panelist on April 18, 1993). "Talk media is to the dominant media institutions what Ross Perot is to the dominant political institutions," he said. "It is the portion of the media that people trust the most."

As preposterous as Limbaugh's promise was to tell his audience all they would ever need to know, the acceptance of his well-informed opinions by millions of people still went a long way to undermine the ancient and heretofore sacred belief that news and information should best come from the pundits, anchormen, editors, and columnists who composed the old news fraternity.

Speaking before a gathering of journalists at Columbia University, NBC News commentator John Chancellor reviewed why 1992 "was not a good year for the mainstream political press." However, he said, "1992 was a *very good year* for Larry King, Phil Donahue . . . Rush Limbaugh, and dozens of others who would in *no way* be called members of the mainstream political press."

It chafed on Chancellor that "talk-show America—that unspecific, nonthreatening, easygoing world of communication with ordinary folks" had been discovered by the presidential candidates "without the intermediation of professional political journalists. I think ordinary folks are wonderful, the salt of the earth, but ordinary folks are not trained to conduct a serious dialogue with presidential candidates."

But in marked contrast to Chancellor's concerns, a poll released late in 1992 by the Columbia Journalism Review and The Roper Organization showed that, by a two-to-one margin, Americans claimed they received a better understanding of candidates appearing on broadcasts when "ordinary listeners," rather than "regular newspeople," posed the questions. This preference appeared rooted in the finding that ordinary folks asked more of the questions that respondents wanted answers to. Not surprisingly, 59 percent of those polled said that candidates' visits to call-in talk shows in 1992 were a good thing for the political process.

In a poll conducted by the *American Journalism Review* and released in March of 1993, talk media received an even more resounding vote of approval: 90 percent of the respondents said they felt that "public understanding of the issues and candidates" during the 1992 campaign was improved by "non-journalists conducting radio and TV talk and call-in shows." A total of 88.2 percent agreed "that the public and the political process benefited from the call-in shows."

Not that Limbaugh himself had exposed his few guests, such as Bush, Quayle, and Buchanan, to callers' questions. He did the questioning himself. He played by his own rules of engagement. He served as his own spin doctor. As he was fond of saying, he did not field calls to his show in order to give vent to public sentiment, but rather to make himself look good. Indeed, an outside research study prepared for Limbaugh's syndicator found that his audience liked listener calls to the radio show far less than they did his views on political and social issues. "I tell you what is interesting to me," Limbaugh said. And besides, he was convinced that only 1 percent of his listeners even bothered to phone anyway.

But it was a sign of how far Limbaugh had come in the public debate that at times he was automatically assumed to be exerting influence toward specific ends.

When Clinton's first nominee for attorney general, Zoe Baird, set off a backlash over her admission that she had hired illegal aliens and failed to pay Social Security taxes for them, some in the media accused Limbaugh of whipping up the frenzy of angry calls to Washington lawmakers. Wrote New York *Daily News* columnist Lars-Erik Nelson: "Baird's withdrawal showed, once again, how easy it is to spook Congress. Just put Ralph Nader and Rush Limbaugh together, generate a few thousand telephone calls, and Congress flees in terror."

At first, Limbaugh laughed at Nelson's assertion—particularly that the columnist would link him to Nader, who was certainly no fan. For in fact, Baird's infraction had not been one of the hot issues raised by callers to his show. When a TV news crew visited the radio studio to tape a sampling of opinion about the embattled nominee, there were few calls about her until Limbaugh expressly asked for some.

"I do not urge people to make phone calls [to congressmen]," he said on the air. "I didn't give out phone numbers during the House bank scandal. All I ever do is enunciate what I think to be the truth in the case."

That may be, Ted Koppel, a Limbaugh listener himself, told him later on "Nightline." But, the newsman said, "You don't have to hand out a telephone number to suggest to your audience, look, if you have half a brain, you're going to let folks in Congress and folks in the White House know how you feel about these things."

Absolutely true, Limbaugh conceded. He was flattered that people paid attention to his views. However, he sought to emphasize that "I have what I do in perspective." Specifically, he would never run for public office because he was a member of the media, an entertainer, "and if what I do has influence, that's—that—it really is not the reason that I'm doing this."

Maybe.

But woe to those who would incur this entertainer's wrath.

EPILOGUE

It was an especially busy period of playing to the multitudes. Besides his own daily radio show, he appeared on one TV program to question the estimates of homelessness in America, he visited the "Today" show to decry the distribution of condoms in public schools, and he sat for an interview with *Time* magazine.

Then he was off to Kansas City for a weekend appearance in his never-ending "Rush to Excellence" tour. KMBZ-AM, the station that had dumped him in 1984 after only ten months on the air, was now a proud affiliate bringing him back to town as a ratings hero. All was forgiven between them.

So he arrived a day early to rendezvous with old friends over dinner. Afterward, as he folded himself back inside the limousine, he had an idea. He instructed the driver to head out to Overland Park.

It was dark now, an autumn night, but he was determined to have a look at the house in which he had lived for most of his ten tough years in these parts. A half-hour on the road and the limo was threading its way through a Kansas neighborhood unaccustomed to such an extravagant display.

Where was it? Where was that house to which he had returned from three firings? In which he had counted his quarters and singles during the eternal gaps between paydays? To which he had brought one bride and then another, both of them now gone from his life?

He wasn't sure. He couldn't tell in the darkness. Or the present owner might have changed the color, maybe altered the place somehow so as to mask its former appearance.

Another turn and the limo was now humming along West 99th Terrace. There. Back up, back up, he told the driver.

Yeah, that was the one. Where his gadgets cluttered the tabletops and his magazines carpeted the floors. Where he brooded time and again over his stymied career, only to move on to Sacramento and the success that launched him within reach of all this—the limo, the fame, the millions, the interview with *Time*, the "Rush, Rush, Rush" chanted by the crowds whenever he crossed a stage.

He had the limo idle in front of the house. He sat and looked and probably remembered: Roxy, and Michelle, and the radio stations that didn't work out, and the tedious days in ballpark anonymity, and the daunting expectations of his father, and the years of nagging frustration.

And the million miles he had traveled since.

Stay tuned . . .

INDEX

NOTE: '*RL*' means '*Rush Limbaugh, III*'